# JESUS *the* JEW

Reality, Politics, and Myth—A Personal Encounter

Second Enlarged Edition

IGNACIO L. GÖTZ

ISBN 978-1-0980-1284-7 (paperback)
ISBN 978-1-0980-1285-4 (digital)

Christian Faith Publishing, Inc.
832 Park Avenue
Meadville, PA 16335
www.christianfaithpublishing.com

Printed in the United States of America

*Truth blushes at nothing except at being hidden.*
—Tertullian

# CONTENTS

# ACKNOWLEDGMENTS

A book like this is the fruit of many years of diligent study and quiet contemplation. Writing it has been like a long journey to a far and distant place where I knew I wanted to get but the getting to which has taken more years than anticipated. I have had many guides along the way in the form of excellent teachers, among whom I must pay special tribute to Jules Volckaert, my New Testament teacher and the organist at the seminary, whose extraordinary commitment to the exactness and the truth of the text, even when controversial, was exemplary; and to Peter De Letter, Jacques Dupuis, Joseph Neuner, Joseph Pütz, Philip Phenix, Henry J. Perkinson, and Gérard Gilleman (who at some point was also my spiritual director). From them I learned the value of scholarship and hard work, the commitment to the truth, and the promise of patience. Of course, I do not hold them responsible for my conclusions, nor would I expect that they would agree with them, but I do hope they would be proud of the use I have made of exegetical and theological methods.

The works of Walter Wink, Marcus Borg, Bart Ehrman, Elaine Pagels, John P. Meier, Jane Schaberg, among many others, have been inspirational.

The staff of the library at Kill Devil Hills, North Carolina, were enormously helpful in obtaining all kinds of books I needed for my research. This Second Edition includes many additions and the documentation pertaining to them. Taylor Birk, Publications Specialist for *Christian Faith Publishing*, has been my steady guide in this venture, and to her I owe a tremendous debt of gratitude.

Quotations from the Bible come from the Holy Bible. Revised Standard Version (New York: Thomas Nelson & Sons, 1959); the

New English Bible, New Testament (Oxford: Oxford University Press, 1961); *The Complete Gospels*, ed. Robert J. Miller (San Francisco, CA: Harper San Francisco, 1994); *The Anchor Bible* (Garden City, NY: Doubleday & Co., 1964–). All quotations from the New Testament have been checked against the Greek text, and in many cases, they have been modified. Many translations are entirely my own. The Greek text is that of Joseph M. Bover, SJ, ed., *Novi Testamenti Biblia Graeca et Latina* (Madrid: Consejo Superior de Investigaciones Científicas, 1943).

# INTRODUCTION

*A faith that requires you to close your mind in*
*order to believe is not much of a faith at all.*
—Rev. Patricia Templeton

This book is a straightforward account of my encounter with Jesus the Jew, with his historical reality as well as with the stories or myths that were told about him. By myths I do not mean falsehoods or imaginary tales; myths are narratives about facts or events (or both) that were told in order to preserve their memory and to explain them in some way. Mythology is the telling of stories (Greek *mythos* [story] + *logein* [to tell]). Myths are as factual as a scientific or mathematical formula, but they use words instead of abstract symbols in order to preserve the memories. Some people claim that myths are truthful, not factual, because they are statements or propositions of which truth (or falsehood) can be predicated. They say this also to avoid entanglement in questions of factuality and literalness; but others maintain that events or facts do give rise to myths, even though we may have forgotten what these facts were and when they occurred. The problem, then, is to discern the fact behind the story, and mythologists spend their careers doing just this. Either way, Christian myths are significant stories about the historical encounter with Jesus. Like all stories, they are interpretations of facts, and therein lies the rub!

Bultmann applied "form criticism" to the New Testament, claiming that we had an obligation to expunge myths and legends from the accounts of the Gospels in order to arrive at an *Urtext*, as far as this was possible. Only then would we have the basic facts of the life of Jesus.

The early Christian community regarded Jesus as a mythological figure.

> It expected him to return as the Son of Man on the clouds of heaven to bring salvation and damnation as judge of the world. His person is viewed in the light of mythology when he is said to have been begotten of the Holy Spirit and born of a virgin, and this becomes clearer still in Hellenistic Christian communities where he is understood to be the Son of God in a metaphysical sense, a great, pre-existent heavenly being who became man for the sake of our redemption and took upon himself suffering, even the suffering of the cross. It is evident that such conceptions are mythological, for they were widespread in the mythologies of Jews and Gentiles and then were transferred to the historical person of Jesus. Particularly the conception of the pre-existent Son of God who descended in human guise into the world to redeem mankind if part of the Gnostic doctrine of redemption, and nobody hesitates to call this doctrine mythological.[1]

As is clear from this example, Bultmann considers myths to be stories designed "to explain phenomena and incidents which are strange, curious, surprising, or frightening," in terms that are reassuring and comforting, that is, in terms of realities such as gods and demons that have control of the affairs of the world.[2] We ourselves do this often when we reassure a frightened child with the words, "Don't be afraid—everything is in order, everything will be all right,"[3] imply-

[1] Rudolf Bultmann, *Jesus Christ and Mythology* (New York: Charles Scribner's Sons, 1958), pp. 16–17.
[2] Ibid., pp. 18–10.
[3] Peter L. Berger, *A Rumor of Angels* (Garden City, NY: Doubleday & Co., Inc., 1969), p. 68.

ing that there is a transcendent order in the universe that oversees all and cares for all.

The mythology of the Gospels, Bultmann contends, hides and conceals a deeper meaning that can only be possessed when one *demythologizes* the stories and sayings. Such stories and sayings need not be eliminated altogether, but they must be interpreted. Thus, Bultmann's method is one of hermeneutics or analysis of the texts.[4]

———※※———

But there is more. It is important for us to understand that the mythology of the Gospels was adapted by the early Christians from their own contemporary mythologies in order to explain the historical Jesus. These early Christians were not doing history; they were *mythologizing*, telling stories from their own traditions that they thought explained who Jesus was and what he had said and done.

Edward W. Said has shown that Westerners have approached the Orient with their own biased perspectives, and therefore have interpreted the cultures of India, Japan, and the Middle East, in Western terms rather than their own terms. Western scholars have studied and interpreted the writings, traditions, and iconography of the Orient in their own terms, and the result has been a picture in which the Western scholars and the general readership could find themselves and not be confronted by something "wholly other." This has not been always the result of deception; it has more often than not been due to lack of self-consciousness, an ignorance of the fact that one was superimposing one's own categories of interpretation on the facts of other cultures. The picture that has emerged, however, has been false though friendly.

If one applies the categories of demythologization and de-Orientalization to the accounts of the Gospels and other writings done by the non-Jewish converts to Christianity, one encounters a similar

---

[4] Bultmann, *Jesus Christ and Mythology*, p. 18. But see Kevin Vanhoozer, *Remythologizing Theology: Divine Passion, Action and Authority* (Cambridge: Cambridge University Press, 2010).

mythologization that was done by them, and which generated a series of written texts that are couched, or dressed up, in language that is foreign to the original Jewish traditions that Jesus and his family, and his immediate Jewish followers, were trying to preserve.

The clearest example is the divinization of Jesus, something that would have been normal to the Gentile converts from Greece and Rome, but which give us, then, a biased picture of Jesus and his teachings.[5] Demythologization, then, must be applied specifically to the Gentile writers who preserved whatever they preserved in their own language and using their own mythologies and traditions. The search must be not merely "for Jesus," but for the *Jewish* Jesus.

---

Wanting to be historical requires an effort. Myths and stories, while preserving the facts that gave rise to them, often acquire a life of their own, so that the facts are forgotten. There is a tendency to take the stories as fact, as far as this is possible. This happened in the case of Greek myths, for example, and since the stories seemed to be so extraordinary by themselves to modern readers, people tended to dismiss them as pure flights of fancy, forgetting the facts they enshrined. This is why the word "myth" came to mean something unreal, something not factual. This is why, too, it is so important to anchor myths to the historical realities that gave rise to them.

The same thing has happened in the case of Jesus. The myths and stories about him, often rationalized as theologies, have tended to obliterate the historical person, the Jew from Palestine. They have often taken a life of their own, so that for many people, Jesus is like the character of a story that is more real than real life. Jesus is believed in like Gandalf or Clark Kent are believed in, as a character in a story called "Gospels." Gandalf died and rose again, and Clark Kent came down from the heavens and became the putative son of earthly parents, in order to save humankind. Like them Jesus becomes a fictional character who may have a foundation in historical fact that

---

[5]   Bart D. Eherman, *How Jesus Became God* (New York: HarperCollins, 2014).

is unknown to us. When historical foundations are unknown, forgotten, or neglected, fancy, even if it is called theology, becomes truth. One example may suffice. For anthroposophists, Jesus is the most recent manifestation of eternal and immortal spirit, who has been approximating our times through successive appearances as Osiris, and then Buddha, each time in a distinctive way. As with the Marcionites, Jesus comes to save us from the world, not from sin. He is not truly imbedded in the world—he is not *of* the world, certainly not of the *Jewish* world—but pure spirit, divine. Here the real, historical Jesus, the Jew from first century Palestine, recedes into a fanciful and obfuscating realm removed from earthly realities.[6] The same happens with many Christians for whom Jesus is Christ the Savior, *le bon Dieu*, the Son of God, the coming Messiah, all theological categories that obliterate the Jewish man who had parents, brothers and sisters, friends and followers, enemies, and who, like so many other preachers that threatened the stability of the Roman occupiers of Palestine, was put to death charged with sedition.

My own encounter with Jesus makes a decided effort not to sacrifice anything human on my part; that is, I bring to the encounter reason, emotion, and belief. I meet him with eyes and ears open to whatever may be the full truth of his life, wherever this may be found, and however it may have been preserved.

This book does not claim to be a life or biography of Jesus in the traditional sense of the term. Many such lives have been writ-

---

[6]  See Rudolf Steiner, *The Gospel of St. John* (New York: Anthroposophic Press, 1962), and *Christianity as Mystical Fact* and *The Mysteries of Christianity* (West Nyack, NY: R. Steiner Publications, Inc., 1961). One should note that Steiner, as the ancient Gnostics did, reinterprets the texts of the Gospels in light of his system. This reinterpretation is not always original, and it sometimes mistranslates the Greek texts to suit his purpose. When the Gnostics did this, there was no orthodoxy, and the texts and the entire message of Jesus were being interpreted differently by different writers. The *Gospel of John*, with its myriad of Gnostic resonances, is an example of this variance. Steiner's system must appear very unorthodox to anyone ignorant of ancient Gnosticism. I should add that Steiner's anti-Semitism parallels the development of the same feeling in the academic community influenced by the writings of Harnack, who was a contemporary of Steiner's.

ten over the centuries, beginning with Tatian's *Diatessaron* in the second century, but especially in the last two hundred years; one should mention Renan, Lebreton, Vilariño, Papini, Grandmaison, Lcal, Goodier, Prat, Karl Adam, Bornkamm, Anderson, Flusser, John Dominic Crossan, but none of them are completely satisfactory because we do not possess sufficient and reliable historical facts about the life of Jesus, and therefore all such lives are reconstructive interpretations.[7] They are more like historical novels. Also, I am keenly aware that today scholars have come to a general agreement regarding the impossibility of completely recovering "the historical Jesus." It took nearly a century to arrive at this conclusion, but the struggle to discover the "real" Jesus was worth the effort, because paradoxically, it brought us closer, truly, to what Jesus probably was, said, and did. The reason we are closer to the real Jesus despite the fact that the Gospels cannot give us the historical Jesus is that our studies have unearthed the culture of the people of Jesus's time, of which he is just a marginal protagonist, and this culture gives us the historical Jesus. In other words, we have now so much information about the Jews at the time of Jesus that we need not rely on the Gospels as our primary sources regarding him. To the contrary, the Gospels, being tendentious documents of the faithful, contain the ways in which the historical Jesus is disfigured, deprived of his Jewishness, and divinized.

This book, then, makes no claims to be a biography of Jesus. On the other hand, it does not accept what most preachers and theologians say about Jesus as "the truth" about him. Theirs is often a tendentious interpretation, a *revision* of the person of Jesus such as began even while he was still alive. At the same time, I take whatever we know about Jesus seriously. My book strives to look at *all* the sources at our disposal, and it makes an effort to understand these sources and to wrest from them as much meaning as possible. In order to do this, it relies on the scholarly research of thousands of men and women over the centuries who have devoted years of their

---

[7] For a fuller bibliography, see Michaele Nicolau, SJ, *De revelatione Cristiana* (Madrid: Biblioteca de Autores Cristianos, 1958), III, 4, No. 769 *ff.*, pp. 495–499.

lives to the study and elucidation of manuscripts of all sorts. I also invoke in support of my commentaries the writings of people of different religious traditions. This is one thing I learned from studying the Mediaeval Christian writers: even though we stereotype them as quaint and narrow-minded, they employed whatever writings and ideas they could find in their pursuit of the truth. Aquinas himself, in his *Summa* alone, refers to more than thirty different non-Christian authors, and often borrows from them. Still and all, however, this book is not a full account of everything that is known about Jesus. It is partial, a partial account born out of my own concerns and my own predilections.

---

When I began to study the gospel records of the life of Jesus more than fifty years ago, I was guileless enough to think that I would find them transparent, that the gospels would give me the complete Jesus as he was, and that the sayings attributed to him were the *ipsissima verba*, the very words he had uttered. But I soon realized that such a belief was totally misguided and naive. As I learned Greek and Hebrew, the primary biblical languages of the sources, as well as Latin, the language of the Vulgate and of the Western Fathers and Mothers of the Church, I soon discovered that translators often interpreted as they translated, and that their interpretations frequently misconstrued the meaning of passages and words. Italians say that translators are traitors *(traduttore traditore)*, and this is paramountly true of biblical translations. Translators have their own preferences, which all too often they do not hesitate to let slip into their translations. But even without this, the work of translation involves choices. There are some 5,700 manuscript sources of the Christian part of the Bible alone, with more than 300,000 variant readings that differ among themselves, and one has to choose the most reliable texts to translate. None of this is easy work, or work that can be accomplished well without training.

I was also shaken out of my naivete by the contemporary commentaries of women theologians and exegetes—Rosemary Radford

Ruether, Elisabeth Schüssler Fiorenza, Mary Daly, Elaine Pagels, Karen King, Jane Schaberg—for in their books they brought out perspectives and details whose existence I had not even suspected, although they seemed to be so clear and obvious once they were pointed out.

Finally, I became aware that the literature about Jesus encompassed a great deal more than the canonical books of the Christian Bible. As I read and studied those other sources, a whole world opened up to me that mesmerized and enchanted me at the same time. I learned to appreciate this polymorphous world as it revealed to me more and more things about the Jesus I was trying to encounter and the people who had lived in his company. As Bart Ehrman says, "The one thing that nearly all scholars agree upon…is that *no matter how* one understands the major thrust of Jesus's mission, he must be situated in his own context as a first-century Palestinian Jew."[8] This is *very* important because early theologizing and the political realities of the Jewish revolt removed Jesus from this context and made a Christian out of him. The same error is still prevalent among those who overemphasize his divinity at the expense of his Jewish humanness. In fact, one may wonder if this very emphasis on Jesus as "the son of God" is not a sign of a disguised anti-Semitism.

For these reasons, I must say that I accept as valid source literature any and all writings that center on the life and sayings of Jesus and that seem to have been put together for the express purpose of enshrining and transmitting such traditions about Jesus as existed at the time. After all, most of the noncanonical sources were excluded for often trumped-up doctrinal and political reasons, not because they were unhistorical. The interrelationships between the different sources is a matter of continued scholarly debate, and I will not be

---

[8] Bart D. Ehrman, *Misquoting Jesus* (San Francisco: HarperSanFrancisco, 2005), p. 187. Speaking at a meeting on Easter Day 1914, Martin Buber asserted that "we Jews knew him [Jesus] from within, in the impulses and stirrings of his Jewish being, in a way that remains inaccessible to the people submissive to him," namely, Christians. See Martin Buber, "Dialogue," in *Between Man and Man* (New York: Macmillan, 1965), p. 5.

involved with them here,[9] but I will make use of the multiple sources in an effort to give to my readers as truthful a picture of Jesus as I can muster.

———————— ✤ ————————

One of my professors quipped once—I think he was quoting from Michelangelo's diaries—that there are three classes of people in the world: those who see, those who see when they are shown, and those who do not see. This division seemed adequate to me at the time, and for years I was quietly content to class myself among members of the second group. But slowly, after many years, and after multiple and often painful experiences, I began to realize that there existed a fourth category, that of *those who do not want to see*—something to the effect that none are more deaf than those who do not want to hear. I have been concerned with members of this group ever since I discovered them.

I taught for many years an undergraduate course on the history of ideas in the Western tradition. The curriculum included, of course, an overview of the Hebrew Bible and some detailed recounting of the rise of Judaism from Abraham to the time of the Babylonian Exile. I strove to present to the students the results of contemporary scholarship with as much care and delicacy as I possibly could but without sacrificing the conclusions of modern biblical research. Over the years I found some resistance to this scholarship from Evangelical Christians and some Orthodox Jews, and once only, I ran into a complete refusal to even discuss the matter at hand. The student in question asserted that she had been commanded by her rabbi not to attend my lectures. Since the course was required of all sophomores, the dean solved the problem by having the student enroll in a section of the course taught by the Jewish chaplain, himself a rabbi; but for a

---

9   See an excellent and succinct account of these sources in Bart D. Ehrman, *Misquoting Jesus* (San Francisco, CA: HarperSanFrancisco, 2005), chapter 1. Also David Laird Dungan, *A History of the Synoptic Problem* (New York: Doubleday, 1999).

student to be forbidden to even entertain the results of biblical scholarship in a college course was a very startling and painful experience.

On another occasion, I presided over a symposium that assembled at the university in order to discuss some aspects of the writings of Maimonides. The occasion was the celebration of the 850th anniversary of Maimonides's birth. Several papers were read, and then a well-known rabbi rose to offer a general reply. He approached the podium, opened a heavy leather-bound volume, read a sentence from it in Hebrew, and then said, "It says here that the Torah must not be discussed. Maimonides is Torah, therefore he must not be discussed. Good afternoon." And he stalked out of the room to the consternation of those present.

One more item. Just recently, the newspapers reported that a well-known televangelist referred to the state of Israel as "God's land." I immediately asked myself, Which God? The Canaanites of old believed that their God had given them the land of Canaan—their Scriptures said so—and they made this claim many years before Abraham ever set foot there (if he ever did!) and before YHWH promised *him* the same land. To which God, then, does the land belong? Why should one God's gift be more valid than another's? How does one decide? These are reasonable questions that scholarship can entertain, though perhaps it cannot resolve. But to state unhesitatingly that Palestine is "God's land" ignores history, geography, archaeology, and comparative religion; in other words, scholarship. This is sad, because merely understanding the conflicting stakes would go a long way in the prevention of prejudice and the hatred of those who hold different opinions.

My point is that even today there is a significant segment of the American population that will avoid at all costs the encounter with scholarly research as it pertains to the Bible. This seems to me repugnant, particularly in a university community dedicated to the pursuit of truth wherever it may be found, and especially, also, among the religious leadership that ought to know better. It seems to me repugnant, too, because without scholarly research, we run a very serious danger of giving in to bias and obscurantism, both of which have been at the root of persecutions and pogroms. The Inquisition had recourse to burnings at the stake rather than confront questioning, and for many centuries, divergent views expressed in writing were placed in an *Index librorum prohibitorum*, books that Roman Catholics were forbidden to read. Even today, Roman Catholic priests whose writings are to be published must seek an *imprimatur* from their local bishops; that is, a permission to print that guarantees the orthodoxy of the published work. Not that Roman Catholics have the monopoly of controlled orthodoxy; even some Evangelical Bible schools require oaths of allegiance to one and only one interpretation of Scripture from both their students and their professors. Today thousands upon thousands of people attend so-called megachurches where they are fed versions of Christianity and interpretations of the Bible untouched by any scholarship. And many of the preachers in these congregations glory in their "inerudition" in the same way as unlettered friars boasted of their ignorance at the time of the Reformation. Erasmus said of them that they brayed like donkeys in church, even though they made a good living out of the generosity of their congregations.[10]

Not too long ago a noted leader of the Southern Baptist Convention was reported as saying that "God does not hear the prayer of a Jew." Aside from being a proof of unbelievable religious prejudice, this statement showed an extraordinary degree of ignorance, for after all, historically, Jesus himself was a Jew! Why such fear of scholarship, considering that St. Paul advised his Roman Christians to present to God a "rational offering" (*logiken latreian*) or, as Fitzmeyer translates, "a cult suited to your rational nature" (*Romans* 12:1)?

It seems to me that to fear scholarship is to fear to be found wanting either in matters of fact or in forms of interpretation. The fear, and therefore the avoidance, and even the rejection of scholarship has at its basis a cult of the self even at the expense of truth. Evangelicals and Fundamentalists who reject scholarship when it comes to the Bible have placed themselves in that "City," which St. Augustine described as the antithesis of the "City of God" because it is based on the love of self, and no matter how much they pretend to

---

[10]  Erasmus, *In Praise of Folly* (Baltimore, MD: Penguin Books, 1973), pp. 53–54.

reject the reasoned truth for the sake of God, they in fact reject God for the sake of themselves.[11]

At bottom, then, the rejection of biblical scholarship is an ethical matter, because it turns the self, and not reason, into the ultimate criterion of truth essentially divinizing the self as if it were God. As Crossan puts it, "it is not morally acceptable to say directly and openly that our story is truth but yours is myth; ours is history but yours is lie,"[12] without having solid and well-argued reasons for saying so. I once heard Joseph Campbell say, with obvious sarcasm, that "myth is other people's religion!" This is what Fundamentalists and Evangelicals say when they reject scholarship and yet affirm the truth of their beliefs without a reasonable basis. I should add that as traditionally understood, this was the sin of Lucifer, who loved himself more than he loved his God.

To the rejoinder that reason itself must be subordinated to the word of God, one must answer that this, precisely, is the point that scholarship shows us, that all religions claim to have scriptures that enshrine the word of God, and that without scholarship, one cannot know how to adjudicate such claims and treat them with the degree of fairness to which they are as entitled as we are entitled to ours.

The rejection of scholarship leads inevitably to a kind of religious solipsism that goes unnoticed simply because it is so prevalent and because so many people fall into it unawares. It leads to the simplistic idea that only one is right, that only one's religion is revealed, that only one's beliefs are true, simply because one says that this is the case. The rejection of scholarship makes one's religious posture painfully arteriosclerotic.

---

[11] St. Augustine, *The City of God* XIV. 28. Edward Farley claims that "Fundamentalisms arise within the modern epoch when religious leaders so work to protect the perennial (authoritative) mediations of religion from the modern that the mediations become themselves the concern of religious faith"— that is, that it becomes more important to believe what Fundamentalist leaders say than what the Scriptures teach. See Edward Farley, "Fundamentalism: A Theory," *Cross Currents* 55: 3 (Fall 2005), p. 397.

[12] John Dominic Crossan, *The Birth of Christianity* (San Francisco: HarperSanFrancisco, 1998), p. 28.

I am very much concerned about people like the Fundamentalists and Evangelicals who have been denied access to the scholarship surrounding the Christian scriptures. I feel that they have been shortchanged and that as a consequence their Christian lives have been impoverished. They have been invited to a banquet under false pretenses and served tainted food. They have been promised wine and offered vinegar instead. And, for the most part, they do not even know this because they have been taught that scholarship is the devil's lure and that they should avoid it like the plague. "It's a matter of faith," they say. Yes, but not a matter of faith *only*, for there are texts, manuscripts, historical people and events. All these are facts that must stand scrutiny independently of faith.

It should be pointed out, too, that Jesus was rather harsh on preachers and their clerks who withhold learning from their followers: "Damn you! Clerks and Pharisees, impostors!" (*Matthew* 23:13), he said; and he explained: "They have taken the keys of knowledge and have hidden them. They have not entered [the Kingdom], nor have they allowed those who want to enter to do so" (*Gospel of Thomas* 39:1–2). Elsewhere (*Apocalypse of Peter* 79:30), Jesus calls them "dry canals," incapable of carrying the waters of life to their parishioners.[13] In other words, Jesus was aware that the Pharisees and the legal scribes that clerked for them and who were also members of the Sanhedrin, kept the people in a self-serving state of ignorance. On the other hand, Jesus saw himself as the true image of God and also as the way to the realization of this image (John 14:6), to the finding of this truth. How could he not bless those who inquired,

---

[13] This criticism applies equally to the thousands of Sunday school teachers who dare walk into classrooms with hardly any scholarly preparation at all. How would we feel about a person with no scientific training whatsoever walking into an atomic submarine and pretending to run it? Yet what we consider ludicrous and foolhardy in science, we countenance without scruples in Bible studies! Celsus had already criticized Christians for believing that "the most stupid and uneducated yokels" could learn moral philosophy (Origen, *Contra Celsum* 6, 1–2, quoted in Meeks, *Origins of Christian Morality*, 102–103).

who knocked at the door of knowledge, with the solemn promise that the door would be opened to them (Matthew 7:7)?

It is my hope that this book will help open the promised door just a chink, so that the radiance within may begin to streak out and illumine the lives of all the seekers.

# A PERSONAL NOTE

When I was younger, I was very much into the traditional Christian view of Jesus as God and Son of God. I was a good student of Christian theology, and I had mastered all the little intricacies of the established dogma. Even before my theological studies, I believed, naively of course, in the divinity of Jesus. But it was the human figure of Jesus that attracted me the most. I read several lives of Jesus, including Prat's and Renan's, always looking for the personal traits of Jesus. Kazantzakis's *The Last Temptation of Christ* interested me enormously, as did Giovanni Papini's *Life of Christ*. I did not take to the popularizations by Jim Bishop and Fulton Oursler, which I thought too sugary and unscholarly and nothing like Jack Miles's *Christ*. Kahlil Gibran's *Jesus* was different, and so was Bruce Chilton's *Rabbi Jesus*. Lately, John Meier's monumental *A Marginal Jew* and Walter Wink's *The Human Being* have been most helpful, not merely because of their scholarship but primarily due to the honesty of their stances. And from all these readings I came up only with a consistent image of Jesus as a straightforward man who strove earnestly to be good to people. *Pertransiit benefaciendo* ("he went about doing good") (*Acts* 10:38) was the sum of my conclusions, the incontrovertible fact about Jesus that I came to hold as *his* truth. This, too, I found later, was the truth of Jesus that Tertullian wanted to preserve against the misunderstandings of Marcion, except that in the process, he forgot that Jesus was a Jew.

In the monastery I gave considerable attention to the Christian practice of living consciously in the presence of God and of acknowledging my faith as often as the opportunity presented itself. My favorite *mantra* was, "Lord, I firmly believe that you are Christ, the

Son of the living God." I recited this *mantra* often, and invariably when I entered church or chapel and genuflected before the tabernacle that *miris sed veris modis* contained the sacrament of the very Body of Jesus.

The four-year course in theology required the students to participate in two special seminars and to write a graduation thesis in one of them. In one of the seminars, I decided to concentrate my studies on Tertullian (*ca.* 160–230), the Latin Church Father who basically created the theological terminology that has remained in use for eighteen hundred years. In the other seminar I undertook the exploration of early credal formulas. As I conducted my studies, it was impossible not to be sidetracked into germane areas that contributed enormously to my understanding of the Patristic times. Thus I tried to elucidate the origin and meaning of the expression "Light from Light" in the Nicene Creed as well as the appearance in third-century Christianity of the belief in the virginity of Mary. I read voraciously, making use of my knowledge of Latin and Greek and of the wonderful seminary library to which I had unlimited access, even to books that were then kept in "Hell" (as the repository of tomes placed in the *Index librorum prohibitorum* was called), a restricted precinct secured by lock and key, but which I was permitted to visit at will.

It was thus that I entered the realm of first-century Judaism and Christianity. It was thus, too, that I began to understand that Christianity had not been formed in one instant by either Jesus's Jewish family or Paul, and that the doctrinal development into what most Christians believe today was rocky, not always clear, and very often brought about by sheer political intrigue, negotiation, and even force.

I learned, for example, that there were some twenty or thirty gospels, not just four, and that they had been in use throughout two or three hundred years, until the four canonical ones had come to be the standard ones, and their exclusive use mandated. I learned that churches gave preference to certain gospels rather than others, that the church of Alexandria, for instance, treasured the "Secret Gospel of Mark," a gospel for those Christians who had a more developed understanding of the new faith, and which therefore was not available to all and sundry. Tradition had it that Mark himself had written both gospels attributed to him, reserving the secret one for those proficient in the knowledge and practice of the faith. I learned, too, that Christianity had been preached in India before it was preached in France and Spain, because the apostle Judas Thomas, the twin brother of Jesus (or of other brothers and sisters), had gone there to evangelize the Indians and had been martyred there. In fact, a Christian community founded by Thomas had thrived there and continued to exist, though splintered, in the region of Malabar. I learned that the *Gospel of Thomas*, a text containing only sayings of Jesus and attributed to this Judas Thomas, had been discovered already at the end of the nineteenth century and then, complete, among the manuscripts found at Nag Hammadi in Egypt. I learned that Paul had written actually only about six or seven letters, the rest being forgeries written by people who had used his name as a way to gain a hearing for their own divergent views. I learned that the *Book of Revelation* was a Jewish eschatological text written already during Jesus's time and adapted later by Christians who tampered with the original text in order to make it fit their musings about the end of time. Christians became very adept at this sort of adaptation. They adopted the prophecies of the Hebrew Bible and interpreted them as referring to Jesus; Virgil's *Fourth Eclogue* was read to mean the birth of Jesus; and new lyrics were written for popular tunes so that Christians could sing them.

I learned many other things, and I am learning more still, for I have continued to read and study the gospels and whatever textual materials I can lay my hands on. Many of the recent scholarly books have confirmed the insights I gained some fifty years ago, insights that have become clarified, explained, and supported by a scholarship that the immense majority of Christians do not have access to, not because it is not available to them, but because their leaders do not allow them to approach these sources at the origin of Christianity.

I have learned, also, that the gospels themselves do not contain objective accounts of the life and sayings of Jesus. As I said earlier, they are records of Jesus's life filtered through the minds and hearts of the people who knew Jesus directly as well as of those who did not but who joined the nascent community. The gospels are records kept by believers for believers, copied down during periods of intense anti-Jewish sentiment, and therefore they are as biased as any historical narrative about a person or event is biased. Through the middle of the twentieth century, scholars tried to recover "the historical Jesus," studying the conditions of his life, the life-situations (*Sitz im Leben*) that gave rise to sayings. But the latter part of the century came to realize that such a search for the historical Jesus was nullified by the fact that many sayings reflected a theology already at work, an interpretation within a faith community (*Sitz im Evangelium*), and often contained even formulas that were already being employed in rituals. For example, the famous expression of the centurion attending the crucifixion hearing Jesus expire, "Verily, this man was a son of God," could only have been preserved by a believing community, since for the centurion it could only have meant something like, "Truly, this was quite a man." After all, emperors were often deified after their deaths.[14] Moreover, *Mark* 15:39 places this statement on the lips of a Gentile centurion, which immediately raises the question of how the statement should be interpreted—as Jewish Christians would, or as Gentiles would.

---

[14] Virgil (70 BCE–19 CE), in *Eclogue I*, has Tityrus attribute his ease and luxury to "a god"—namely, Augustus.

# The Gospel Texts

I said above that there are some 5,700 extant manuscripts of the New Testament alone, with more than 300,000 variant readings. Moreover, there is a great difference between the oral traditions behind the Gospels and the edited documents that were produced from them.[1] A simple example will illustrate this: no one mentions Jesus ever going to the bathroom. Therefore, establishing what Jesus said and did is not an easy matter, and preachers who naively speak as if it were are either ignorant or gravely mistaken. They traipse gaily where scholars fear to tread.

Tradition has it that there were four main gospels, *Matthew*, *Mark*, *Luke*, and *John*, and four actual writers were usually credited with authorship. *Matthew* was attributed to Jesus's disciple of the same name, who supposedly wrote in Hebrew (or Aramaic, more likely), and who was the first one to set down an account of the Master's life. This Gospel seems to have been translated into Greek shortly after its appearance, probably after 70 CE.

*Mark* was written by a Gentile (probably Roman) convert, as the name suggests. It was written in Rome before the Jewish uprising in Palestine in 66 CE, and it represented the traditions that Peter and his followers preserved.

*Luke* comprised traditions treasured by those who made up the entourage of Paul. Luke himself was a Gentile convert, probably a Syrian; he wrote in Greek, and also after 70 CE.

---

[1] James Charlesworth, *Jesus within Judaism*, p. 59.

*John* was supposedly written by the apostle John, "the beloved disciple," son of Zebedee, but we really do not know who wrote it. While it contained some narratives of events, it was mostly a mystical interpretation of the life and sayings of Jesus. However, since it recounted some stories that cast Peter and Thomas in an unfavorable light, the public reading of it in the churches of Rome (loyal to Peter) was forbidden,[2] and it was not popular in Syria because of what it said about Thomas.

The versions of all four canonical Gospels we read today are not the original ones, because these were altered by copyists again and again. We know this because we know that in ancient times, copies of any writings had to be done word for word by scribes who might make mistakes, or might add or subtract as they saw fit. Moreover, the original writers themselves may have produced more than one narrative. In the case of Mark, we have the *Secret Gospel of Mark*, supposedly a version of the original written by Mark himself when he lived in Alexandria after the death of Peter, containing additional materials and explanations. These additions, inserted in different places throughout, often clarify matters left unclear in our canonical versions.

---

From the beginning, both Christians and Gentiles found problems with the Gospels. There were discrepancies among them, and the chronologies were askew.

*John* was the worst offender, and from the start, there was a tendency to exclude his accounts whenever they conflicted with those of the other three Gospels. Moreover, there was the question of textual dissimilarities: *Mark* was very short, almost like a summary of *Matthew*, while *Luke*, which was more expansive, contained materials that were not found in *Matthew*. Discussion of these matters began quite early, often under pressure of Gentile critics, and it has continued until the present day.

---

[2]   Dungan, *A History of the Synoptic Problem*, chapter 3.

Moreover, *Luke* 1:1–3 acknowledged specifically that there were other accounts of the life and sayings of Jesus that the author did not deem accurate, and he claimed that his own book was going to set the record straight.

Papias (*ca.* 75–140), Bishop of Hierapolis, a city in Asia Minor, who wrote about all these things, also mentions other sources of the life of Jesus, such as Andrew, Philip, Thomas, and James.[3] We know today that there was a *Gospel of Thomas* written quite early and attributed to Judas "Thomas" ("the Twin"), brother of Jesus; he also may (or may not!) have written the *Letter of Jude*; there is James, probably James "the Just," another brother of Jesus, who probably wrote the letter that bears his name and is now included in the New Testament canon;[4] there is a *Gospel of Philip* discovered at Nag Hammadi, but the identity of the author is much in doubt,[5] the date of redaction appears to be late second century, and the content bears unmistakable trademarks of Valentinian Gnosis. Still, the fact remains that barely thirty years after the death of Jesus (James was executed in the year 62, Paul and Peter around 64–65), there were several accounts of the exploits of Jesus circulating among the faithful and claiming to represent the authentic message of the Master.

Such accounts proliferated until the Council of Nicaea in 325 officially established the canon consisting of the four gospels, *Acts*, and the letters that still figure in it. Shortly after the Council ended, Athanasius, archbishop of Alexandria and one of the most important theologians of the time, sent an Easter letter to all the churches of Egypt ordering the faithful to reject the "illegitimate and secret books"[6] that were still circulating. As a result, some of the faithful,

---

[3]  Eusebius, *Historia Ecclesiastica* 3. 39. 1.

[4]  There are many problems with the attribution of these letters, not the least of which is the fact that Jesus and his brothers were probably illiterate, as were most Jews at the time. The *Letter of Jude*, especially, displays literary accomplishments of some merit. Of course, they may all be literate translations of uncouth originals.

[5]  Marvin Meyer, ed., *The Nag Hammadi Scriptures* (San Francisco, CA: Harper-San Francisco, 2007), p. 159.

[6]  Athanasius, *Festal Letter*, 39.

including possibly monks, hid a few of these "secret" books in a big jar and buried them. These codices constitute the scriptures found near the town of Nag Hammadi, Egypt, in December, 1945. This means that as late as the middle of the fourth century, many scriptures besides the canonical New Testament were still in circulation and were being used in Christian, even monastic, circles.

———— ✤ ————

However, things are seldom simple and straightforward. In Palestine, besides the Jews who spoke Aramaic and Hebrew and stuck to their religious and cultural traditions, there were the Romans (and a smaller number of Greeks) who spoke Latin and Greek (*koine*), some of whom were members of a kind of ruling class. There were also Hellenizers, generally Jews who were bilingual and who were attracted by the foreign culture of the occupiers. They often compromised in religious matters, or were less observant, for they sought accommodations wherever they could find them. We often ignore such details, but it is easy to understand that in a social milieu in which going to the baths and exercising, all in the nude, was the order of the day, circumcised Jews stood out like a sore thumb, and many of them sought to enlarge their prepuces so as to blend more easily with the uncircumcised Romans (*1 Maccabees* 1:11–15). This Greek and Roman bias against the circumcised was not a sexual but, rather, an aesthetic matter: to the Greeks, circumcision was an ugly mutilation. As it happened, many members of the priestly class were counted among the Hellenizers.[7]

Jesus's message appealed to all these groups, and converts came into the movement from all of them, perhaps first among the Jews, but later among the Gentiles and Hellenizers, who soon became

---

[7] Paul himself, despite his youthful zeal for Judaism, may have been a Hellenizer: he had Roman citizenship, spoke Greek, sided with the Gentile converts to the movement, and preached a Gospel that suited them best. On the social consequences of circumcision, see David M. Friedman, *A Mind of Its Own: A Cultural History of the Penis* (New York: The Free Press, 2001), pp. 13–17. See also Hans Jonas, *The Gnostic Religion* (Boston: Beacon Press, 1963), pp. 8–9.

more numerous. The urge for separation from the revolutionary Jews (as I shall show below), therefore, was different for the Jewish Christians and for the Gentile Christians (who obviously were not Jewish) and for the Hellenizers (many of whom had some sympathy for the Jewish uprising). Relations between all these groups had not always been cordial, and they often vented their dislike of each other in open diatribe and even violence.

A clear hint of the differences between Christian convert groups is given in *Acts* 6:1, which speaks of the disagreement between those who spoke Greek and those who spoke Aramaic or Hebrew. The dispute was solved by establishing a committee with members from both sides of the issue, Greeks and Jews (to judge by their names: *Acts* 6:5–6).

Stephen was a member of this committee. He was probably a Hellenized Jew who had converted to the new faith.[8] His Greek name would indicate this, though as a Jew he could still refer to Moses and Aaron as "*our* ancestors" (*Acts* 7:39). And while traditionally Stephen's confession of the divinity of Jesus (*Acts* 7:55–57) has been taken as the reason for his being stoned to death, the obvious reference to *Daniel* 7:13 contains also a political threat to the Hellenizer priests and elders who were sitting in judgment over him: power will be taken from them and returned to the ordinary people, the autochthonous Jewish remnant in the land. The political climate of the times clamors for such a consideration.

During the War, Josephus mentions how the Greeks living in Caesarea Maritima and other cities welcomed the victorious Roman troops under Vespasian with blessings and congratulations born of a hatred of the Jews and a wish for the revolutionaries to be punished;[9] but even the Gentile converts to Christianity harbored a certain self-satisfaction at the fact that they, and not the Jews, had become the new "chosen" people.[10]

---

[8] Fitzmyer calls him "a converted Hellenist." See Joseph A. Fitzmyer, *The Acts of the Apostles* (New York: Doubleday, 1998), p. 350.

[9] Josephus, *Jewish War* 3, 409–411.

[10] Robert Murray, SJ, *Symbols of Church and Kingdom: A Study in Early Syriac Tradition* (Piscataway, NJ: Gorgias Press, 2004), p. 41.

Some of this animosity is at play also in the dispute between the Gentile converts in Galatia and the visiting Jewish converts who appeared to be preaching a different Gospel from the one proclaimed by Paul (*Galatians* 1:6 *ff.*). Paul was no longer a practicing Jew (*Galatians* 1:13), and his converts in Galatia were, in all likelihood, Gentiles who were being challenged by these visiting Christians derogatorily called Judaizers because they were thought to represent an effort among the Jewish converts to maintain their preeminence by requiring the practice of certain Jewish customs such as circumcision and the regulations regarding food; but these matters had been settled fairly early in favor of the Gentile converts (*Acts* 11:1–18, *Colossians* 3:11), who then assumed that theirs was the only true orthodoxy, and continued to call Judaizer any one who preached a Gospel different from their own. And yet, in fact, the Gospel of the visitors to Galatia, members of the Church of Jerusalem presided over by James, the brother of Jesus, was (minus circumcision and kosher) a purer version of what Jesus had preached and died for.

The fact is that Paul, who may have been a Hellenizer, refashioned the simple message of Jesus, often without acknowledging that his pronouncements were his own, though he sometimes wrote explicitly that his advice was his own, not Jesus's. Thus, for example, in allowing converts to divorce their heathen wives (*1 Corinthians* 7:12–16), he did not claim this to be the view of Jesus; but in many other instances, his theology clearly stepped beyond the boundaries of Jesus's message without any explanation or justification of this fact.

------ ✷ ------

Matters became more complicated when the Jewish Revolt against the Romans began in 66, culminating in the destruction of the Temple and of much of the city of Jerusalem in 70 CE. There were by then well-established Christian communities in Rome, Alexandria, Jerusalem (which fled to the Galilee), Antioch, Edessa, and India, and the membership was probably made up mostly of Gentile converts who had comparatively little to fear from the Roman authorities. The remnants of the early Jewish followers of

Jesus, including his family, weakened by their loss of a social base, do not seem to have endured much beyond the beginnings of the second century.[11] The original writings disappeared, only copies remained; and of those made in Greek during the second century, only fragments are extant. When Fundamentalists and Evangelicals proclaim the inerrancy of the Scriptures, they completely ignore this fact.

Questions about the discrepancies of the accepted Gospel texts continued, and in the second century, Tatian (*ca.* 110–185), a pupil of Justin Martyr (*ca.* 100–165), composed a harmony of the four basic texts, which he called *Diatessaron*. It was designed to show how the four accounts fitted together and were in tune with each other so that a continuous narrative could be read. In this way he hoped to show that the objections were groundless.[12]

While this effort was underway, a more radical answer to the constant objections and criticisms appeared in the person of Marcion of Pontus (*ca.* 85–144), a Christian scholar. Marcion's approach was revolutionary. In order to establish that Christianity had nothing to do with Judaism, he jettisoned the entire Hebrew Bible and most of the New Testament. He proclaimed a Gospel without name, though in fact it was based largely on *Luke*, and he rejected many of Paul's letters. His program was to eliminate discrepancies by insisting that Jesus was not Jewish but a spiritual being sent by the good God of the Bible, not the Creator God of *Genesis*. This wholesale reinterpretation of the historical Jesus succeeded because it solved the scriptural problem created by inconsistencies, and it stressed the independence of Christianity from Judaism, a public relations ploy that allowed the new faith to survive and prosper.[13]

Marcion's effort to efface the Jewishness of Jesus was prepared by Paul, who had already insisted that Jews and Gentiles were equal before God, and who had begun the movement to divinize Jesus. *John*, too, continued this trend by beginning with a paean to the divine

---

[11] Hans Jonas, *The Gnostic Religion* (Boston: Beacon Press, 1963), pp. 15–17.
[12] Dungan, *A History of the Synoptic Problem*, pp. 38 *ff.*
[13] Dungan, *A History of the Synoptic Problem*, chapter 5.

Word, which was then identified with Jesus, and then by affirming that the Word had simply become "flesh," not *Jewish* flesh.[14]

Marcion was rebuked by Tertullian, whose *Adversus Marcionem* is a mountainous defense of the physical reality of Jesus. Tertullian, however, retained Marcion's claim that Jesus was a divine spirit, the son of the good God. Jesus was a real person, with a real body, born of a real mother, but in all this, the Jewishness of Jesus was underplayed, as if it did not matter. In the late second century, another brilliant critic of Christianity, Celsus (second century), picked up where Marcion left off and delivered another violent attack against the Jewishness of Jesus. According to Origen (185–253), who wrote a book against his views, Celsus claimed,

> It is an absurd idea that the God of the universe would send a Savior to humanity through the Jewish race. If God...wanted to deliver the human race from evils, why on earth did he send his (divine) spirit into (such) a corner (as Judaea)?... Do you not think it is...ludicrous to make the Son of God to be sent to the *Jews*?[15]

Such attacks continued even after Christianity became the official religion of the Roman Empire, so much so that Augustine (354–430) was prompted to come out with his own concordance of the Gospels, *On the Harmony of the Evangelists* (400), precisely "because of those who falsely accuse the Evangelists of lacking agreement."[16] He wrote, besides, extensive commentaries on several books

---

[14] Christians generally take for granted that the word "flesh" (*sarx*) means body, human body. The Latin has "man" (*homo*). The meaning would be that the Word became human. But there are plenty of Gnostic influences in *John*, and for the Gnostics, "flesh" was bad. The Word becoming "flesh" would have meant a Fall, in a pejorative sense. It may be that this crucial passage of *John* 1:14 contains a subtle hint of anti-Semitism.

[15] Origen, *Contra Celsum* 6, 78, quoted in Dungan, *A History of the Synoptic Problem*, p. 54.

[16] Augustine, *Retractationes*, 42.

of the Hebrew Bible and the New Testament. Augustine's method of answering the criticisms was the one that Tatian had originally developed. It consisted in an effort to harmonize wherever possible, and through ingenious devices, to produce a coherent narrative that was, itself, the answer to the critics.

---

Matters appeared settled this way for a thousand years, until Erasmus (1469–1536) decided to publish an edition of the Gospels in Greek. This work appeared in 1516. It was based on the best Greek manuscripts Erasmus could find, but it soon became evident that the manuscripts used were not very old, mostly from the late Middle Ages, and that they contained a large number of inaccuracies, divergent readings, and lacunae. Two things happened: it became clear that no true understanding of the Gospels would be possible until the original Greek texts could be consulted, and therefore an intense search began for these elusive manuscripts. No originals have been discovered dating back to the first century. The second century has produced only a few fragments. Most manuscripts date from the third and subsequent centuries.

Today, after almost five hundred years of painstaking research, some agreements have emerged. In the German- and English-speaking world, priority of authorship is generally given to *Mark*. *Matthew* and *Luke* are taken to be elaborations of *Mark*, with additions from their respective traditions. They also appear to contain materials from an unidentified "sayings" Gospel termed *Q* (German *Quellen*, "source"). *John*, too, bears traces of another unknown source. French and Spanish scholars are less concerned about these matters and continue to discuss questions of divergence along the lines of the old "harmonies" pioneered by Tatian in his *Diatessaron*.

Of greater concern is the understanding of the effects the heated politics of the first three centuries had on the whole issue of the integrity of the Gospels. As indicated above, the public relations effort to disentangle the nascent sect from the Jewish revolutionaries who were battling the Romans led to an anti-Semitism that has pervaded all levels of Christian society. As a result of this, it is realistically impossible to know today with any kind of certainty what the original texts of the Gospels and the letters contained, since they may have been expurgated of most of their Jewish content. In addition, the Jewish gospels themselves (Ebionites, Nazoreans, Hebrews), or what has come down to us from them, bear the unmistakable stamp of the anti-Semitism of those who commented on them, usually to dismiss them. As a result, it is nearly impossible to ascertain what the first Jewish followers of Jesus really taught (and by implication, what Jesus himself believed), because their writings have been generally suppressed, lost, or altered in translation so as to eradicate their Jewishness. As Dungan remarks,

> The powerful anti-Jewish reaction that swept through western Christianity beginning in the mid-second century, [affected] many Christian practices including the copying of the Gospels. It is only in Tatian's *Diatessaron*, a few very early Greek papyri, and the Syriac and old Latin translations that we can still detect the faint, original Jewish echoes of many of Jesus's saying— turns of speech and specific teachings—that were modified in all later copies of the Gospels.[17]

One may entertain the hope that further studies of the development of Christianity in Syria and India may reveal more of the original faith of the first Jewish followers of Jesus. They were truly the heirs of his message. What we know today as Christianity, and what we have known for two thousand years, is the elaboration of the faith by Gentile theologians who disregarded the Jewishness of the Founder, of his family, and of his immediate followers.

---

[17] Dungan, *A History of the Synoptic Problem*, p. 43.

# A Historical Note

During the late Middle Ages, the Inquisition, under King Ferdinand's direction, sought to rid Spain of open heresy through the elimination of unconverted Jews, Judaizing *Conversos*, and anyone suspected of Judaizing acts or tendencies. After several years of persecution, torture, and endless imprisonments, the Jews were finally expelled. King Ferdinand signed the edict of expulsion on March 30, 1492. A remnant of over one hundred thousand Jews left Spain. Spain achieved religious unity, as the king intended, and as a corollary, it became free to develop a view of Jesus and a Christianity disconnected from Judaism.

Jews were also expelled from England (1290), from France (1306), from Flanders (1370), Cologne (1424), Strasbourg (1439), Erfurt (1458), and Nüremberg (1498), and thousands were periodically tortured and murdered under the most outrageous pretensions. For centuries, and nearly everywhere, they were subjected to what Durant calls "the deliberate degradation of an entire people, the merciless murder of the soul."[18] Eventually, centuries later, Hitler would seek to finish what King Ferdinand had begun by eliminating all the Jews of Europe. He did not succeed, even after the extermination of some seven million Jews. But from the perspective of history, the Inquisition and the Holocaust were but another effort to remove Jesus from his Jewish roots by destroying the race from which he had sprung. Marcion had merely eliminated the Jewish Scriptures; King Ferdinand and Hitler strove to obliterate the Jewish race so that no evidence of Jesus's racial origins would remain.

---

[18] Will Durant, *The Reformation* (New York: Simon & Schuster, 1957), p. 738.

CHAPTER

2

# The Life

## Preamble

It happens sometimes, and unexpectedly, that a person's facial expression, mannerism, tick, or sudden movement, discloses a resemblance to a parent; there is a revelation, as it were, of the physiognomy of the person's mother or father. This ephemeral disclosure, this fleeting glimpse of what the parent looks like, causes us to say, inwardly and to ourselves, "*That* is what his mother looks like!" "*That* is what her father looks like!" The experience is so quick, and the recognition so elusive, that it is there and it is gone in almost no time at all.

It is the same with the historical Jesus. The Gospels are records of the life of Jesus written by believers for believers. They are part recollection and part interpretive accounts, memories and musings, almost theological in their intention, and therefore one errs if one takes them solely as historical narratives of the events in Jesus's life. This is the reason scholars today maintain, almost unanimously, that we cannot recover through them "the historical Jesus." Albert Schweitzer (1926) had warned us of the impossibility of this quest nearly a century ago, but it has been hard for us to really accept this conclusion. In fact, thousands upon thousands of preachers still keep alive the illusion of historicity when they intone, Sunday after Sunday, the words "Jesus said" or "Jesus did," referring to the Gospel accounts. The only thing we are really empowered to say is that *tradition* has it that Jesus said or did such and such, or that we *believe* he did so and so. But old habits die hard, and I myself am sometimes guilty of this inaccuracy.

Still, in the middle of the twentieth century, scholars were able to make a distinction between what they called "life situations" (*Sitz im Leben*), narratives that seemed to capture a historical moment, and "gospel situations" (*Sitz im Evangelium*), statements that seemed to be later interpretations. Today, scholars like Marcus Borg distinguish between a "pre-Easter Jesus" and a "post-Easter Jesus," a distinction that reflects the earlier manner of speaking; they separate those narratives that seem to reflect a memory of historical events from those that are metaphorical interpretations of the same,[1] and while the distinction is valid, it is often difficult to decide which is which.

Along the same lines, it has become customary to emphasize that statements made by Jesus about himself, or statements made by others about Jesus, had probably a *functional* meaning at the time, even though we, especially after Nicaea, take them to have a *substantive* one. For example, Jesus's statement, "I am in the Father and the Father is in me" (*John* 14:10), would have meant for Jesus that his will was attuned to that of God and that he, therefore, behaved as God would have him behave; while for us, the statement conjures up an affirmation that Jesus knew himself to be the second person of the Trinity, a ludicrous and anachronistic idea, since Jesus, as a good Jew, would have been repulsed by such an interpretation. However, none of these distinctions, valid as they are, mean that we have captured the historical figure of Jesus.

Much less have we discovered the historical Jesus when we impute to him the theological and exegetical thoughts *we* have developed about him and his message over the past two thousand years. Many scholarly commentators, in their zeal to understand the historical Jesus, write as if Jesus had thought all kinds of complex and abstruse theological thoughts during his life. I think they do this when they are misguided by their belief that Jesus was God. Had Jesus been God, it would be plausible to affirm that he knew all this

---

[1]  Marcus J. Borg, *Jesus* (San Francisco, CA: HarperSanFrancisco, 2006), pp. 25 *ff.*

theological stuff before it was even invented by scholars in order to answer their own questions. But this would be far from historical. These elaborations could not have been wrought by the simple, if bright and intelligent Jew from First Century Palestine. One needs to be realistic about this. Jesus could no more have thought the answers to eschatological and scriptural problems than he could have developed the theory of quantum mechanics. We simply have to rein in our fantasies. He was an illiterate laborer, like most of his Jewish contemporaries, even though, like many of them, he had some expectations about the coming liberation of the people from the heavy yoke placed upon them by the Romans and their collaborators, and he expressed these expectations well enough to gather a following.

I should add that the study of the historical Jesus follows essentially the same criteria employed in the search of any historical figure. All biographers, whether of Socrates or Augustine, ask basically the same methodological questions: are there multiple attestations of the same data, are the sources reliable, is there coherence among the details of the life, are the historical facts (at least some of them) such that they might be embarrassing to the subject in question?[2] But even with the scrupulous application of these criteria, the most one can expect is an approximation to the historical figure, never complete accuracy, and never the full disclosure of the person. We cannot have this fullness even of people living right now, much less of those who lived hundreds of years ago. Therefore, as Meier explains, "the historical Jesus is not the real Jesus. The real Jesus is not the historical Jesus,"[3] since the totality of the person overflows the boundaries of historical facts.

And yet…

And yet there are instances when the barest glint of a historical moment may catch our eye in the accounts of events and the records of conversations supposedly held by Jesus.[4] There are ephem-

---

[2]  John P. Meier, *A Marginal Jew*, 3 vols. (New York: Doubleday, 1991–2001), vol. 1, p. 168.

[3]  Ibid., p. 21.

[4]  Marcus Borg, in *Jesus*, p. 304, puts it this way: "It is possible to glimpse at least a bit of the pre-Easter Jesus. What we can see is, at the minimum, interesting,

eral moments when we are compelled to say, "*This* is what must have happened," "*This* is what he must have said." There are not too many of these revelatory glimpses, but there are enough, and they occur often after years and years of impartial acquaintance with a text and protracted meditations upon it. Mary Magdalene's straightforward report that the corpse of Jesus had been removed from the tomb (*John* 20:2) is one such instance. What follows is construct, but her words are fact.

I have sought to explicate instances such as this momentary insight into the historical reality of Jesus and to retrieve them, or extricate them, from the mass of partisan interpretive allusions that envelop them in the text. The result is a bare-bones and incomplete picture of the Jesus who walked the land of Palestine two thousand years ago, a Jesus that still commands my allegiance because he was, after all, the incarnation of what God wants us all to be.

# The Life

While Rome was enjoying the Augustan Peace, an event took place in one of its provinces that would revolutionize the world: Jesus was born in the spring or early summer of the year 4 or 6, certainly before the death of Herod the Great, since Herod is specifically mentioned in the gospels as being alive. Then, again, it could have been in the year 12, according to calculations based on the appearance of Halley's Comet. At any rate, his birth would have taken place in the late spring of the year because pregnancies usually began in the fall after the harvests were in and there was enough money for a wedding feast.[5] The celebration of the birth on December 25 came about much later as an effort to counter the orgiastic festivities of the Roman Saturnalia, which were celebrated in late December. The commercialization of

---

and for many, of great value."

[5]  Of course, if Mary was pregnant as the result of a rape, all bets are off. See next note.

Christmas in recent years would seem to negate the very reason the celebration of Jesus's birth was moved to December.

The tradition that his birth marks the beginning of the so-called Christian (now Common) Era rests on an error made by Dionysius Exiguus in 1287 AUC (*ab urbe condita*, "from the founding of the City [of Rome]") (in 533 by our reckoning) when he calculated backward to 754 AUC the date of Jesus's birth: it should have been 750 or 748.

That Jesus existed is hardly questionable.[6] Josephus, the Jewish historian (37–95 CE), mentions him, and so do Roman historians Suetonius (60–140 CE), Pliny the Younger (*ca.* 62–113), and Tacitus (*ca.* 55–117). The earliest reference to him may be Paul's *First Letter to the Thessalonians*, generally dated around 49 or 51 CE. Noteworthy is the fact that already in it we find evidence of a theologizing foreign to the Jewish faith.

Tradition has it that Jesus was born in Bethlehem of Judea, but this is probably an effort to have Jesus be born in "the city of David," so as to connect him to the Davidic line, an important factor if he was to be deemed a messiah. Jesus was probably born in Nazareth, and he could have been born in the little town of Bethlehem in the Galilee, near Nazareth. His mother was Mary, and his putative father was Joseph, who seems to have had some apprehension about marrying Mary (to whom he was betrothed) because she was pregnant—and not by him. The basis for this assertion are the pertinent statements in *Matthew* and *Luke*, which may reflect an early tradition that after her betrothal to Joseph, Mary was raped by a Roman soldier named Panthera.[7] Since she was pregnant before marriage, Joseph had to

---

6   Bart D. Ehrman, *Did Jesus Exist?* (New York: HarperCollins, 2012).

7   See Origen, *Contra Celsum* I, 28 and *ff.* Other sources of the story, and analysis of the texts, in Jane Schaberg, *The Illegitimacy of Jesus* (San Francisco: Harper & Row, 1987), and James D. Tabor, *The Jesus Dynasty* (New York: Simon & Schuster, 2006), chapters 3 and 4. According to this tradition, Jesus would have been a *mamzer*, a Jew whose paternity is suspect. The evidence is persistent, though not absolutely convincing.

   The tradition of the "virginity" of Mary (that she did not conceive Jesus through intercourse, that her hymen was not broken at his birth, and that she had no other children after Jesus) may also have arisen as an effort to counter the accusation of illegitimacy. Some early apocryphal texts mention it; *v.gr.*,

exercise the option given him by the law, to either repudiate her or take her in as his wife. Reassured by an angel, he chose the latter. But the accusation of illegitimacy would be hurled at Jesus in envy or in spite as his fame grew,[8] and so his family may have countered with the claim that his birth, anyway, had been blessed by a holy spirit.[9]

Jesus probably grew up just as any other Jewish kid. Tradition has it that his father was a carpenter and that Jesus himself was one, though the Greek word *tekton* means simply "laborer." It is more likely, given the terrain and the scarcity of wood in Galilee, that he was a stonecutter or mason. The *Infancy Gospel of Thomas* and the *Infancy Gospel of James* contain many stories about Jesus's extraordinary powers, but also depict him as a willful and sassy child, difficult to manage and prone to get in trouble. Even the canonical gospel account of his staying back in the Temple unbeknownst to his parents after the Passover visit, records an unpleasant exchange with them more in line with the *Infancy Gospels* view than with the pious picture of later legend.

There were other brothers in the family, and their names are given as James, Joses, Judas, and Simon (*Mark* 6:3; *1 Corinthians* 9:5); and there is mention of sisters, though given the male chauvinism of the times, their names are not noted (*Mark* 6:3 and *Matthew*

---

the *Ascensio Isaiae* xi.7–9, the *Gospel of James* 19, 2, the *Odes of Solomon*, 19, and Clement of Alexandria reports a legend that, after Jesus's birth, Mary was found to be still a "virgin" (*Stromata* vii, 16). This erroneous belief happened when the Hebrew word *almâ* ("young woman") in *Isaiah* 7:14 was translated as *he parthenos* ("virgin") by the Septuagint and then as *"virgo"* by the Vulgate.

On the other hand, there is clear Docetist influence in this belief, and so it was countered strongly by Tertullian, Cyprian, and Origen. The belief has persisted till this very day despite strong scriptural evidence to the contrary.

It may have continued also because it supported the anti-Semitism that became so important to the nascent sect, as was explained above.

[8]  See *Mark* 6:3 (and *John* 8:41), which implies he was only Mary's son, not Joseph's.

[9]  In the Greek text, the article is indefinite. Therefore any translation as "the" Holy Spirit represents a theological bias and is not supported by the grammar. Moreover, the expression *"the* Holy Spirit," which is a clearly anachronistic reference to a Trinitarian doctrine, would have been totally baffling to Mary.

13:56).[10] Judas is probably the Judas "Thomas," twin brother[11] of Jesus or of another brother or sister, who is believed to have evangelized South India and is the presumed source of the *Gospel of Thomas* and, possibly, of the *Letter of Jude*. James is the future leader of the Jerusalem church, the likely author of the *Letter of James*, whose ossuary was claimed to have been discovered recently. Simon, sometimes called "the Pious," led the Jerusalem community after the death of James in 62 CE. Some scholars identify Joses (or Joseph) with Matthew, though this is much less certain, especially since the finding of an ossuary with his name on it in the Talpiyot Tomb in Jerusalem. The four brothers were members of the original Twelve Apostles.

It is impossible to say with any kind of reliability that Jesus was literate, that he knew how to read and write. The *Infancy Gospel of Thomas* describes a difficult relationship with a teacher, but such a story must probably be discounted as mere legend. On the other hand, the gospels narrate a couple of instances in which he read the Torah at the synagogue meeting (*Luke* 4:16–21), and also that once he wrote something in the dust at his feet that the pharisees could read and understand (*John* 8:1–11), though he may have just been doodling as a sign of his indifference to what the pharisees were trying to achieve. But given the overwhelming illiteracy of the people among whom he lived, it is hard to fathom how he would have come by these skills.[12]

---

[10] Tradition has it that the sisters were named Mary and Salome. See *Gospel of Philip* 59:6–11, *Protoevangelium of James* 19–20, and Epiphanius *Panarion* 78: 8–9. Together with their mother, Mary, they were present at the crucifixion of Jesus.

[11] *Thomas* means *twin* in Aramaic, as *didymos* means the same in Greek.

[12] I have translated *katagraphô* in John 8:6 and *graphô* in 8:8 as "doodling" on the strength of the fact that most Palestinian Jews at the time of Jesus were illiterate. Also, *katagraphô* can mean "making pictures" or "scratches," though it may also be used in the sense of "writing words." See Chris Keith, *The Pericope Adulterae, the Gospel of John, and the Literacy of Jesus* (Leiden: Brill, 2009), and Catherine Hezser, *Jewish Literacy in Roman Palestine* (Tübingen: Mohr Siebeck, 2001). For me, the fact that only 3 percent or so of ordinary Jews at the time of Jesus were literate weighs more than Keith's elaborate technical analysis, which anyway could not have been known to the author of the *pericope*.

As a young man, Jesus came to the River Jordan to be "baptized" by John the Baptizer (*Mark* 1:9), a fiery preacher who was urging the people to repent from their sins and turn their hearts to God. There were several other baptizing groups along the Jordan, and we do not know for sure why Jesus chose John. It may be because they were related somehow; Elizabeth, John's mother, was Mary's "kins-woman" (*Luke* 1:36), but at any rate, it was to John that he came. Jesus obviously considered himself a sinner, for he willingly underwent the cleansing rite. As he emerged from the waters of the Jordan, the Gospels describe an experience in which Jesus felt especially loved by God, and which may have had a profound effect on the rest of his life, though it is impossible to know how they came by this knowledge. That the oral tradition regarding this event was garbled may be seen by the fact that the Gospel narratives are at odds among themselves. *Luke* 3:22 has God address Jesus directly: "Today I have become your father"; Mark 1:13 also has God speak to Jesus: "You are my son in whom I am well pleased"; *Matthew* 3:17 has God address those present: "This is my son in whom I am well pleased." Given these discrepancies, it is clear that we may be dealing with a legend.

At some point, Jesus began to preach a new message, especially to the rich and prosperous in Galilee, and whether he carried this ministry for three years or for a little over one year, it is impossible to tell. The pity is that most of the records concern this very brief period in his life and do not detail how he lived his life as a young man, how he sought to incarnate God's humanness in the daily give-and-take with family, friends, neighbors, and customers. In other words, the years during which a person shapes his or her life, during which the foundation is laid for one's mature years, are a total blank for us. These were difficult years, with lots of political and military happenings all around, like the destruction of Sepphoris, just four miles away from Nazareth, in 4 BCE.[13] We would like to know what he thought during these years, what he meditated on, what he sang,

---

[13] John Dominic Crossan, *God and Empire* (San Francisco, CA: HarperSanFrancisco, 2007), pp. 109–110.

what he whistled, how he danced, how he entertained himself, what practical jokes he played on his brothers, his sisters, and his friends, what he did when he had a cold, who was the first girl he ogled, the first one he kissed, how he handled frustration, what wages he earned, did he have wet dreams, erections (all without sin), and so much more, all of which remains wholly unknown to us.

A major decision seems to have been to go up to Jerusalem to present his message to the authorities. Here he was embroiled in the bitter disputes among the various religious groups, Pharisees, Sadducees, adherents to what Josephus calls the Fourth Philosophy,[14] and Essenes. His message was not well received, though the real reasons for the rejection are not clear. He was accused of blasphemy, meaning, perhaps, that he claimed an authority against that of the priests, and that on this authority he challenged their male dominance, their male chauvinism, and the social reforms they and the Romans were imposing on the region.[15] He was condemned to death and crucified by the Romans, probably between the years 30 and 32. He died for his own particular version of what it meant to be a Jewish man. He was about thirty-eight years old when he died.

———— ✦ ————

For the Romans, crucifixion was a punishment reserved for the lower classes, slaves, and foreigners, never to be meted out to citizens, and while the Romans did not invent this form of execution, they refined the cruelty of its application with a sickening attention to detail.

There were many variations depending on place, custom, and the whim of the executioners. By the time of Jesus, the condemned man commonly carried the crossbar to the place of execution, not the entire cross (as Jesus is often depicted doing). Usually, the upright stake was permanently in place, and sometimes prisoners were affixed

---

[14] Josephus, *Antiquities*, 18, 3–9 *ff.*

[15] Richard A. Horsley and John S. Hanson, *Bandits, Prophets, and Messiahs* (San Francisco: Harper & Row, 1985), pp. 52–63.

to it alone, arms nailed or tied above the head. The upright sported a small wooden block (*sedile*) at the height of the buttocks for the prisoner to sit. This gave rise to one of the euphemisms for crucifixion, "to ride the cross" (*equitare crucem*). This block was not added out of humane considerations but in order to prolong the life of the prisoner and thereby lengthen the agony. The arms were affixed to the crossbar with ropes and/or nails through the wrists. The feet, too, were tied to the post and sometimes nailed, singly or upon one another.

Death occurred after several days, normally as the result of exposure and asphyxiation caused by the weight of the body depressing the lungs and cutting off the air supply. Prisoners sometimes tried to raise themselves on their nailed feet or on a footrest (*suppedaneum*) attached near the bottom of the upright, in order to be able to breathe, so their legs were often broken to render their efforts futile. Since crucifixion took place outside the city, the bodies were exposed to predators, dogs, vultures, and crows.

There is not a word in the Gospels about the shape of Jesus's cross. We do not know if it was *commissa*, the crossbar being placed on a V-shaped notch at the top of the upright, or *immissa*, with the crossbar fitted into a notch cut high up the upright. No Gospel account specifies whether Jesus was tied or nailed (or both) to the crossbar.[16] An early source of the passion narratives, the *Gospel of Peter* 6:1, mentions nails being removed from the hands as the corpse was taken down, but since the body could not have hung from the nailed hands alone (they would have been torn), the statement does not seem historical. The passages in *John* 20:27 and *Luke* 24:40 are late and seem to be constructed answers to doubts expressed (personified in the person of Thomas), rather than statements of fact.[17] A lot of the later Christian iconography comes from the legend of Saint

---

[16] See Raymond E. Brown, SS, *The Death of the Messiah*, 2 vols. (New York: Doubleday, 1994), vol. 2, § 40, #3, p. 949.

[17] See Raymond E. Brown, SS, *The Gospel According to John*, 2 vols. (Garden City, NY: Doubleday & Co., 1970), vol. 2, pp. 1031–1032. They are part, also, of a tendency of *John* to belittle Thomas, perhaps because his Gospel was seen as a competition.

Helena (*ca.* 248–328), the mother of the Emperor Constantine the Great, who, after her conversion in 313, supposedly sponsored the excavation of Jesus's cross in Jerusalem, where she also found three nails. From this legendary event, too, came the innumerable fragments or relics of "the true cross" that became so popular during the Middle Ages.[18]

—❖—

Obviously, Jesus did not die at thirty-three years of age. Before Christians took seriously the results of scholarly research, thousands of homilies were preached on the mystical significance of Jesus's age, which people assumed to be thirty-three. But there are no grounds for accepting this dating error.

Similarly, because many Christians took for granted that Jesus was divine, his death was invested with a significance beyond all measure, as if his torture and crucifixion had been exceptional in every respect. But according to Josephus, the Romans crucified some six thousand people in Palestine before the year 70 CE, though very few skeletons of crucified people have been actually found. Moreover, neither Jews nor Romans nor Jesus's own followers believed he was divine at the time of his death. We know this because of their own comments, and because we know that the belief in Jesus's divine sonship arose later, as a result of the evangelization of Hellenes and Romans who brought with them their own religious beliefs. For all of the immediate followers and the spectators at the crucifixion, Jesus was a marginal Jew who had become uppity and had preached a message that, if implemented, would have upset the *status quo* of the male Temple leadership. The crucifixion of Jesus was neither more nor less cruel than that of any other Jew who was put to death under Roman domination.

Nor was it worse than the execution of Socrates in 399 BCE, soberly narrated by Plato in his *Phaedo*. In fact, as executions go,

---

[18] See J. W. Drijvers, *Helena Augusta: The Mother of Constantine the Great and the Legend of Her Finding the True Cross* (Leiden: Brill, 1991).

the murder of Hypatia in 415, the young woman and Neoplatonist teacher at the Museum School in Alexandria, at the hands of a rabble of Christian monks, was excruciatingly more painful;[19] and the horrific martyrdom of al-Hallâj in 912 almost defies belief, such was its cruelty and savagery.[20] Christian pietism is understandable up to a point, but the unhistorical exaggerations born out of a stubborn refusal to broaden one's horizons is pretty much unforgivable.

---

The mystery of the Word made flesh is a mystery only because the theologians say so; Jesus, the Jew, was no mystery!

---

[19] Edward Gibbon, *The Decline and Fall of the Roman Empire* (Chicago: Encyclopaedia Britannica, 1952), chapter 47, volume II, p. 139.
[20] Louis Massignon, *The Passion of al-Hallâj*, 4 vols. (Princeton: Princeton University Press, 1982).

CHAPTER

3

# The Virgin Birth

It was at a meeting in Chicago in 1895, when Fundamentalism was created, that belief in the virgin birth of Jesus became one of the five "fundamentals" that all Christians should adhere to.

It should be stated right from the beginning that the earliest sources, the reconstructed *Signs Gospel*, the *Sayings Gospel Q*, the *Gospel of Thomas*, the *Gospel of Mark*, and the letters of Paul, say absolutely nothing about Jesus's birth, much less about a divine conception. Such claims appear only in the later gospels of *Matthew* and *Luke*. The *Gospel of John*, even though much later, also says nothing about Jesus's birth.

Roman Catholics believe that the virgin birth is affirmed in scripture and that it is a universally accepted tradition. This belief is not a defined dogma, but according to many, to deny it is heresy. The first passage of scripture alluded to in support of the belief is *Isaiah* 7:14, which is quoted in *Matthew* 1:23: "The Lord God himself will give you a sign: See, the young woman is pregnant and about to give birth to a son; she will give him the name Immanuel." The second text is from *Luke* 1:35. When Mary questions the angel's announcement that she will become pregnant, because she is not married, the angel replies, "A holy spirit will come upon you and the power of the Most High will cast its shadow on you; and for that reason the child to be born will be holy, and will be called son of God." When Joseph, who was engaged to Mary, considers breaking the engagement, an angel tells him not to do so because "a holy spirit is responsible for her pregnancy" (*Matthew* 1:20). On the basis of these texts it is affirmed that Mary conceived Jesus without having had intercourse with a man; that in giving birth to him, her hymen was not broken; and that she had no other children. In other words, conception and birth were miraculous.

I should add that virginal births were claimed in antiquity for many great figures.[1] Suetonius, for example, in his *The Twelve Caesars*, retells the story of the virginal conception of Augustus by his mother, Atia;[2] and in India, the conception of the Buddha by his mother, Queen Maya, is also believed to have been virginal. In India, too, Krishna was conceived virginally by his mother, Devakî.[3] In the Hebrew Bible, the births of Isaac (*Genesis* 21:1–2) and Samuel (*1 Samuel* 1:1–20) were described as the result of God's special intervention, but not as virginal. Moreover, by the time of the writing of *Luke* and *Matthew*, many Greeks and Romans had joined the new movement. To them, claiming a virginal birth for Jesus would have placed him in opposition to, and on at least the same level as, Augustus.[4]

In the Christian tradition, Zeno of Verona († 371) may have been the first to proclaim Mary's triple virginity: "O great mystery! The virgin Mary conceived without corruption, after conception brought forth as a virgin, and remained a virgin after giving birth."[5] These words disclose a major reason for the belief, namely, that sex "corrupts," an idea foreign to the Jews but widespread among the Gentile converts because of Gnosticism.

The Gospels themselves say that Mary had other children, both boys and girls, and the names of the boys are given, though not those of the girls (*Mark* 6:3 and *Matthew* 13:56), at least not directly. In

---

[1]  For a partial list, see Raymond E. Brown, *The Birth of the Messiah* (New York: Doubleday, 1993), pp. 522 *ff.*

[2]  Suetonius, *The Twelve Caesars*, "Augustus," 94.4.

[3]  See A. C. Bhaktivedanta Swami Prabhupâda, *KRISHNA, The Supreme Personality of Godhead* (London: The Bhaktivedanta Book Trust, 1986), chapter 2, p. 24.

[4]  John Dominic Crossan, *God and Empire* (San Francisco, CA: HarperSanFrancisco, 2007), p. 106.

[5]  Zeno of Verona, *Lib.* II, *tract.* 8, 2; M L 11, col. 414.

fact, Jesus may have had a twin brother, Judas Thomas (that is, "the twin," in Hebrew), who was sometimes called specifically "the Twin" (*didymos* in Greek), though it is not specified whose twin he was. Mary may have been pregnant before she got officially married to Joseph (though they were betrothed) because she was raped by a Roman soldier named Panthera.[6] Custom gave Joseph the choice of marrying her or breaking the engagement. Being reassured by the angel, he married her without further qualms.

The text from *Isaiah* that is adduced as proof of virginal conception does not refer to Mary at all. To begin with, the Hebrew word ‹almâ means only "young woman." If a virgin were meant, the word used would have been *bìtûlâ*. The confusion may have originated when the Septuagint translated ‹almâ as *he parthénos*, which the Vulgate later translated as *virgo*. In the Greek of the second century BCE, *he parthénos* meant "young woman," not necessarily "virgin." Two hundred years later, the Vulgate translated it more literally as "virgin."[7] Moreover, Christian commentators took the words in *Isaiah* to be a prophecy of the virginal birth of Jesus, without really understanding that Isaiah was giving a sign to Ahaz, a prophecy that would be fulfilled within a short period of time. Early commentators ignored this fact and took the text out of context. They could only countenance a prophecy about the birth of Jesus. Tertullian, for example, wrote about this text:

> Now, a sign from God would not have been
> a sign unless it had been some novel and prodi-
> gious thing. Then, again, Jewish cavilers, in order
> to disconcert us, boldly pretend that Scripture

---

6  See Origen, *Contra Celsum* I, 28 and *ff.* Other sources of the story, and analysis of the texts, in Jane Schaberg, *The Illegitimacy of Jesus* (San Francisco: Harper & Row, 1987). This is an ancient tradition, though the evidence appears slim to many scholars yet convincing to others.

7  Such confusions were not rare. When St. Augustine commented on the *Genesis* story of the creation of Eve, he read that God infused an *ecstasy* in Adam. "Ecstasy" was one term for sleep common at the time of the Septuagint translation. Still, he understood it to mean simply "sleep."

does not hold that a virgin, but only a young maiden, is to conceive and bring forth. They are, however, refuted by this consideration, that nothing of the nature of a sign can possibly come out of what is a daily occurrence, the pregnancy and child-bearing of a young woman. But a virgin mother is justly deemed to be proposed by God as a sign.[8]

Tertullian did not take into account that the very fact that Isaiah knew the young woman was pregnant would have been a sign in itself. Ibn Ezra, followed by Rashi, identifies the "young woman" as the Prophet's wife, and Immanuel as his second son.

Some early apocryphal texts mention a virginal conception and birth. The *Ascensio Isaiae* xi.7–9 says: "After two months of days, while Joseph was alone in the house with Mary, his wife, it came to pass that, when they were alone, Mary looked in front of her eyes and saw a small babe, and she was dazed. And after that, her womb was found as formerly before she had conceived." St. Ignatius of Antioch, in *Ephesians* 19, and with obvious Gnostic reference, writes that "hidden from the prince of this world were the virginity of Mary and her child-bearing." Justin Martyr, in his *Dialogus cum Tryphoeo*, 66, comments, "Of all the carnal descendants of Abraham no one was ever born of a virgin, or even claimed to be so born, except Christ." The *Gospel of James* 19, 2, in direct reference to the text of *Isaiah*, says, "A new sight have I to tell you: a virgin has brought forth, which her nature allowed not." So also the *Odes of Solomon*, 19, and Clement of Alexandria reports a legend that, after Jesus's birth, Mary was found to be still a "virgin."[9] But all these texts originated in traditions where the Hebrew Bible was known only in a Greek translation, where the

---

[8] Tertullian, *Adv. Marcion.* III, 13, 3–5. Using the Hebrew Bible as a precursor of the New Testament, claiming that the prophets had spoken about Jesus; that is, using the past to serve the interpretation of the present was a common trend among writers of the period. See Doron Mendels, *The Rise and Fall of Jewish Nationalism*, p. 45.
[9] Clement of Alexandria, *Stromata* vii, 16.

authors did not know Hebrew, and where they were Gentile converts to Christianity.

The belief that Mary's conception was virginal, and that the birth of Jesus did not break her hymen, suited perfectly the new interpretation of the reality of Jesus that was being spread among the Gentiles in the later decades of the first century. If Jesus was divine, the son of God, it was no wonder that he had been conceived miraculously and that his birth, too, had been extraordinary. Also, this was a neat way to "prove" that Jesus was not Jewish: he had simply appeared in front of Mary as any God would do. As the tradition grew, the Greek texts concerned with conception and birth were misinterpreted, especially because Latin lent itself to the mistranslations, since it has no articles at all. For example, the angel's words to Mary in *Luke* 1:35, which in the Greek text read, "*A* holy spirit will come upon you," were mistranslated to say, "*The* Holy Spirit will come upon you," implying that the Holy Ghost, the third person of the Trinity, would be the impregnating agent. In Greek, however, the phrase is clearly indefinite; to translate it as "the" is due to the translator's bias. It is surely remarkable that such an error in translation is still being perpetrated. Moreover, Mary would have been dumbfounded by any reference to the Trinity, however veiled.

It happened, also, that the symbolism of a neuter spirit (*pneuma* is neuter in Greek) impregnating a woman, Mary, superseded the Hebrew/Aramaic *ruâh*, which is feminine, thus obviating the difficulty posed later in the *Gospel of Philip* 55:24–25: "Some say the Holy Spirit inseminated Mary. They are wrong and do not know what they are saying. When did a woman ever get a woman pregnant?"

But the belief in the virginal conception and birth ran into an unexpected obstacle. The Docetists and other Gnostics began to use it as proof that Jesus did not have a real physical body, but only an apparent one. If he was divine, they argued, it would not make sense for him to assume a human, physical body, since the physical and the material are evil. If Jesus "looked" human, it was because, in fact, he had an "apparent" body (Greek *dokeô*, "to appear, to seem"). Consequently, the body that died on the cross was an apparition, a phantasm, a ghost. God-Jesus did not die on the cross, since this crucified body was not Jesus, and God cannot die anyway. Therefore, God entered Mary's womb and came out of her without damaging her hymen; this happened "as water runs through a pipe."[10] As far as the crucifixion is concerned, the resurrected Jesus tells his brother, James, "I am the one who was in me. Never have I experienced any kind of suffering."[11]

Tertullian could not stomach this. The physical, human reality of Jesus was being compromised, and he could not tolerate it. Therefore he denied that Mary had remained a virgin at the birth of Jesus: "She was a virgin as regards the [abstinence] from a husband, not as regards the bearing of a child."[12] Against the Valentinians, he argued that the very objective of the incarnation had been to take on human flesh:

> Otherwise, why did the spirit of God descend into a woman's womb at all...? For God could have become spiritual flesh without such a process; indeed, he could have done so much more simply outside the womb than inside it. He had then no reason for enclosing himself within one if he was to take nothing from it. However, he did not descend into a womb without a reason. Therefore he received flesh from it; for else, if he received nothing from it, his descent into it would have been without reason.[13]

Accordingly, Jesus's was no painless birth, nor was Mary spared the dolor of parturition: "According to the laws of corporeal substances... after ten months of torture...shaken suddenly by pain...he was pushed out."[14] Mary's hymen was torn, not on her wedding night (as is the nor-

---

[10]  Irenaeus, *Adversus Haer.* I, 7, 2.

[11]  *First Apocryphon of James* V, 31, 15–20, in Robinson, ed., *The Nag Hammadi Library*, p. 245.

[12]  Tertullian, *De Carne Christi* XXIII, 2.

[13]  Tertullian, *De Carne Christi* XIX, 5.

[14]  Tertullian, *Adv. Marcionem* IV, 21, 11.

mal case), but upon the birth of her son. "She became a wife," Tertullian says, "when she brought forth her son" (*in partu suo nupsit*).[15] Many other writers of the times, Irenaeus and Origen among them, sided with Tertullian in order to safeguard the truth of the physical humanity of Jesus. Ephraem the Syrian, for example, wrote, "Glorious and hidden was his entering, vile and visible his coming forth, for he was God in going in, and man in coming forth."[16] And again, very graphically: "Who will not marvel at the glorious mother crouching to give birth… in everything equal to every other mother?"[17]

When the Docetist threat passed, the belief in the virgin birth returned, and it still holds among Roman Catholics, Evangelicals, and Fundamentalists. In many Protestant denominations, the tradition of Jesus's virginal conception and of a birth that left Mary intact is interpreted metaphorically.

---

It should be added that belief in the virginal conception and birth of Jesus has made Christians neglect the real family of Jesus and the contributions the members made to the Christian cause. The four brothers of Jesus, James, Joses, Judas (the "twin"), and Simon, are numbered among the Twelve Apostles. The two sisters, Mary and Salome, were present at the crucifixion with their mother, Mary. James "the Just," Jesus's brother, succeeded him in the leadership of the Jerusalem community. His letter is included in the Christian Bible. Simon, another brother, succeeded James when he was executed in 62 CE. In other words, the entire family continued the traditions started by Jesus, kept his message alive, preached it, defended it even unto death, and passed it on to future generations. All this

---

[15]  Tertullian, *De Carne Christi* 23, 3.
[16]  St. Ephraem the Syrian, *Hymn. De Nativitate Christi in carne*, I, 22.
[17]  St. Ephraem the Syrian, *Hymn. De Beata Maria*, V, 4.

history, and much more, was lost because of an insistence on the unhistorical claim of the triple virginity of Mary.

———— ✻ ————

Quite a few years ago, Mitterer[18] tentatively asked for a rethinking of this whole issue in light of modern biology. He made the following points:

> The Fathers and the Scholastics interpreted Mary's perpetual virginity as involving a miraculous process of birth, because they considered that the integrity of the hymen constituted an element in physical virginity. This reason does not seem valid: on the one hand, the hymen may be broken by a mere accident; and on the other hand, there have been cases of sexual relations where the hymen has remained intact. An unbroken hymen, then, is not an element but only a sign, and a doubtful one at that, of physical virginity. This consists in absence of sexual intercourse and absence of the male seed. At the same time, the full concept of physical motherhood seems to require the active, muscular co-operation of the mother in the bringing forth of her child. The conclusion may be drawn from these observations that the miraculous process of birth with the consequent preservation of the hymen is not required for Mary's virginity and seems in fact to be opposed to her genuine and complete motherhood.[19]

---

[18]  A. Mitterer, *Dogma und Biologie der heiligen Familie nach dem Welt bild des h. Thomas von Aquin und dem Gegenwart* (Wien, 1952).

[19]  Summary by C. Davis, in *Clergy Review* (London), 41 (1956), pp. 545–546 and 701–703. See also W. Dettloff, OFM, "Virgo-Mater: Kirchenväter und moderne Biologie zur jungfraülichen Mutterschaft Mariens," *Wissenschaft und Weisheit* (Düsseldorf) 20 (1957), pp. 221–226.

He should have added the misreadings of the pertinent texts as primary culprits for the erroneous belief.

This is a valiant attempt to reinterpret the tradition, but there is more. At the time that the legend of the virgin birth was born, the existence of the female egg was unknown. The fetus, it was thought, came solely from the male, and the woman was merely a receptacle for the man's seed and a nurturing environment until it germinated. In the ancient non-Christian examples of virgin birth, the male god sexually intruded into the woman's womb and deposited there the seed of the future hero.

All this was overturned by the scientific discovery of the female egg in the early years of the nineteenth century. After this discovery, to claim a virginal conception would entail the supposition of some kind of divine semen that would have been united with Mary's egg in her womb in order to produce a fetus—in other words, some kind of artificial insemination divinely performed; if this were not the case, Jesus could not be said to have a real *human* body, nor could he be proclaimed "born of the virgin Mary," as the Nicene Creed has it. Proponents of the virgin birth continue to ignore such bizarre implications of their belief.

The conclusion is very clear. If the legend of the virginity of Mary, as traditionally retold, is not required for Christian belief (as Mitterer asserts), and if it is based on unlettered understandings of conception and birth, then the way is open for a symbolic interpretation of the tradition, as many believe today. More to the point, we should ask why such a view was proposed in the first place, by whom, and for what reasons. Answers to these questions might get us closer to a real understanding of Jesus's birth, life, and death.

———— ❊ ————

According to the Gospel of Luke, Mary *chose* to conceive Jesus out of wedlock (*Luke* 1:34-38), a proposition made by a visiting angel. It was only later that Joseph agreed to marry her. Many contemporary Christians who believe this, refuse to acknowledge a similar right to choose for women who decide to have an abortion.

CHAPTER

4

# Resurrection

One of the articles of faith of the Fundamentalists and of Christians generally is the belief in the physical resurrection of Jesus. In fact, the Nicene Creed intones convincingly that Jesus "rose from the dead on the third day." Even though it is more accurate, theologically, to say that God raised Jesus from the dead, these are the words of the Creed. Most of the statements in the gospels and the letters regarding the resurrection insist that he *was raised* (by God) rather than that *he rose*, but linguistic niceties are often ignored in translations and commentaries.

The question is, of course, what can all this mean? Did Jesus actually return to physical life, the physical life that we are leading right now? When the women reported that the corpse was not in the tomb, the story was deemed "foolish" (*Luke* 24:11). Mary Magdalene only reported that the body had been taken away, which was a reasonable assumption when they did not find it (*John* 20:2). The disciples on the way to Emmaus explained that some people claimed the tomb had been found empty (*Luke* 24:23), and this is about all that can be ascertained from a historical point of view. This "empty tomb" has been offered as proof that Jesus did rise physically, since his body was not found in the tomb, and it has never been found; and the Shroud of Turin has long been known to be a clever if pious hoax (though some are trying to revive interest in it); and the Talpyot tomb, right now, only holds interesting possibilities; but these are conclusions and interpretations.

To explain the disappearance of the corpse, a few have claimed that Jesus's body was taken out of the tomb "at night" by Joseph of Arimathea and Nicodemus, but the evidence is nonexistent, really, and it is based on a misreading of the text.[1] The corpse could have been legitimately transferred to a "family tomb," but the evidence is meager, though this point has not been researched thoroughly.[2] Moreover, it has been claimed that Jesus appeared to many of his followers who conversed with him and actually, as his brother Thomas did, touched him; but, these stories are clearly "invented" to prove a point, and the apparitions did not convince all those present; so, again, one must inquire into the meaning of all of this, for therein lies much of the mystery of Christianity.

At the time of the death of Jesus, and for centuries before and after, Jews, Greeks, and Romans believed that after death, any departed soul could appear to the living and be recognized and even hold converse with them, but none of those dead souls would have been thought to be "real" in the same way as we all are real right now. According to Crossan, the ancient world "was filled with gods, goddesses, and spirits who assumed divergent shapes and figures, who assumed and changed bodies as we assume clothes and change styles."[3] When Jesus died, the souls of many dead people appeared to many citizens of Jerusalem (*Matthew* 27:52–53), and when Jesus showed himself to several of the disciples, they thought they were seeing a ghost (*Luke* 24:37). According to the *Sophia of Jesus Christ* 90.14–92.6, "the Savior appeared [to them], not in his previous form, but in the invisible spirit." And going back several centuries, everyone knew that Saul had tricked a witch into conjuring up the ghost of the dead prophet Samuel and had held converse with him

---

[1]  Michael Baigent, *The Jesus Papers* (San Francisco: HarperSanFrancisco, 2006).

[2]  James D. Tabor, *The Jesus Dynasty* (New York: Simon & Schuster, 2006), *passim*. The discovery in 1980 of a family tomb containing ossuaries purporting to be those of Jesus, his mother Mary, Mary of Magdala, and other family members, must wait for thorough DNA analysis and other authentication.

[3]  John Dominic Crossan, *The Birth of Christianity* (San Francisco, CA: HarperSanFrancisco, 1998), p. 37. See Geza Vermes, *The Resurrection* (New York: Doubleday, 2008), chapter 2.

in order to ascertain from him the future of his kingship (*1 Samuel* 28:14).

Moreover, the story of a messiah who will rise from the dead after three days existed already before Jesus, and is attested in a tablet dating to the late first century BCE and found in Jordan, near the Dead Sea, in the last decade of the twentieth century. This story may refer to a certain Simon, a servant of Herod who claimed kingship after the death of Herod in 4 BCE, and who led an uprising. He was beheaded by the Romans under Gratus.[4] His followers may have developed the story about his future rising from the dead in order to maintain his influence. Therefore, the motif of a messiah who is to undergo suffering, death, and resurrection, existed before Jesus; it was not first invented in reference to Jesus, but may have been applied to him by followers acquainted with this tradition.

Further, ancient literatures abound in examples of such apparitions. Slain Patroklos appeared to his friend Achilles;[5] Odysseus, upon his visit to the underworld, beheld the ghost of his own dead mother (of whose demise he had not been informed) as well as the souls of many of his comrades-at-arms; and he even held converse with long-dead Tiresias, whose guidance he sought in the matter of his return to Ithaca.[6] Aeneas, too, when he in turn visited the underworld, encountered the souls of his father, Anchises, of many of his soldiers who had perished in battle, and of Dido, the Queen of Carthage, "still fresh from her [self-inflicted] wound," whom he had betrayed in his haste to get to Italy, and who, despite his entreaties, refused to speak to him.[7]

The ghost of the murdered Caesar appeared to Brutus, his assassin, twice, shortly after his death and later before the battle of Philippi.[8] Scipio the Elder appeared to his grandson, but none of these people who were favored with visions of the dead would have

---

[4]   Josephus, *Antiquities* 17. 273–276.
[5]   *Iliad*, XXIII. 60.
[6]   *Odyssey* XI.
[7]   Virgil, *Aeneid*, Book VI.
[8]   Plutarch, *The Lives of the Noble Grecians and Romans*, "Brutus."

claimed that these were *alive!*[9] On the other hand, such apparitions were not pathological incidents, nor were they delusions or hallucinations, all of which can be readily identified for what they are when they occur. Also, they were not considered extraordinary, since pretty much anybody could have them. In the cultures in which they occurred, such visions were taken for granted. Not that they happened daily or at whim, but that they might occur in specific circumstances and for good reason.

In the culture of the Native Americans, this too was the case, especially during the time of the "vision quest," the search for the meaning of the young person's life, which was the duty of every young male.

It may be that, in the case of Jesus, his soul or ghost was seen by many, but those who saw him thus, regular Jews that they were, would not have claimed that Jesus was physically back with them. Assuming, *arguendo*, that Jesus's encounter with his brother Thomas (*John* 20:24–29), who doubted anyone had seen his brother's ghost, did, in fact, take place, this may have been more a matter of identification, of ascertaining that the apparition was *of Jesus*, than of physical proof of resurrection. After all, many people did not recognize Jesus when he appeared to them, so there must have been some cause for doubt. Since he was Jesus's brother, Thomas may have been reluctant to acknowledge that his own brother's ghost had been seen by so many, and wanted to make sure by inspecting the remnants of the torture on the ghostly body of Jesus. In fact, the disciples considered these sightings so ordinary that they went back to work plying their trades (*John* 21, *Gospel of Peter* 14:2–3). But, as I said above, this incident may have been simply a concoction of *John* to put down Thomas, whose *Gospel* was a competitor.

This is one reason the discovery of a tomb and an ossuary supposedly containing traces of the remains of Jesus, if ascertained, would not undermine Christianity at all, because although popularly misunderstood, the resurrection does not entail the physical, bodily, rising of Jesus (as the Fundamentalists claim), but only a *real* one, such as may

---

[9]  Geza Vermes, *The Resurrection* (New York: Doubleday, 2008), p. 16.

have been experienced by his followers. It may be salutary to ponder that Buddhism, Jainism, Confucianism, and Judaism, faiths that are older than Christianity by some six hundred years at least, all thrive still, yet none believe that their founders rose from the dead!

But from the more or less common experience had by the disciples, the ghost of Jesus was hypostatized, turned into a real, substantial thing like any other in the world. Apparition was turned into bodily reality, and the myth of the physical resurrection of Jesus was born. All this is important because emphasis on the physical resurrection of Jesus, emphasis on the miracle, on the extraordinary event as *super*natural, has clouded the deeper meaning of the rising of Jesus and has helped many shirk the responsibilities that would come with his resurrection; because the real thing about the resurrection of Jesus is not whether or not he is in heaven, but whether or not he has been reborn in us, raised again in our hearts and, more importantly, in our lives. It is so easy to be sidetracked by miraculous events and miss the really crucial happening that may be about to take place in our lives.

---

In one of his sermons, John Donne said the following about Paul's conversion experience: "*Saul* was struck blind, but it was a blindness contracted from light; it was a light that struck him blind… That powerful light felled *Saul*; but after he was fallen, his own sight was restored to him again."[10] But note that even though Paul was actually struck down by light, his experience was primarily auditory: he *heard* Jesus's voice, but for some reason, people tend to fix on the light rather than on the words. True, in his letters, Paul says that he *saw* Jesus (*ôphthê kamoi* "was seen by me"; *eôraka* "I saw"), but this visionary mode may be a conflation of the hearing and the vision of light. At any rate, in the three speeches he made, as narrated in *Acts*, he speaks only of *hearing* (*ekousen phônen, ekousa phônen*).

---

[10] John Donne, St. Paul's. Christmas Day in the Evening. 1624; in *The Complete Poetry and Selected Prose of John Donne*, ed. Charles M. Coffin (New York: Random House, 1952), pp. 500–502.

Two thousand years before Donne, Plato had explained that one can be blinded, or fail to see, because there is no light at all, or because there is a superabundance of light, as happens when we walk from a dark room into the brilliant light of the sun.[11] Perhaps more pertinently, St. Gregory of Nyssa explains in reference to Moses's experience that what is apprehended in the light is that God's divine nature is invisible, that is, a darkness; we have, therefore (he says) "a resplendent darkness";[12] but this interpretation is irrelevant in the case of Paul, because what really mattered to him was the *implication* of the dialogue he had with Jesus—*that Jesus was alive!*—not the blinding light. Paul's conclusion from his brief dialogue with Jesus was the significant thing, and this would be true whether he saw Jesus or only conversed with him.

Paul came by his own experience of light on his way to Damascus, and this experience was much more a mystical blinding than we are usually wont to admit. Luke, the presumed author of *Acts*, makes this very clear in his narrative about Paul's imprisonment under Governor Felix. As Paul tells the story, he had returned from Damascus to Jerusalem and was visiting the Temple in order to pray, when he fell into a trance (an *ecstasy*, according to the Greek text!), which would seem to indicate that Paul was in the grip of some mystical experience. He was apprehended in the Temple, and later on, he was brought into the presence of the new governor, Festus, and of King Agrippa and his wife, Bernice. Paul narrates to them in great detail the story of his experience on the way to Damascus, and as he was doing so, Festus suddenly stood up and shouted, "Paul, you are raving. Too much study is driving you mad!"[13] Paul remonstrates and, turning to King Agrippa, who was Jewish, asks him, "Do you believe in the prophets?" In other words, Paul places his "madness" on a par with the ecstatic trances of the Prophets. In fact, the whole episode is clothed in language reminiscent of the *mania* of the maenads in Euripides's *The Bacchae*. Festus exclaims, *"Mainê, Paule!"*

---

[11]  Plato, *Republic* VII. 518A.

[12]  St. Gregory of Nyssa, *Vita Moysi*; MG 44, 377A.

[13]  *Acts* 26:24.

(You are mad, Paul), and Paul replies using the same language, "*Ou mainomai*" (No, I'm not mad). This is not a fortuitous use of language: Luke employs words that appeared in *The Bacchae*. When Dionysus escaped from the jail to which Pentheus had confined him, he advised the king "not to kick against the pricks," because "you are a mortal, he is a god."[14] These are the very words Jesus addresses to Paul: "It is hard for you, this kicking against the pricks."[15] As Wilson writes, "The mania into which Paul has been led, Luke wishes to suggest, is precisely comparable to that mania which took possession of the initiates into a mystery. Just like Pentheus confronted by a god-man, Paul could not kick against the pricks. Henceforth, he is possessed."[16]

By recalling the ecstatic experiences of the Prophets, Paul places himself within their orbit of influence. Divested of their fireworks, those are experiences of union with the divine, pure, and simple, with the *mysterium tremendum*. Plotinus will write later that "we ought not to say that the seer will *see*, but he will *be* that which he sees, if indeed it be possible any longer to distinguish seer and seen, and not boldly to affirm that the two are one."[17] This is precisely the reaction of Paul to his encounter with Jesus.

Paul spoke with Jesus. Furthermore, on his way to Damascus, he experienced Jesus as identified with the people he, Paul, was persecuting; that is, he experienced Jesus as somehow *alive*, and he says this clearly to the Galatians (to whom he is writing), referring explicitly to the Damascus experience: God "chose to reveal his Son to me."[18] Further on, in the same letter, he exclaims, "The life I now live is not my life, but the life Christ lives in me,"[19] for which fact, of course, Christ must be somewhat alive. This identification experi-

---

[14] Euripides, *The Bacchae*, line 796.
[15] *Acts* 26:14.
[16] A. N. Wilson, *Paul: The Mind of the Apostle* (London: W. W. Norton & Co., 1997), p. 76.
[17] Plotinus, *Ennead* VI, 9, 7 (Dean Inge's translation).
[18] *Galatians* 1:16. The revelation can be both auditory and/or visual.
[19] *Galatians* 2:20. See Claude Tresmontant, *Saint Paul and the Mystery of Christ* (New York: Harper & Brothers, 1962), p. 41.

ence becomes, then, the way to follow Jesus, that is, *as mystically one with him*. As he tells the Philippians, "Have *the same mind* that was in Christ Jesus."[20]

Gerard Manley Hopkins gives voice to Paul's mystical hearing in a poem equally suffused with mystical insight:

> Í say more: the just man justices;
> Keeps gráce: thát keeps all his goings graces;
> Acts in God's eye what in God's eye he is—
> Chríst. For Christ plays in ten thousand places
> Lovely in limbs, and lovely in eyes not his
> To the Father through the features of men's faces.[21]

If Christians are *deified* by the grace of the Father, *spiritualized* by the action of the Spirit, then they are likewise *Christified* by their existence "in Christ." Thus, St. Athanasius can claim, "I have become flesh of the Word"[22] and Gregory of Nazianzus can state that "purification renders us divine,"[23] so that "once in this state, God may deal with us more familiarly, as with relatives, united and known to us as God to 'gods' (if the expression be not too daring!)."[24] The various expressions Paul uses throughout his letters have this mystical union as background. Although he heard the voice of Jesus, after the mystical experience, he identified Jesus as the Christ, and this is the term Paul uses consistently. Believing in Christ, as John Herman Randall Jr., writes, is "an intensely personal and practical religious experience. Believing in Christ is no mere intellectual assent, and

---

[20] *Philippians* 2:5; emphasis added.
[21] Gerard Manley Hopkins, "As Kingfishers Catch Fire," in *Hopkins: Poems and Prose* (New York: Knopf, 1995), p. 18.
[22] *"Tou Logou gegona sarx"*: Athanasius, *Contra Arian.* III, 34; MG 26,396.
[23] *"Theoeideis."*
[24] *"theos theois enoumenos"*: Gregory of Nazianzus *Orat.* 38,7.

acceptance; it is utter absorption."[25] But in consequence, the Jesus of history gives way to the Christ of faith, and Paul does not give us any significant information about Jesus's life, even though he had met Peter and James (the brother of Jesus). Unwittingly, Paul becomes one of the first to neglect/deny the Jewishness of Jesus, which is one of the things that made his letters appeal to Marcion.

Paul spent years elaborating this view. The framework of the redemptive system he proposed and preached parallels those of many mystery cults, where the pattern is one of descent and ascent, death and resurrection. As Randall writes, "The means of salvation for Paul is a personal, mystical 'union in faith.'"[26] This slant toward the mystical and away from the historical, allowed the later interpretations of the Gnostics to take a foothold within the burgeoning Christian community, and even to create an obstacle that had to be overcome by the refinements of the Councils.

———— ❧ ————

On his way to Damascus, bathed in a coruscating light, Paul hears the words uttered to him by Jesus, a Jesus who he knows was put to death by the Roman soldiers at the instigation of the Sanhedrin about three or four years before. Jesus, therefore, he reasonably concludes, must be somewhat alive, at least spiritually, or mystically. This Jesus becomes for Paul "Christ," to whom he insistently refers in his authentic letters. From then on, Paul is going to lead a life in which he sees himself similarly identified with the risen Christ, the resurrected Christ, but this identification is with a *mystically risen Christ*, not with a physically resurrected Jesus. After Damascus, Paul chooses to live at the level of the mystical, not the level of the physical.[27] His insistence that Jesus has, indeed, risen, cannot be taken to mean that Jesus has risen *physically*, since this is not how Paul

---

[25] John Herman Randall, Jr., *Hellenistic Ways of Deliverance and the Making of the Christian Synthesis* (New York: Columbia University Press, 1970), p. 148.

[26] J. H. Randall, *Hellenistic Ways*, p. 155.

[27] Wendy Doniger O'Flaherty, "Inside and Outside the Mouth of God: the Boundary between Myth and Reality," *Daedalus* 109, No. 2 (1980), p. 97.

has actually experienced him: he never *saw* Jesus or met him "in the flesh." Writing to the Corinthians around 56–57 CE, Paul details what he is preaching as the traditional message (*kêrygma*) that he had received, and he includes the reports that Jesus had been raised, or resurrected, but he does not specify whether or not this resurrection is physical or involves the body.[28] Paul's continuous advice that we must have in ourselves the *mind* of Jesus, translates *his own mind* in which he heard mystically the words of Jesus mystically resurrected. The entire context of Paul's almost obsessive talk of resurrection is mystical, not physical, but it was later interpreted as the latter by people who had not experienced the former and who chose to live at the level of the physical, or to encounter Jesus as Christ at this level. For them, therefore, there *is* a question of the physical resurrection of Jesus such as did not occur to Paul. Nowhere in his writings does Paul claim that Jesus was physically resurrected: this is not the reality in which he lives the life of Christ. But for most of his followers through the centuries, this has been the reality in which the Christ has been believed to have been resurrected, a physical reality; therefore, the issue of the physical resurrection of Jesus has continued to agitate the minds of believers to the present day.

Two observations. To some extent, the physical resurrection of Jesus becomes a matter of *belief*, since there is no empirical evidence of Jesus's corpse, although some intriguing sarcophagus has been discovered in the Talpyiot tomb in Jerusalem. Christians, therefore, can in good conscience believe that Jesus was raised bodily from the dead because no physical evidence exists to the contrary. But this, in a sense, makes it easier for Christians to go on living their ordinary and often sinful lives without any change in their "minds," contrary to what Paul asked the Philippians to do. That Jesus was raised meant something different for Paul. Christ's life lived in him *mystically*, and that was the only way he could countenance the resurrection of Jesus. This means his entire life had to change, because the resurrection of Jesus was for him a mystical *fact*. The mystical

---

[28] Joseph A. Fitzmeyer, SJ, *First Corinthians* (New Haven, CT: The Anchor Yale Bible, 2008), p. 547, on *1 Corinthians* 15:3–10.

reality he had experienced imposed on him a different kind of obligation to change and to

> Act in God's eye what in God's eye he was—
> Christ. For Christ plays in ten thousand places
> Lovely in limbs, and lovely in eyes not his
> To the Father through the features of men's faces,

as Hopkins wrote. This mystical realm in which Paul heard Jesus speak had harsher requirements than the belief in a physical resurrection. And this is the reason the belief in the physical resurrection of Jesus has been the predominant mode in which to understand the resurrection: *it is easier to just believe that Jesus was raised physically than to live mystically conjoined to him by the power of the mystical experience,* as Paul did from then on. The martyrs of Lyons (*ca.* 177) knew this when they saw Jesus in their dying sister Blandina.[29] Saint Augustine knew this, and so did Saint Francis Xavier. Saint Francis of Assisi knew this, too, and so did Martin Luther. Saint Thomas Aquinas knew this when the mystical light overpowered him toward the end of his life so that he could write no more, and Saint Teresa of Ávila was impelled by this knowledge to peregrinate incessantly founding her convents. Saint Thérèse of Lisieux knew this when the Groom possessed her mystically on the day of her solemn profession; and Mechtilde of Magdeburg knew this when she heard Jesus tell her mystically, "Nothing can come between me and thee!"

*The belief that Jesus was raised physically from the dead is the lesser part of being a Christian.* However much Søren Kierkagaard may have exaggerated, he got this exactly right. As Dupré puts it, "When Christianity becomes a 'doctrine,' it becomes detached from God and petrified."[30] For, as Luther is reputed to have said, people

---

[29] Eusebius, *Historia Ecclesiastica* V, 1, 41.
[30] Louis Dupré, *Kierkegaard as Theologian* (New York: Sheed & Ward, 1963), p. 102.

without spirituality become their own exterior.[31] Kierkegaard himself confessed that his task had been "to liberate people from the conceit that they are Christians."[32] Imagine what he would say to Evangelicals who think that adultery is a mulligan, or to Fundamentalists who cannot forgive the trespasses of their neighbors.

---

During the 1960s, at the New York World's Fair, a movie was shown in the Mormon Pavilion that became a *cause celèbre* and a subject of heated controversy. The film in question, *The Parable*, depicted Jesus as a circus clown, murdered by colleagues and spectators, but come alive again in the lives of his circus friends. This is, perhaps, as close as one may be able to come to the real meaning of the "resurrection" of Jesus. In the words of Dominic Crossan, "Bodily resurrection has nothing to do with a resuscitated body. And neither is bodily resurrection just another term for Christian faith itself [as the Fundamentalists would have us believe!]. Bodily resurrection means that the *embodied* life and death of the historical Jesus continue to be experienced, by believers, as powerfully efficacious and salvifically present in this world. That life continued, as it always had, to form communities of like lives."[33]

A proof of the inadequacy of the resurrection as conceived by Fundamentalists and traditional Christians is the inability of such a belief to stop wars, deceit, crimes of pride and greed, and so forth. For as long as Christians have held that all they had to do was believe in a risen Jesus who would save them from eternal damnation when the time came, they did not have to change anything, *really*, in their

---

[31] Quoted by Erik H. Erikson, *Young Man Luther* (New York: Norton, 1958), p. 135.

[32] Søren Kierkegaard, *Efterladte Papirer*, 232, quoted in Walter Lowrie, *Kierkegaard* (New York: Harper Torchbooks, 1962), vol. 2, p. 557.

[33] Crossan, p. xxxi. I have argued elsewhere that the belief in the Resurrection of Jesus is a male invention intended to preclude belief in a cyclical renewal of life as would be easily understood by women. See Ignacio L. Götz, *The Culture of Sexism* (Westport, CT: Praeger, 1999), pp. 61–67.

own actual lives. As long as belief remained just that, belief, without the embodiment of the actual life of Jesus in the lives of the believers, nothing could be accomplished. And this has been the case. Two thousand years of Christianity have not made the world more peaceful, more kind, more gracious, more humane. Just the contrary: the Crusades, the Holocaust, the two Great Wars (let alone all the regional European wars), global colonialism, and the depredation of forests and wetlands and tundras—all have been perpetrated by Christians. Not that Christians have a monopoly on cruelty, but that they bear one awful responsibility for the atrocities perpetrated in the name of a crucified Jesus whom they have failed to resurrect in their own everyday lives.

----->*<------

Some scholars, like Marcus Borg and John Dominic Crossan, insist that the most important thing about the resurrection is not the *factuality*—was Jesus raised from the dead or not?—but its *meaning*; after all, the fact of the resurrection, if it happened at all, was not witnessed by anyone, and the stories of the apparitions are just that, stories of apparitions. In this sense, the best thing that could happen to Christianity would be the discovery of the remains of the dead Jesus, or at least his ossuary; that, and the authentication of his physical remains. If this happened, then Christians could address themselves to the real issue, the *meaning* of the resurrection stories.[34]

Borg and Crossan suggest that a major component of the meaning is the recognition that Jesus is still alive in the lives of many who have been stirred by his teachings and inspired by the example of his life. The narratives of the apparitions of Jesus were metaphorical expressions of the experience his followers had of his continued inspiration. They seemed to say that the truth that the Kingdom of God dwelled already among us was proven by the fact that thousands

---

[34] Borg and Crossan, *The Last Week*, pp. 197 *ff.* An obstacle to this authentication quest is the fear among the powers that be that, if it happened, they would lose control of the very lucrative business of ordering people's lives.

of people professed to follow the example of Jesus's life and to devote themselves to actualizing in their own lives the image of God that Jesus himself sought to actualize with a passion that ultimately cost him his life. Paul understood this well when he wrote, "Christ was raised to life, the *first fruits of the harvest of the dead*" (*1 Corinthians* 15:20, emphasis added). Obviously, chronologically, Jesus was not the first one to be raised: Elijah raised the dead son of the widow from Zarephath (*1 Kings* 17:27); and his disciple, Elisha, raised the dead son of the Shunemite woman (*2 Kings* 4:18–37). Jesus himself was said to have raised Lazarus (*John* 11:43–44), the daughter of Jairus (*Mark* 5:39–42), a young man from the village of Nain (*Luke* 7:11–17), and *Matthew* 27:52 says that many who had died rose from the dead when Jesus expired on the cross. The point, therefore, is not that Jesus was the first dead person resurrected,[35] but that the Kingdom of God is already present among us—so present, actually, that the general resurrection of all people from the dead, in which the Pharisees believed, which Muslims affirm, and that Maimonides explained,[36] is already taking place,[37] though only some wise ones can recognize such a wonder in the exemplary lives of the righteous.

It might be interesting to speculate what would happen to Christianity if the body of Jesus was discovered; not the body itself, which would obviously have turned to dust after so many centuries, but earthly remains of it, like DNA—for example, in the ossuary of the Talpiyot tomb that bears his name. This DNA might be compared to that of members of his immediate family discovered in the same tomb. If serious doubts were raised about the resurrection, what would happen to Christianity? How would Christianity confront

---

[35] Geza Vermes, *The Resurrection*, chapter 3.
[36] See Maimonides, "Essay on Resurrection" (1191), in *Epistles of Maimonides: Crisis and Leadership*, trans. and ed. Abraham Halkin (Philadelphia: The Jewish Publication Society, 1985), pp. 211 *ff.*
[37] Borg and Crossan, *The Last Week*, p. 209.

evidence denying the resurrection, or at least casting aspersions on any unhistorical understanding of it?

In *The Brothers Karamazov*, there is an episode that somehow illustrates the quandary that might arise. Father Zossima, the revered priest and elder and the spiritual father of Alyosha, has died, but unlike some of his saintly predecessors, his corpse has not exuded a sweet fragrance after death. No, the smell of decomposition began to come from the coffin more quickly than usual in such cases, and this fact created a crisis, not only for Alyosha, but also for others, for whom it became a stumbling block. Some thought it unseemly that the corpse of a reputed holy man should stink; some showed delight in what they thought was the exposure of peasant beliefs; some came to the monastery merely out of curiosity; others showed prideful contempt for what they considered a superstition. For Alyosha himself, the event was a turning point; his ideas were turned not only by the stench of the corpse but by a kind of vision that he endured while he was in the cell, kneeling before the silent and already stinking corpse of "his saint," whom he thought he heard praising a life of kindness to others but lived outside the monastery; for all the earth was the theater of God's play. When he awoke, he stood up, walked out of the cell, and resolutely strode away from the monastery.[38]

The story of Rabbi Akiba and his ascent to Paradise also illustrates the possible kinds of reactions to the historical debunking of religious superstitions. Of the four men who ascended with him to Paradise only to find that what they had believed was false, one died on the spot, one went crazy, one lost his faith, and only one, Rabbi Akiba, left Paradise unperturbed. He had already come to terms with the truth of the Divine, which needs no extrahistorical effects in order to exert its powerful influence on our lives.

In another case, when in 1929 Krishnamurti announced that he was no one's teacher, and that his only concern was to set people absolutely and unconditionally free,[39] many of his erstwhile follow-

---

[38] Fyodor Dostoevsky, *The Brothers Kamarazov*, Part III, Book VII, Ch. 1*ff.*

[39] Mary Lutyens, *Krishnamurti: The Years of Fulfilment* (New York: Avon Books, 1983), p. 15.

ers were unable to continue as his disciples, claiming they could not understand his new language of abstractions. Others accused him of escaping his responsibilities as a leader, which included, they said, advising people of their spiritual progress (or lack thereof) along the spiritual path. Many of his followers disowned him, and for the next fifty-seven years refused to acknowledge him.

Of course, these were comparatively small responses, numerically speaking, nothing like the intellectual upheaval resulting from the sack of Rome in 410, the fall of Toledo in 1085, the realization that the earth is not at the center of our solar system, the publication of Darwin's *Origin of the Species* in 1859, and of Einstein's theory of relativity in 1916, the liberation of Auschwitz at the end of World War II, or the explosion of the atomic bomb over Hiroshima in 1945.[40]

———※———

Finally, we must also consider the fact that belief in the resurrection of Jesus played an important role in the de-Judaizing of Jesus. This belief in the resurrection appears very early, first in the writings of Paul to the Thessalonians around 52 CE, barely twenty years after the death of Jesus. It appears, too, in *Mark*, the earliest of the canonical Gospels; it is present in all the other Gospels, with details being added to the story as the decades go by. In *Luke* 24:52, Jesus ascends to heaven on the same day of his resurrection, so that no further account of his existence on earth needs to be given. Thus, the divinity that appears as Jesus returns whence it came after rising from the dead. No physical remains are found, no corpse, no ossuary (though recently there have been doubts about this). No trace of a Jewish man who was born, lived, and died in Roman-occupied Palestine in the early decades of the first century CE.

Against this background, *John* will be able to maintain that Jesus was a divine being (the Word) who came down from heaven,

[40] James Burke, *The Day the Universe Changed* (Boston: Little, Brown & Co., 1985).

74

took human flesh for a while, and was taken back up to heavenly glory; and Marcion will be able to claim that this man who appeared as Jesus was not a *real* Jewish person but a spirit seemingly clothed in human flesh.

Belief in the resurrection literally abstracts Jesus from his earthly setting. Whatever he strove to be and do concretely during his life is negated, obliterated, sublimated into the amorphous spiritual.

## A Historical Note

Christians tend to think of the resurrection of Jesus as a unique event in history, but the fact is that the resurrection theme is older than Christianity by some two thousand years. Sumerian goddess Inanna, Queen of Heaven and Earth, descended to the underworld to visit her sister, Ereshkigal, Queen of the Nether regions. But what was meant as a friendly visit ended in tragedy: Ereshkigal "fastened on Inanna the eye of death," and Inanna was annihilated, turned into a mere piece of raw meat hanging from a hook in a butcher's shop. The god Enki, however, raised her from the dead and restored her to her former glory. It will be recalled, too, that Osiris was murdered and *dis*-membered by his jealous and evil brother, Set, and that his wife, Isis, *re*-membered him (all but his phallus, which could not be found!), restoring him back to a sort of eternal life in the Egyptian underworld.

The Greeks believed that Zeus, in one of his sexual escapades, and disguised as a serpent, had got Persephone pregnant. The child that was born, Zagreus, was horned. He was a playful toddler who climbed on his father's throne, made fun of him, and mimicked him by holding the lightning in his tiny hand. Hera, however, was enraged and ordered the Titans to slay the newborn child, but Zagreus fought valiantly, turning himself into all kinds of shapes, that of old Kronos, that of a youth, a lion, a horse, a serpent, and a bull. In this last form, he was finally slain. But, in at least one version of the story, Zeus swallowed his heart, and when he got Semele, a human, pregnant in another of his escapades, the child that she bore was Dionysus, the resurrected Zagreus, who strutted into ancient Thebes announcing to one and all, "I am the son of God!"[41]

Eliade explains the role of the resurrection motif:

> Dionysos was the son of Zeus, and his appearance in the religious history of Greece was a spiritual revolution. Osiris, in the same way, was the son of the sky (a goddess) and earth (a god); the Phoenician Aleion was the son of Ba'al, and so on. In every case these divinities had a close connection with vegetation, with suffering, death and resurrection, and with initiation. All of them are dynamic, able to feel suffering, redemptive. Not only the Aegean and Eastern mystery religions, but also the main streams of popular piety took shape around these gods, in name gods of vegetation, but primarily dramatic gods, taking on the destiny of man himself, like him experiencing passion, suffering and death. Never had god been brought so close to man. The Dioscuri helped and protected mankind; the savior-gods even shared mankind's sufferings, died and rose from the dead to redeem them. The same "thirst for the concrete" which was forever thrusting the sky gods—with their remoteness, their impassibility, their indifference to the daily struggle—into the background, is shown in the importance given to the "son" of the sky god—to Dionysos, Osiris, Aleion and the rest. The "son" often invokes his heavenly father; but it is not his paternity that explains the all-important part he plays in the history of religion, but his "human-

---

[41] Euripides, *The Bacchae* 1. When I first heard those words at a live performance of the play, I was stunned. Here was the same claim that Christians have made for Jesus in a play performed in 405 BCE in Athens.

ity," the fact that he definitely shares the lot of mankind, even though he passes beyond it in his periodic resurrection.[42]

Thus, despite the theologians' assertions that the resurrection of Jesus is a unique event, the mythological data disprove their claim and, at the same time, provide a matrix in which to place the Christian belief. What belief? That even though executed by the powers, Roman and priestly, Jesus and his vision rose again in the lives of those who had known him, and he has been victorious, for the most part, for the past two thousand years. This is miracle enough, if we could only see it.

According to *Luke* 24:5, we must look for Jesus among the living in whom he has been raised, those who follow his lead in the pursuit of justice even unto tribulation and death.

---

[42] Mircea Eliade, *Patterns in Comparative Religion* (Cleveland, OH: Meridian Books, 1963), pp. 98–99. In his letter to the *Philippians* 2:6–11, Paul quotes a beautiful kenotic hymn in which he commends to us the example of Jesus, who being in the form (*morphê*) of God made himself human even unto death, and has now been raised by God to his pristine divine condition. The same sentiment is found in the story of Dionysus, who announcing his advent to the citizens of Thebes, explains how he has "put off the God and taken human shape" in order to bring solace to the people (*Bacchae* 1–45). Except for a reference to Jesus at the beginning and at the end of the hymn, and a probably intercalated phrase about the cross, the hymn could have originally referred to Dionysus. Paul makes it refer to Jesus, the new Dionysus, an assimilation that would have been understood by the Hellenistic converts at Philippi, where many ancient cults were still practiced. See Stephen L. Harris and Gloria Platzner, *Classical Mythology*, 2nd ed. (Mountain View, CA: Mayfield Publishing Co., 1998), p. 445.

CHAPTER

5

# On Miracles

The Gospels and other accounts of the life of Jesus mention a number of "miracles" that Jesus is supposed to have performed. These "miracles" are then taken as proof that he was divine, the incarnate Son of God.

But note that *Q* and the *Gospel of Thomas*, probably the two oldest records of the life of Jesus, have no narratives of miracles or otherworldly events. As Bishop Spong writes, "There are no miracle stories in either *Q* or *Thomas*. There is also no story in either of a supernatural birth or supernatural ascension. There is not even an account of the crucifixion and resurrection. There are no parables. There is nothing that presents Jesus in the supernatural theological language that later was to surround him."[1] And if we look at Paul, whose writings are the first canonical Christian documents we have, there are also no miracles, "no reference to a miraculous birth," and, as Spong comments, Paul "says that Jesus 'was born of a woman, born under the Law' (*Galatians* 4:4). There is no hint of the concept of virginity in Paul's use of the word *woman*. He seems to be referring to a normal birth, one no different from that which happens to any other person. He later says that Jesus was 'descended from David according to the flesh' (*Romans* 1:3). That hardly sounds miracu-

---

[1]  John Shelby Spong, *A New Christianity for a New World* (San Francisco, CA: HarperSanFrancisco, 2002), p. 86.

lous."[2] In other words, miracles were not part of how the early followers of Jesus saw him.

There are several kinds of miraculous stories in the Gospels. Meier distinguishes three general types: exorcisms, healings (including raising of the dead), and nature miracles,[3] a cataloguing accepted by most authors. In terms of numbers, there are roughly six accounts of exorcisms, seventeen of healings, and eight of so-called nature miracles. This number does not include parallels.[4] But what counts as a miracle—that is, as a "startling deed" (*paradoxa*),[5] a "wonder" (*thauma*)? What deeds are characterized as "miracles"? For obviously not all of Jesus's actions were so labeled. This is a determination of fact. Meier suggests that there are really only four criteria useful in this determination. I will detail them briefly here.

First, and most importantly, there is the criterion of *multiple attestation*; that is, is the event recounted in several Gospels? Second, there is the criterion of *coherence*: do the various sources present the event in more or less the same light, in more or less the same circumstances, with more or less the same purpose? Third, there is the criterion of *discontinuity*, not as useful then as it might be today. This criterion asks if the deed or event was exceptional, if it stood out of the ordinary; but in Jesus's time, many such events were recorded in more or less local narratives entirely different from his. Many miracles are detailed in *Pirke Aboth* V, 8. Apollonius of Tyana (first century CE) was said to have worked miracles, and so did Honi the Circle Maker, Hanina ben-Dosa (first century CE), Ananias (who restored Paul's eyesight), Simon Magus, and even the Emperor Vespasian.[6] Against this prolific background, the only thing one can say that was special in the case of Jesus is that some belief or trust in Jesus was presupposed in the Gospel narratives, an attitude lacking in other similar accounts. However, such distinctive marks cannot pass muster under

---

[2]  Ibid., p. 87.
[3]  John P. Meier, *A Marginal Jew: Rethinking the Historical Jesus* (New York: Doubleday, 1994), vol. 2, pp. 509 *ff.*
[4]  John P. Meier, *A Marginal Jew*, vol. 2, p. 618.
[5]  See Josephus, *Antiquitates* 9. 7. 6 §182.
[6]  Suetonius, *The Twelve Caesars*, "Vespasian" 7.

strict critical analysis. Fourth, there is the criterion of *embarrassment*, which looks at the fact that some accounts of miracles are included even though they did not cast Jesus necessarily in a favorable light.[7] This is a criterion of authenticity because generally, people do not tell stories that might result in a loss of respect, or worse, for their leaders.[8]

Now, these criteria merely authenticate the specific deeds and events characterized as miracles. They certify that an event is indeed historical and considered a miracle at the time. They do not prove that the events were "miracles" (violations of the laws of nature, signs of clear divine intervention) any more than proving that Augustus existed and was deemed the son of God proves that he was truly divine. In other words, a further question must be asked, namely, whether or not any of these actions would qualify as acts that, in our modern parlance, broke or exceeded the laws of nature. But, as I have said before, such an understanding of miracle would impose on events from two thousand years ago an understanding not warranted from the historical circumstances and beliefs of the people who lived at the time of Jesus. Once the historicity of the narratives is determined, we have no right to interpret the facts according to our own views, not any more than we have the right to claim that a Jew at the time of Jesus was tall or short according to *our* modern standards of height.

In the matter of the miraculousness of Jesus's miracles, we must refrain from weaving a web of interpretation different from what passed as miracle at that time. The miracle stories were recounted for those who shared an understanding of miracle as something merely "startling" or "wonderful" or "significant"; they were meant for people who simplemindedly had no idea about *laws of nature* and their scientific application. To go beyond this is like wanting to produce gold from lead.

———— ➤✖◄ ————

7   See *Mark* 3:20–30 and *Matthew* 12:22–32.
8   John P. Meier, *A Marginal Jew*, vol. 2, pp. 619–631.

Moreover, there are several other considerations that must be taken seriously when dealing with the so-called miracles. To begin with, as I mentioned above, the terms used in Greek and Latin do not mean what they do to us today. "Miracle" (*thauma* in Greek, *miraculum* in Latin) means simply a wonder, something to wonder at. We often express the sense of wonder by saying, "This was wonderful!" "This is amazing!" Such evaluations have nothing to do with the suspension of the laws of nature, which is involved in *our* meaning of miracle.

Second, the Jews had a very different conception of "miracle," one that, again, had little or nothing to do with the suspension of the laws of nature. For the Jews, a "miracle" was something that happened when you needed it to happen. It might be the simplest and most ordinary occurrence, but it happened when you needed it, that was all. Fleeing the Egyptians (assuming there was an Exodus!), the Israelites needed to cross the marshy and reedy land (*jam suf*) north of the Red Sea. The waters suddenly receded because, unbeknownst to them, Santorini, the island volcano on Thera, north of Crete, had exploded with the usual consequence of tsunamis and dust clouds and pumice. But for the Israelites, the recession of the waters happened when they needed it, and the waters' return a few hours later happened, again, when they needed it in order to overwhelm the pursuing Egyptians. Similarly, when Deborah and Barak went to battle against the Philistines, there was a thunderstorm, and the river Kishon overflowed its banks, creating a mess of mud in which the Philistine chariots were mired, thus giving the Israelites an easy target (*Judges* 5:21). Nothing "miraculous" here, just a natural occurrence when you needed it. But what *was* significant, and what we all too often lack (therefore requiring unnatural happenings to qualify as miracles) was that the Israelites had the faith to see the hand of God even in the ordinary events that graced their lives. In modern times, in *Fiddler on the Roof*, the tailor Motel Kamzoil rejoices because Tzeitel agrees to marry him, and he sings "Miracle! Miracle!" But there is nothing miraculous (unnatural or supernatural) in a woman's agreeing to marry the man she loves, just the eyes of faith seeing the hand of God in this ordinary event.

81

Third, I take exception to Meier's definition of miracle, which includes events that are the result of special interventions of God "doing what no human power can do."[9] This definition brings again the preternatural or supernatural element that I believe is unwarranted and prejudicial to a historical understanding of the marvels that Jesus wrought. Moreover, it is circular: it defines as extraordinary what needs to be proven so!

Fourth, as I mentioned above, the Gospels are not the only accounts containing "miraculous" stories of healing and the like.[10] Such stories appear in other cultures. In the Hindu lore, for example, Sita was proved to have remained faithful to her husband Rama by a miracle—walking through fire—and her life was therefore spared.[11] The sixth Buddhist patriarch, Bodhisattva, was believed to have crossed the river Yangtse, swollen and roaring down the canyons, floating on a slim bamboo reed. The Greeks believed that Asklepios performed "miraculous" cures at Epidauros, the medical center and temple dedicated to his memory.[12] In fact, it is narrated that Asklepios himself brought back to life a dead man, a feat that angered Zeus, who in his wrath struck him down. This precipitated a nasty encounter between Zeus and Apollo, whose son Asklepios was said to be. In another story, the sculptor Pygmalion, who was a devotee of the goddess Aphrodite, saw the statue of Galatea, which he had sculpted and with which he had fallen in love, brought to life by the favor of the goddess.

Josephus mentions in *Antiquities* 18. 63–64 that Jesus "wrought surprising feats," and even though some scholars suspect Christian

---

[9] Ibid., p. 512. Meier may be prompted to define miracles in this way by his official religious affiliation as a Roman Catholic priest. His book, after all, carries an "imprimatur," which means it conforms to official Catholic teachings. But defining miracles the way he does begs the question, which is, really, whether or not God has suspended the laws of nature in a specific instance.
[10] Meier deals with this issue in volume 2, chapter 18.
[11] Valmiki, *Ramayana*, 6.103–6.
[12] See Lynn R. LiDonnici, *The Epidaurian Miracle Inscriptions: Text, Translation, and Commentary* (SBL Texts and Translations 36; Atlanta: Scholars Press, 1995).

interpolations in this passage, the fact is that the Jews of Jesus's time could see many events and occurrences as worthy of wonder, and detect the hand of God in them, without necessarily claiming that they were unnatural or beyond nature (in our sense of the term).

Fifth, miracles always require interpretation, and interpretation depends on the mentality of the observer and his/her culture. The so-called raising of Lazarus, if it had been simply the recalling of a dead and stinking body back to life, should have been enough to "convert" everybody present. This did not happen. In fact, the story may be an allegory foretelling the resurrection of Jesus himself. Also, it was not the only such event, as the *Secret Gospel of Mark* narrates, and the effect was also very different. Crossan defines miracle as "*a marvel that someone interprets as a transcendental action or manifestation.*"[13] The problem, however, from a historical point of view, is to determine which events actually elicited the interpretation, and why. Crossan again: "To claim a miracle is to make an interpretation of faith, not just a statement of fact. The fact open to public discourse is the marvel, something that is assessed as neither trickery nor normalcy,"[14] and about which there may be disagreement on factual and historical grounds. A contemporary example might involve the reported miracles at Lourdes and Fatima, and those still required by the Catholic Church for the beatification of dead holy people.

---

Sixth, biblical narratives do not label what they describe: the naming is ours. They do admit that they are signs, or deeds of power, but nothing beyond the ordinary. Calling an event a "miracle" in the sense that God has abrogated the laws of nature in favor of a particular individual or cause *explains* what the event is. But this is precisely what the narrator does *not* want to achieve: the event must remain as something merely to wonder at (which is the original meaning of the Latin word *miraculum*), as something factual yet unexplainable. The

---

[13] Crossan, *Birth of Christianity*, p. 303.
[14] Crossan, *Birth of Christianity*, p. 304.

naming is *our* doing, and *our* mistake; the narrator simply presents the facts and makes no judgments beyond marveling, thus avoiding the error and preserving the mystery.

Why is this a mistake? Because by claiming that something is a "miracle," people intend to invoke God as its source and thereby appear religious, but in doing so, they unwittingly deny God's involvement because they explain what is not to be explained, but only wondered at.[15] It is like offering a scientific explanation for the wonder of a sunset.

The preceding should make clear that contemporary Americans have a very warped notion of miracle. They seem to believe that any and all occurrences not immediately and easily explainable are the results of a direct intervention of God. God, they seem to believe, is just waiting to intervene on their behalf. He is as Jim Carrey depicted him in the film *Bruce Almighty*, ready to hit the return key on his divine computer and thereby grant every request made to him by people all over the world. God is like a powerful and rich daddy who grants every wish of his children even if they are naughty, not nice.

Recently I heard a gentleman confess on TV that a particular event that was being discussed was "a miracle." Why so? He answered fervently, "Because I believe in the power of prayer." Which means that he believes in a God whose almighty power is at the service of every human request; that is, a God who is *not* almighty, since he is subject to the power of prayer; a God who is *not* all-merciful, since he is partial to some, not others; a God who is like a magician, ready to perform an astonishing trick on demand. Saying "I believe in the power of prayer" with great conviction is not a sign of piety, as the gentleman thought, but of a pitiful if petulant ignorance.

The thing is not whether or not God can do everything we impute to him as miracle; the thing is the conception of God that

---

15 See Ludwig Wittgenstein, *Tractatus Logico-Philosophicus* (London: Routledge & Kegan Paul, 1961), No. 6. 372.

is implied in such claims and attributions. For believers there is no denying that "the earth is God's and all there is in it," but equally there is, or should be, a reluctance to countenance a conception of God as a busybody, a kind of wholesome Puck traipsing "through brush, through briar," to minister to our every need.[16]

———※———

A story from the Taoist tradition might help to bring all this to the fore:

> One disciple said: "My master stands on one side of the river. I stand on the other holding a piece of paper. He draws a picture in the air and the picture appears on the paper. He works miracles."
>
> The other disciple said: "My master works greater miracles than that.
> When he sleeps, he sleeps.
> When he eats, he eats.
> When he works, he works.
> When he meditates, he meditates."[17]

Thomas Merton said essentially the same thing: "How I pray is breathe."[18]

———※———

There is a vicious circle in the modern belief in miracles, especially as used in the canonization process: miracles are invoked to prove the saintliness that is presupposed for the miracles to be miracles.

---

[16] Shakespeare, *A Midsummer-Night's Dream*, Act II, Scene 1.
[17] From *The Fire of Silence and Stillness*, Paul Harris, ed. (Springfield, IL: Templegate Publishers, 1997), p. 10. Also in Paul Reps, *Zen Flesh, Zen Bones* (Garden City, NY: Doubleday Anchor, n. d.), No. 80, p. 68.
[18] Thomas Merton, *Day of a Stranger* (Salt Lake City: Gibbs M. Smith, 1981).

# 6

# Who *Was* Jesus?

It is clear, then, that there is very little that can be called historical about Jesus. Chapter 2 pretty much said it all. But who *was* Jesus? According to the received tradition, and in the beautiful imagery of a baptismal hymn in the ancient *Odes of Solomon*, a letter came floating down from heaven. People strained their arms and hands to catch it, but of itself, it took abode in the womb of the humble maid of Nazareth. "And the Word became flesh and dwelled among us" (*John* 1:14). Jesus, in the minds of most Christians, is God incarnate. The incarnation has been deemed to be a mystery that takes place in the stillness of a divine silence.[1] It is a mystery so profound and manifold, so wrought in wonder and implication, that the human mind feels stunned and dizzy, unable to estimate, however faintly, the richness of its eternal truth. Moreover, this mystery has been understood to be so full of paradoxes that it is no wonder that faith in the incarnate Word became the touchstone of orthodoxy at the beginning of Christianity, "for this is indeed an unbelievable communication and commingling, a paradoxical fusion of opposites. He who is, becomes; the Infinite is created and contained in space; the Word becomes reachable by the senses; the Invisible is seen; the Inaccessible, touched; the Timeless steps in time; the Son of God becomes the son of man."[2] It was in the stillness of that secret moment in which eternity touched time that God made it possible for us humans to hear

---

[1] St. Ignatius of Antioch, *Ad Ephes.* 19:1.
[2] St. Gregory of Nazianzus, *Orat.* 38, 1.13; MG 36, 31, 325.

his word in a way we could understand. Hindus, Greeks, and Jews, so the tradition explained, had been afraid of the awesome vision of God. The Israelites had even pleaded with Moses, "Don't let us hear the Lord speaking: it will cost us our lives!" (*Exodus* 20:19–21). Yet, now, all this might was bent down unto our lowliness. We did not need to shrink from God any longer, because the radiance of his face was veiled in order to protect us (*Exodus* 34:29–35). So, in humility, in the ordinariness of a human garb, he could address us and continue to reveal himself to us. For, the belief was, "daily in the virginal womb—that is, in the souls of the faithful—he is conceived by faith!"[3]

---

But this beautiful view of the incarnation was not devoid of political consequences. It made Jesus divine first, and only human because of historical—that is, accidental—necessity: there *had been* a man called Jesus. But to many after Jesus's death, it seemed that this man did not have to be Jewish. In fact, it was better for all concerned if any trace of his Jewishness was removed from the incarnation, and so it was. Moreover, the incarnation placed the burden of salvation on God alone. Jesus, God incarnate, substituted himself for our sins, and that was that. This is what theologians call "substitutional atonement." Surely we were supposed to pray, to abstain from sin, to strive to lead exemplary lives, but still everything revolved around God's grace, God's favor to us, won by Jesus's death. God was to save us, not we ourselves.

Christian theology is a romantic effort to avoid responsibility for serious personal change. "It's in the hands of God," "it's the merits of Christ," not our own efforts, our own change, our own conversion. Most likely, this is not Jesus's own view but what theologians have concocted, and it is a beautiful theory. It saves us the trouble of working on ourselves. It is a way out without seeming to be so, so we

---

[3] Venerable Bede, *In Luke* 2, 6; ML 92, 330.

feel good about it and about our faith, because we think it behooves us to believe all this "for our salvation."

We still recite in the Nicene Creed that Jesus came "for us and for our salvation," but Jesus probably did not have any of this in mind. He was a Jew, and therefore he would not have had any such things in mind. "To save us" meant, if anything at all, to indicate to us what *we* should do to save ourselves, to extricate ourselves from our sins, from our faults. Jesus saved us only in that he set for us an example of what we can do to imitate God, to actualize the divine image of humanity in our own lives. We can save ourselves by living as Jesus did, even unto death.

———————✦———————

I should add that, already in ancient times, the Gnostics (Christians who also espoused other current religious views) disagreed with the traditional interpretation of the birth and death of Jesus as "substitutional atonement." They did not think it was a saving act at all, because what had died on the cross was merely a fleshly ghost, a phantasm, not a personality both human and divine. As Jesus tells Judas in secret, by betraying him, "you will sacrifice the man that clothes me" (*Gospel of Judas* [56]), thus freeing the immortal spirit. What saves us, then? It is this knowledge, this *gnôsis* that we are spirits trapped in matter. As Marvin Meyer puts it, for the Gnostics, "Jesus is primarily a teacher and revealer of wisdom and knowledge, not a savior who dies for the sins of the world. For Gnostics, the fundamental problem in human life is not sin but ignorance, and the best way to address this problem is not through faith but through knowledge."[4]

Today, knowledge is hard to come by in many self-styled Christian environments. In this the Gnostics were right: we have to know what lies behind the appearances of daily life and beyond the

---

[4]  Marvin Meyer, "Introduction" to *The Gospel of Judas*, ed. Rodolphe Kasser, Marvin Meyer, and Gregor Wurst (Washington, DC: National Geographic, 2006), p. 7.

obfuscations of preachers. But we also have to act. An old Spanish proverb counsels, "Pray to God and pick up the hammer!" The house of God will not be built without the hammer, nor will our salvation be effected without our efforts. Jesus showed us how to save ourselves by what he did throughout his entire life, not just by his death on the cross.

------※※------

When the disciples were worried about their lives as followers of Jesus—what would happen to them, and would they be put to death as Jesus had been—Mary of Magdala reassured them by reminding them that Jesus had already prepared them to lead truly human lives.[5] Ehrman reminds us that to be truly human means to accept the teachings of Jesus[6] and, I would add, *to model them in our own lives.* Regardless of the Gnostic leanings of this *Gospel of Judas*, the importance of the imitation of Jesus emerges clearly; and, interestingly, this truth is mediated to us by a woman.

------※※------

A view of Jesus as divine is one of the answers to the question of this chapter, "Who *Was* Jesus?" It is often based on the Prologue that opens the *Gospel of John*: "So the Word became flesh and pitched his tent among us" (*John* 1:14).[7]

For nearly two thousand years, Christians have identified "the Word" with the second Person of the Trinity, a belief which, of course, did not exist at the time that *John* was written. Since this second Person is believed to have come to dwell among us as Jesus, Jesus has

---

[5]  *Gospel of Mary* 5:8.

[6]  Bart D. Ehrman, *Peter, Paul, and Mary Magdalene*, pp. 242–243. See *1 Corinthians* 11:1.

[7]  As I explained above, becoming "flesh" would have been a bad thing according to the Gnostics. Becoming Jewish "flesh" was even worse. One cannot ignore completely the suggestion that this crucial passage of *John* 1:14 may be a subtle hint of anti-Semitism.

been identified as "the Word." This has been taken to mean that Jesus is divine. The Word was with the God at the beginning; through him (through the Word or through the God?), all things came to be. But this is really an easy and somewhat superficial interpretation of the prologue to John's gospel, a reading almost dictated by the text itself, at least as usually translated. It ignores the enormously rich and varied tradition that saw in this text the exposition of a mystery hidden in God. For, after all, nobody was there to see God in himself, to hear God speaking to himself his inmost word (*logos endiathetos*, as it was called), and nobody was there when God formed the heavens. As God asked a complaining Job, "Where were you when I founded the earth? Tell me, if you know so much" (*Job* 38:4). Still, this is a tradition, and many may ask if we have to give it all up by understanding Jesus as "the human being." The answer is, it is not a question of giving up but of understanding differently, and perhaps more truthfully, and certainly as profoundly, what may have been behind the words of the hymn (it *is* an old hymn, with additions from the writer![8]) that opens John's gospel.

The Word. In Greek, the *logos*: not the *logos* as entity, as the second Person of the Trinity, but as that in God that can be spoken, that can be actualized as, or in, speech. Only mental words can become speech, only images can become paintings or sculptures, only inner stirrings can become music. When we speak, it is not our whole self that becomes speech, but that in us which can be spoken. When we paint or sculpt, it is not our whole self that becomes painting or sculpture, but that in us that can be made plastic or concrete. When we sing or compose music, it is not our entire self that empties itself and dissolves into the sounds but those emotions in us that can be expressed in sound. Saying that "the Word became flesh" does not necessarily have to mean that *God* became flesh, as the traditional interpretation has maintained. It can mean that a part or aspect of God was actualized, that part of God that is the archetype of humanness, that part of God that is an *image* of humanness; for, after all,

---

[8]   See Raymond E. Brown, *The Gospel according to John*, 2 vols. (Garden City, NY: Doubleday, 1970), vol. 1, pp. 3–37.

God created humans in his own image (*Genesis* 1:26). It is not God who becomes but God's inner image, just as it is not our minds that become statues or paintings but only our inner images, the images seen in the sanctity and obscurity of our minds. This is what painters and sculptors do, they body forth what they imagine; and this is what poets do, as Shakespeare said:

> ...as imagination bodies forth
> the forms of things unknown, the poet's pen
> turns them to shapes and gives to airy nothing
> a local habitation and a name.[9]

The Word is the image of God, the image of which *Genesis* 1:26 speaks, the image according to which humans were created. *This* image becomes human, for male and female he created them. And so all humans are the image of God, since the image of God became actual, incarnate, real in them. To see the image, any human image, is to see God, or an aspect of God, and therefore Jesus could tell Philip, "Anyone who has seen me has seen the Father" (*John* 14:9). Humanity is the grammar of a possible expression of God. Thus the miracle of the incarnation repeats itself in each of us, and we participate in this mystery of creation whenever we strive to actualize God's image in our own lives. As James Joyce put it, "In the virgin womb of the imagination the word [is] made flesh."[10]

All this led Nietzsche to claim that we must be the poets of our lives (understanding "poet" in its original meaning of "maker")[11] and Friedrich Hölderlin to state that "humans dwell poetically on this earth."[12] Martin Heidegger interprets this to means that "existence is 'poetical' in its fundamental aspect,"[13] for it is the function of poetry to create visual images that contain the invisible in a vis-

---

[9] William Shakespeare, *A Midsummer-night's Dream*, V, Scene 1, 14–17.

[10] James Joyce, *A Portrait of the Artist as a Young Man* (New York: The Viking Press, 1958), p. 217.

[11] Friedrich Nietzsche, *The Gay Science* (New York: Vintage, 1974), p. 299.

[12] Friedrich Hölderlin, *Werke* (Berlin: Propyläen-Verlag, 1914), Vol. VI, 25, line 32.

[13] Martin Heidegger, *Existence and Being* (Chicago: Regnery, 1949), p. 282.

ible way, something it does through metaphor. Poetic language (or, for that matter, painterly and sculptural language) is not concerned with metaphor for the sake of metaphor but with metaphor in so far as it is the revelation of what remains essentially unknowable and unrevealed in its totality—in this case, what it truly means to be a human being. Our chosen lives, then, are like living metaphors of the mysterious reality of the human image in God. To the extent that this peculiar epiphany of the mystery of humanness is achieved in each life, to the same extent is human life an authentic reproduction of the divine image.[14] "The goal of life," says Crouzel, "is the *homoiôsis theô*, the resemblance [to God] which restores the original similitude."[15] When this resemblance is achieved, one is oned with Jesus's own resemblance, and one

> Acts in God's eye what in God's eye [one] is
> —Chríst. For Christ plays in ten thousand
> places,
> Lovely in limbs, and lovely in eyes not his
> To the Father through the features of [our]
> faces.[16]

The verse from *John*'s gospel says that "the Word became *flesh*." It does not say that the Word became Jesus, although this is implied in the hymn as a whole, at least in the traditional sense. But perhaps the meaning here is that the Word became *human*; that is, what we are, even though we do not know exactly what it is we are. For the human is an undefinable consciousness that exists physically on this earth. We are a mystery. We are that which exists precisely as unfathomable. Consequently, that in Palestine, at a certain historical

---

[14] Cf. Ignacio L. Götz, *The Culture of Sexism* (Westport, CT: Praeger, 1999), pp. 104–105.

[15] Henri Crouzel, *Théologie de l'Image de Dieu chez Origène* (Paris: Aubier, 1956), p. 35.

[16] Gerard Manley Hopkins, "As Kingfishers Catch Fire," in *Poems and Prose* (New York: Alfred A. Knopf, 1995), p. 18. I have changed two words in order to make the meaning gender inclusive.

moment in time this human was called Jesus is really secondary to the fact that the image of God, the word that God spoke to himself intimately about his humanness, was spoken. It became "the spoken Word" (*logos prophorikos*),[17] and Jesus appropriated it just as each one of us can appropriate it to ourselves in our efforts to become human.

———✹✹———

These incarnations are not the exclusive domain of Christianity or Judaism. They are to be found in the lives of great holy men and women, and in more imperfect form in the lives of all of us. Thus, many centuries after the beginning of Christianity, there appeared in Islam the notion of "the Perfect Man" (*al-Insân al-Kâmil*). This was expounded by many mystical writers, among them Nasafî (*ca.* 1250–1322). The doctrine of "the Perfect Man" is attributed to 'Alî ("the Commander of the Believers") by Nûr ad-Dîn Jâmî (1414–1492). It appeared first in Arabic in a text by Jâbir ibn Hayyân (*fl.* eighth century): "Thus the little world [microcosm] is created according to the prototype of the great world [macrocosm]. The little world is man when he has realized his original nature, which was made in the image of God." Mohammed al-Ghazâlî (1058–1111) discussed the idea at length, and so did Ibn al-'Arabî (1165–1240) in his *Fusûs al-Hikam* ("Bezels of Wisdom"), though the *Al-Insân al-Kâmil* of al-Jîlî (1365–1417) is often credited with being the fullest exposition.

The idea is based on a *hadîth* (a saying of the Prophet) reported by Ibn Hanbal, that "God created Adam in His image" (*Genesis* 1:27). Adam, thus, is the "First Man," the universal man, fully conscious of his essential unity with God who created him after his own image. To become "the Perfect Man," then, is to reach the fullness of one's spiritual and human nature; it is to become another Adam.

---

[17] These reflections were inspired by Karl Rahner's "Zur Theologie der Menschwerdung," *Catholica* 12 (1958), pp. 1–16. See also Henri Crouzel, *Théologie de l'Image de Dieu chez Origène* (Paris: Aubier, 1956); and Bernard-Henri Lévy, "We are not born human," *The New York Times*, August 28, 2018.

Jâmî quotes Rûmî: "As you are born from Adam, become like him." Rûmî himself wrote:

> That is why, in appearance, you are the microcosm, but in reality you are the macrocosm. From the point of view of appearance, the branch is the origin of the fruit, but in reality, the branch has come into existence because of the fruit. Had there been no desire or hope for the fruit, would the gardener have planted the root of the tree?[18]

As Jesus for Christians, Mohammed is, of course, the prototypical "Perfect Man" for Muslims. In a *hadîth*, he says, "He who has seen me has seen the Truth" (*al-Haqq*);[19] hence, it follows that to know the Prophet is to know God. However, this view came to appear to many as heretical, as is shown by the martyrdom of al-Hallâj, who was executed precisely for claiming in a moment of mystical ecstasy, "I am the Truth" (*anâ'l-Haqq*).

---

The Prologue at the beginning of *John*'s gospel has another, perhaps more esoteric, provenance. At least, it can be connected with a tradition that originated in Judaism but which found its way into the early oral tradition and the first writings of the followers of Jesus. This tradition is that of Wisdom (*Sophia* in Greek, *Hokhmah* in Hebrew). Wisdom, too, was there "at the beginning," when the world was created:

> *Before the ages, from the first, he created me,*
> *and through the ages I shall not cease to be.*
> *From the mouth of the Most High I came forth,*

---

[18] Rûmî, *Mathnawî* IV.521 *ff.*
[19] Reminiscent of Jesus's answer to Philip, "Anyone who has seen me has seen the Father" (*John* 14:9).

*and mistlike covered the earth.*
*In the heights of heaven I dwelt,*
*my throne on a pillar of cloud.*
*The vault of heaven I compassed alone,*
*through the deep abyss I took my course.*
*Over waves of the sea, over all the land,*
*over every people and nation I held sway.*
*Among them all I sought a resting place:*
*in whose inheritance should I abide?*
*Then the Father of all gave me his command,*
*and he who had made me chose the spot for*
*my tent.*[20]

Wisdom, of course, was the inspiration (the one who "breathed in," or "through") the prophets, including John the Baptist and Jesus. One of the oldest sayings attributed to Jesus says this explicitly: "Wisdom is being proved right by all her children" (*Q 26* = *QLK* 7:35; *Luke* 7:35), and Paul calls Jesus "the Wisdom of God" (*1 Corinthians* 1:24).

In fact, there was a tradition, either begun or elaborated by Philo (*ca.* 30 BCE–40 CE), the famous Alexandrian Jew, that saw the Logos as God's reasoning power, his firstborn, the highest mediator, through whom he made the world. This Logos is identified with Wisdom, and it is Wisdom who has a son who descends into the historical world in order to clear a path for the fallen souls to return to heaven.[21] At his baptism, Jesus would be acknowledged as the son of the divine Sophia, not really of God (*Matthew* 3:17, *Mark* 1:10–11), for, according to Philo, God can have no direct relation to the world. Schüssler Fiorenza summarizes: "Jewish Sophia theology provides the language world and mythological frame of reference that can explain

---

[20] *Sirach* 24:9 and 1–8. See also *Proverbs* 8:22–31, *1 Enoch* 42:1–2, and *Job* 28:12–28. For another esoteric view of the Word, see David Fideler, *Jesus Christ, Sun of God* (Wheaton, IL: Quest Books, 1993), chapter 3.
[21] Elisabeth Schüssler Fiorenza, *Jesus: Miriam's Child, Sophia's Prophet* (New York: Continuum, 1994), p. 138.

the earliest attempts to make meaning out of the ministry and execution of Jesus as well as the meaning-making of the later christological development of the early church."[22]

————⋙⋘————

So, we must come to the realization that those around Jesus, both men and women, seem to have been profoundly affected by him and his teachings, but they had no idea of him as divine. This is clear from their own reports about their beliefs, as recorded in *Luke* 24:19–24 and *Acts* 2–4. According to them, Jesus was simply a man chosen by God, who worked through him; even his "resurrection" was not seen as extraordinary, but only as a portent of what was to come for everyone else. In fact, many of his immediate followers went back to ply their trades immediately after the crucifixion (*John* 21, *Gospel of Peter* 14:2–3). The matter-of-factness of these accounts is due, partly, to the fact that in ancient times the Jews saw the whole world as permeated by God, and therefore did not see such events as "miraculous" (in our sense of the term, as being supernatural). As I explained in the previous chapter, even the Gospels do not speak of "miracles" (in our sense of the term, as something against the laws of nature), but only of signs (*semeia*) and "acts of power" (*dynameis*); the very term "miracle" (Latin *miraculum*, from *mirari*, to wonder) translates the Greek *thauma*, wonder; miracles were something to wonder at. Further, the expressions preserved in the Gospels are clearly faith statements of later believers written down for believers; that is, for those who had the faith to see the hand of God in events that otherwise were ordinary and that many bystanders did not at all see as significant.[23]

---

[22] Ibid., p. 140.

[23] Ferdinand Prat, SJ, *Jesus Christ* (Milwaukee: The Bruce Publishing Co., 1950), I, p. 520. The "miraculous" stories are often accounts exaggerated for the sake of apologetics, to prove a point, or to enhance the personality of Jesus. Even the raising of Lazarus, troublesome to interpret otherwise, must be seen in the tradition of "prophetic symbolism," as foretelling an event to come—namely, the resurrection of Jesus.

For his immediate followers, Jesus was a man, a great man, a charismatic leader, somewhat like the man ("someone like a son of man": *bar enosh*) walking upon the clouds of heaven described in *Daniel* 7:13 and *4 Esdras* 13:3 and 51. But he also suffered as the people of Israel had suffered during the Babylonian Exile, and therefore he was also like the "suffering servant" (*'ebed YHWH*) of *Second Isaiah* 42:1–53:12.[24] This combination of exaltation and abasement fit the traditional heroic pattern wherein the great hero descends even unto death and ascends even unto glory, bringing boons to his fellows. Thus a mythology was created patterned on the descent and ascent of the hero: In the beginning, he was with God; he then descended and pitched his tent among us, and was eventually saved and raised by God to the heavens. The hymn opening *John's* gospel (*John* 1:1–18) is a clear example of this, and so is the *Gospel of Peter*, but there are many, many other similar utterances.

As for Jesus, he spoke of himself nearly always in the third person, and nearly always by means of a peculiar expression, peculiar in linguistic terms and also in what it portended about him. The disciples never used this expression to refer to Jesus: this was *his own* exclusive way of talking about himself. All this would indicate that the expression was not invented by the disciples after Jesus's death, but that it originated with Jesus himself.

Most commonly Jesus referred to himself as "the son-of-the-man," an awkward expression in Greek because of the double article, but an expression used with such insistence that it would be wrong to disregard it. The expression may be translated as "the human being"

---

[24] The Hebrew *'ebed YHWH* (literally *Gottesknecht*, "servant of God") was translated into Greek by the Septuagint as *pais theou* (literally "child of God"), since *pais* can mean both "servant" and "child." It is clearly recognizable in the interpretative *hyios theou* (literally "son of God") of *Luke* 23:47 and *Mark* 15:39.

or "this mother's son" or "my father's son."[25] It may even be seen as a circumlocution for the first-person singular pronoun.[26]

According to the book of Genesis, men and women were created in the image of God. The expression is repeated for emphasis. This would mean that there is a human dimension to God that is mirrored by the two-gendered creation: God created the new creatures to be male and female, man and woman.[27] It should not be surprising, therefore, that Jesus should have striven to incarnate, enflesh, actualize, realize, the humanness of God in his own life, that he should have tried very hard to be as human as he could be. Hence his insistence that he was "the son-of-the-man," the human being. He consistently rejected the title of messiah in favor of the simple one of "*mensch.*" He may have come to realize this when he was baptized by John. He may have had some kind of religious experience or revelation, a "born again" experience, for when he came out of the

---

[25] Rabbinic literature sometimes referred to Jesus as "son of Panthera" (for example, Palestinian Tosephta *t. Hullin* 2.24), and Epiphanius (*Panarion* 78:7) confirms this. The possibility cannot be excluded that "the man" in the expression is the Roman soldier, whose name is given as *Panthera* or *Pantera*, who allegedly raped Mary, and who therefore would be Jesus's blood father. Though by marrying Mary Joseph became his legal father, it may be that Jesus kept the memory of the rapist alive by a continuous reference to him.

There is a record of a Tiberius Julius Abdes Pantera, a Roman soldier stationed in Sidon around the time of the birth of Jesus and transferred later to Germany, where he died in mid-first-century CE. Jesus may have even visited him in Sidon, where Pantera apparently lived, reading this way a cryptic passage in *Mark* 7:24. One reason for the repeated expression "the son-of-the-man" may have been a desire to maintain alive in the Jewish community the brutality of the Roman occupiers.

One more thing: to read this phrase as equivalent to "son of God" is another effort to deprive Jesus of his Jewishness.

[26] James Charlesworth, *Jesus within Judaism*, p. 40.

[27] *Genesis* 1–3 has a subtext, the opposition to the Goddess religion whose symbols must be downplayed. The new male God, YHWH/Elohim, must be as potent as the Goddess. The Goddess embodies the prehistorical experience of people who knew of no connection between sexual intercourse and pregnancy, and who therefore experienced parturition as an extraordinary event in which a human female gave birth to both male and female beings. The new male God must do no less, so he creates both males and females.

water, he was laughing, as the *Gospel of Philip* tells it. And he may have realized then that both men and women shared equally in the divine humanness.

The incarnation, therefore, was not some mysterious happening as was to be explained later by the theologians. The union of two natures, divine and human, in one person, the formula that Tertullian and Pope Leo the Great invented, was an unnecessary complication, still preserved in the Nicene Creed.[28] The struggles to make Jesus "of the same nature" or substance as God the Father (as opposed to being of a "similar" nature) were bitterly fought, not just intellectually but also politically. In the end, the theologians won the day, and every century obscured more and more the simple truth, that Jesus strove mightily to imitate the divine humanness, to incarnate it in his life.

To incarnate God is to enflesh the human dimension of God, to exemplify it concretely, much as later saints would strive to incarnate Jesus in their own lives. Such enfleshment included the possibility of suffering, and Jesus understood this well. The human archetype in God includes the potential to suffer; otherwise, we would not have been able to suffer. It also includes death, and for the same reasons, as Heidegger has shown in our own times. Suffering and death are elements of the human archetype.

Jesus was not perfect, much less divine. His was just an effort to actualize the human image in God. A similar effort was made by Buddha, Mahâvîra, Mohammed, Lao-tzu, Chuang-tzu, Hypatia, Hildegaard von Bingen, and Mother Ann the Christ (founder of the

---

[28] The formula for the incarnation developed by Tertullian and Pope Leo the Great was not initially shared by all, as can be seen by the theological discussions that preceded the Council of Nicaea and subsequent synods, and by the fact that Arianism almost triumphed. This is apparent also from the writings of the Syrian tradition and the "Hymn of the Pearl." The Syrian formulas were more imaginative, poetic, metaphorical, while the Greek ones were more philosophical. They represent the movement from image to concept that took place through the first five hundred years of Christianity in an effort to achieve precision so as to exclude as heretical expressions that did not concur. See Murray, *Symbols of Church and Kingdom*, pp. 310–312.

Shakers). By divinizing Jesus, we have excused ourselves from the obligation of striving to imitate him, who was bent on imitating God.

—⟶✴⟵—

Was Jesus married? We do not know, and we do not know why we do not know. There are no records indicating anything one way or the other. On the other hand, Jesus was never asked to defend his not being married in a culture that favored marriage.[29] Also, if he was not married, St. Paul would have used him as an example to strengthen his recommendation of celibacy in *1 Corinthians* 7:25. This is circumstantial evidence, but it *is* evidence.

If Jesus was not married, this may have been because he was a *mamzer*, a Jew whose paternity was suspect. Such people had difficulty contracting marriage. This also may have been the reason Jesus referred to himself so insistently as "the son-of-the-man," as if he were constantly reminding himself and others of his illegitimacy.

At the same time, there are no writings regarding the sexuality of Jesus. Chilton says that "there is no evidence that Jesus did or did not enjoy sexual contact during his life,"[30] but similarly, there is no evidence that he did or did not go to the bathroom. We assume he did, in both instances, because he was an ordinary human being. In fact, the *Gospel of Mary* 10:10, a late first- or early-second-century text, describes his relationship with Mary of Magdala: "He knew her completely and loved her devotedly." A later text, the *Gospel of Philip* 63:35, goes even further: "Christ loved her more than all the disciples, and used to kiss her often on her mouth;"[31] and in *Gospel of Philip* 59:6–9, she is said to be Jesus's constant partner or companion (*koinoné*).

[29] Michael Baigent, *The Jesus Papers* (San Francisco: HarperSanFrancisco, 2006), p. 107.

[30] Bruce Chilton, *Rabbi Jesus* (New York: Doubleday, 2000), p. 145. Also William E. Phipps, *The Sexuality of Jesus* (Cleveland, OH: Pilgrim Press, 1996).

[31] Admittedly, there are lacunae in this passage, though many scholars subscribe to the translation offered here.

This should not be surprising. The Jews did not regard the sexual instinct as bad in itself. When sexuality was renounced, as in the case of ascetics like John the Baptist and some of the Essenes, it was more for functional reasons than because it was considered evil or sinful. John was an itinerant preacher, and the Essenes lived in constant readiness for what they believed was an imminent Armageddon. There was no point in getting married if you were going to go to war in a jiffy.

Peter Brown retells a legend from the *Babylonian Talmud, Yoma* 69b, according to which the Sages of Palestine once captured the Sexual Drive, and considering its wild nature, they were plotting to execute it. However, they compromised and only mangled it so as to control its force, because they understood that if they killed it, the world itself would disappear.[32]

Steinsaltz says that "Judaism regards the taking of a wife as an important precept, binding on every man."[33] The rationale, as the *Talmud* explains repeatedly, is God's command in *Genesis* 1:28, "Be fruitful and multiply." Not to marry would contravene God's blessing and desires. According to Rabbi Akiva, since man and woman were created in God's image, failure to marry and reproduce would diminish God's image (*Yebamot* 63b). Moreover, if there are no descendants, how will the covenant with God be maintained? (*Yebamot* 64a).

There is a third alternative: Jesus may not have married officially, but his relationship with Mary of Magdala was close, strong, and loving, and it is attested by all the canonical gospels. Theirs may have been a "common law" marriage, and this may not be mentioned because not everybody may have been happy about it; but in truth, we cannot be sure. One thing we *do* know, however, and it is that they loved each other very much and that their love was single-minded, public, and enduring.

---

[32] Peter Brown, *The Body and Society* (New York: Columbia University Press, 1988), p. 62.
[33] Adin Steinsaltz, *The Essential Talmud* (New York: Bantam Books, 1976), p. 142.

I should add that it is totally ludicrous to maintain that Jesus could not have been married because his marriage would have compromised his divinity and his salvation work. Most traditional Christians believe that Jesus was *both* God and man, "truly God and truly man." If he was truly man, then marriage, as a natural human condition, was possible for him. Claiming that he had to be absolutely pure in order to effect the world's salvation and that marriage would have been a stain, implies that marriage is "bad," or sinful; but Christianity has maintained from its beginnings that marriage is good, and that sex within marriage is good too. In fact, many Christian denominations consider marriage a sacrament and claim that Jesus affirmed the sanctity of marriage when he attended the wedding feast in Cana.

Unfounded exaggerations are more detrimental to the faith than fanciful and novelistic considerations.

———— ✦ ————

Mary of Magdala is included by Luke (*Luke* 8:2) among the women who followed Jesus during his ministry. Some of these women had been healed, presumably by Jesus, though in the case of Mary, the text is not explicit: "seven demons had come out of her," it says simply. Today we would say that Jesus had "cured her of an intense malady," or "healed her from a severe disorder," as Meier translates the text.[34] Renan believed that the illness may have been sexual desire,"[35] though his evidence for this diagnosis is meager. The passage in *Tobit* 6–8 in which Tobit successfully exorcizes Asmodeus, the demon possessing Sarah, his intended wife (a jealous demon who had killed seven former husbands on their wedding nights!), is interesting and pertinent, but not convincing. The fact is, we do not know.

*What* was exorcized from Mary, if anything, is difficult to determine also because of the primitive state of medical knowledge and

[34] John P. Meier, *A Marginal Jew* (New York: Doubleday, 1994), vol. 2, p. 658.
[35] Ernest Renan, *The Life of Jesus* (New York: The Modern Library, 1927), p. 253.

the lack of clear etiological description. As Meier writes, "Mental illness, psychosomatic diseases, and such afflictions as epilepsy were often attributed to demonic possession."[36] Exorcisms as cures were common in the Israelite world of the time. Josephus describes one performed by a certain Eleazar and witnessed by Vespasian.[37] Jesus must have entertained the beliefs of his contemporaries that illnesses were caused by evil spirits. In that he was simply a man of his times.

Such attributions are not uncommon even today. Many years ago I was visiting an ancient mosque in Gujarat, India, when I spied a woman walking around the precinct rambling in a loud voice and uttering often incomprehensible noises. From my point of view, she was raving mad. Upon inquiring, however, I was told that she was possessed by a divine spirit who had alienated her mind. Some years later I did a survey of a fairly large and select population all across India, and found, to my surprise, that this belief was held pretty consistently even among well-educated people. When I joined the Jesuit novitiate, we were told never to pray to God to take away our minds—our hearts, our liberty, our health, yes, but never our minds, for fear that an evil spirit might bamboozle us.

If Jesus healed Mary of Magdala as well as some of the other women, it is understandable that they should have followed him assiduously and supported his ministry financially. For Jesus, the healings were certainly part of his messianic mission even if they were described in the language of exorcism.

Centuries later, Christians lumped together other provocative accounts of anonymous women dispersed throughout the gospels and superimposed them on Mary. The image of Mary of Magdala as a prostitute, and then as a repentant hermit, tickled people's imaginations and made for prurient art, and it endured for centuries even though, in fact, it has no foundation in history at all.[38]

---

[36] Meier, *A Marginal Jew*, vol. 2, p. 407.

[37] Josephus, *Antiquitates* VIII, 2, 5.

[38] In her book, *Harlots of the Desert* (Kalamazoo, MI: Cistercian Publications, 1987), p. 16, Benedicta Ward points out that such amalgams were performed "for ends which were not in any way historical." See also Bart D. Ehrman, *Peter, Paul, and Mary Magdalene* (New York: Oxford University Press, 2006), Part 3.

What *does* have a strong foundation in history is that Mary of Magdala was the first one to find out that Jesus's corpse was missing from the tomb in which it had been laid to rest. Whether or not this makes her the first witness to the resurrection of Jesus is an entirely different matter, since it involves an interpretation of the fact of the empty tomb.[39]

———✵———

Ehrman claims that "Jesus is best understood as a Jewish apocalyptic prophet,"[40] though other scholars, like Wink, think that this understanding of Jesus depends on the authenticity of the apocalyptic sayings attributed to Jesus,[41] about some of which there is doubt. Apocalypse refers to a future that is closed up, inevitably so, and which is therefore unchangeable. It sees the end as imminent, but with the belief that it will be followed by a new age in which all evils will be redressed and the good will triumph (*Mark* 9:1 and 13:30, *Luke* 21:34–36). For Jesus, this new age is the Kingdom of God whose coming is so imminent that it is already among us. Hence he can honestly advice his followers to seek this Kingdom first, right now, and above all things, for "the rest" (food, family, etc.), will be provided for later (*Matthew* 6:33, *Mark* 10:29–32). The expectation of a cosmic apocalypse at the end of time, a "Second Coming," is an invention of the later church to cover up the fact that the expected millennium failed to arrive.

Most Christians will probably agree with this picture of Jesus as an apocalyptic prophet. But the thing is that this view of Jesus is not at all unique, nor does it confer upon Jesus's special powers of perception or foresight. The fact is that apocalyptic prophets were common in Palestine at this time because the conditions in which ordinary

---

[39] Bart Ehrman, *Peter, Paul, and Mary Magdalene*, pp. 230–231.

[40] Bart D. Ehrman, *Peter, Paul, and Mary Magdalene*, p. 28. See also his *Jesus, Apocalyptic Prophet of the New Millennium* (New York: Oxford University Press, 1999).

[41] Walter Wink, *The Human Being*, pp. 158–197. See also James H. Charlesworth, *Jesus within Judaism* (New York: Doubleday, 1988), p. 38.

people lived were so dire that expectations of deliverance were ripe, and all that was needed was a charismatic leader or prophet to foment this expectation of imminent deliverance. Apocalypticism usually emerges in response to actual historical circumstances in which penury is experienced, and these conditions existed in Palestine in an almost exemplary manner.[42] Referring to these times, Josephus could write with a hint of sarcasm:

> Impostors and demagogues, under the guise of divine inspiration, provoked revolutionary actions and impelled the masses to act like madmen. They led them into the wilderness so that there God would show them the signs of imminent liberation.[43]

Thus the Qumranites (the Essenes) had walked out of Jerusalem under the leadership of the "Righteous Teacher" into the desert caves around the Dead Sea, there to expect the upcoming Armageddon. They did not pose a threat to the Romans; but where this was the case, Roman reprisals were swift and lethal. Judas of Galilee (around 6 CE), who led people to expect the end of Roman domination and the coming of the messiah, was apprehended and crucified with his two sons.[44]

Josephus also mentions an unnamed prophet who led the Samaritans to Mount Gerizim in the hope that God would restore their prosperity and give them freedom from the Romans. But Pontius Pilate put down this disturbance quickly and ruthlessly, as was his wont.[45] Then, around 45 CE, a certain Theudas, a self-proclaimed prophet, led some people to the river Jordan with expectations of a reenactment of Joshua's triumph. But Fadus, the governor

---

[42] Horsley, *Bandits, Prophets, and Messiahs*, pp. 151–153; Charlesworth, *Jesus within Judaism*, p. 35; John J. Collins, *The Scepter and the Star* (New York: Doubleday, 1995).

[43] Josephus, *The Jewish War*, 2, 259.

[44] Josephus, *Antiquities*, 20. 100–103.

[45] Josephus, *Antiquities*, 18. 85–87.

of Judea at the time, attacked them, captured Theudas, and had him executed.[46]

Josephus also mentions a prophet from Egypt who, in 56 CE, led people to the Mount of Olives outside Jerusalem in order to prepare an attack on the Roman garrison in the city. Felix, the governor at the time, attacked them first, killing most, though a few escaped.[47] Then in 62 CE, there was Jesus son of Hannaniah, who was also caught and executed.[48] Better known, of course, was John the Baptist, who was decapitated not only because he censored Herod Antipas (as the Gospels say), but because Herod feared he would lead an uprising.[49]

Against this background of sociopolitical ferment, it is not difficult to see Jesus as an apocalyptic prophet—not as an exceptional one, but as one in a long list of such prophets and charismatic leaders who maintained alive in the people the expectation of deliverance. There were also bandits of all sorts harassing the Romans and the Jewish authorities, and often defending, even militarily, the poor peasants among whom they lived. In fact, according to accounts of the juridical trials preceding Jesus's execution preserved in all the canonical gospels, Pilate offered the people a choice between Jesus bar Abbas and Jesus of Nazareth (*Mark* 15:7, *Luke* 23:19, *Matthew* 27:17, *John* 18:40). The people chose Jesus bar Abbas, and one may well ask, Why? Well, bar Abbas was a well-known, Robin Hood—like bandit (*lestés*), of which there were many around, for the harsh conditions of the peasant folk under the Romans and their allies, the Temple priests, made the frequent appearance of such generous highwaymen a necessity for survival. In choosing him over Jesus of Nazareth, the crowd preferred a known benefactor of the poor and an enemy of the Romans—that is, a real patriot.

---

[46] Josephus, *Antiquities*, 20. 97–98.
[47] Josephus, *Jewish War*, 2. 261–263; *Antiquities*, 20. 169–171.
[48] Josephus, *Jewish War*, 6. 300–309.
[49] Josephus, *Antiquities*, 18. 116–119.

It must have become clear by now that what we know as Christianity today did not appear one fine day in the first decades of the Common Era, packaged and ready for distribution. Christianity is a construct, and as such, its formation underwent pressures of all sorts for over two hundred years that influenced the outcome. What sort of political and ideological forces were at play during the formation of the Christian tradition?

Already during his own life, Jesus was aware that people were talking about him and expressing differing opinions about his work. At least once he asked his followers about these views (*Matthew* 16:13 *ff.*, *Gospel of Thomas* 13), but the confrontations with Sadducees and Pharisees must have indicated to him clearly that he was a somewhat controversial figure. His dealings with women and with the rich, including tax collectors, made him unpopular in some quarters; the fact that his disciples flouted the Sabbath regulations irked the religious authorities; and that he lectured publicly without authorization from the rabbinate was another source of conflict. He did nothing to diminish the negative views of him even when the fate of his life was hanging in the balance. Some apparently took him to be the expected military savior of Israel, the one who would liberate the people from Roman domination. Judas Iscariot may have held this opinion, and his surrender of Jesus to the authorities may have been prompted by a wish to force Jesus's hand and precipitate a revolt (though the newly discovered *Gospel of Judas* gives a different motivation). When this did not materialize, Judas realized his mistake, but it was too late.[50] As is clear from the story of the disciples on the way to Emmaus (*Luke* 24:13 *ff.*), when Jesus died, disillusionment set in because some of the expectations did not seem to have been fulfilled.

The post-resurrection narratives indicate an effort to rehabilitate the image of Jesus and to tone down his message. The distrust of

---

[50] The view that Jesus was a rebel who consorted with rebels (*lestai*) has some basis in the careful analysis of the texts, for example, *Matthew* 27:38, *John* 18:40, *Luke* 6:15–16. On the other hand, it is not clear whether or not there were Zealots in Jesus's time, though they certainly played a role later in the war against the Romans. Michael Baigent's arguments in *The Jesus Papers* (San Francisco: HarperSanFrancisco, 2006) are weak and trite, interesting but unscholarly.

the women's testimony about the empty tomb reveals the opinion the men harbored about the women, and this despite Jesus's expressed views on the subject. The *Gospel of Mary* records some of the bitter differences within the immediate circle of followers regarding the equality of men and women. In fact, according to some scholars, there was a deliberate effort to suppress the traditions that originated with Mary of Magdala, whom some records depict as the brightest and most devoted disciple of Jesus.[51] In addition, when Paul and Barnabas began their ministry to the Gentiles, disputes arose between them and the leadership in Jerusalem. Some, eventually called Ebionites, believed that Jesus's message was addressed only to Jews, and that therefore anyone desiring to join the newly formed sect should have to become a Jew first. Therefore they wanted all converts from paganism to be circumcised and to observe the *kosher* food laws. Paul had to go to Jerusalem to confront Peter and the rest of the leadership (*Galatians* 2:11), and for years the "circumcision party" hounded him (*Acts* 11:2) and elicited from him angry outbursts. Peter eventually changed his mind with regard to the *kosher* laws. The *Acts of the Apostles* narrates a dream Peter had in which he saw a sheet descending from heaven full of all kinds of edibles, "clean and unclean," and he heard a voice saying, "Peter, wake up and eat!" "No, Lord," he answered, "I will not eat anything unclean." The voice spoke again: "What God has made, don't you dare call unclean!" (*Acts* 10:9–16). Peter understood and thereafter ceased insisting on the observance of the *kosher* laws for the Gentile converts. Despite their judaizing efforts, the Ebionites were in many respects more true to the view that Jesus seems to have had of himself than the views that became orthodox later on.

But, as was mentioned above, another early group, the Marcionites or followers of Marcion (85–144), saw Jesus as totally

---

[51] See *Gospel of Mary* 10:1 *ff.*, *Pistis Sophia*, *The Dialogue of the Savior*, especially 139:12, and *The Sophia of Jesus Christ*. Also Ann Graham Brock, *Mary Magdalene* (Cambridge, MA: Harvard Divinity School, 2003); Holly E. Hearon, *The Mary Magdalene Tradition* (Collegeville, MN: Liturgical Press, 2004); and Jane Schaberg, *The Resurrection of Mary Magdalene Legends, Apocrypha, and the New Testament* (New York: Continuum, 2002).

spiritual and as not even having a real physical body, but only an apparent one. Jesus was deprived of all Jewishness. Thus the Docetist heresy. In support of their views, they often quoted Paul and also the legends that claimed that Mary had become pregnant with Jesus without having been impregnated by a man and that her hymen had remained intact after a miraculous birth. These legends were contained in the *Infancy Gospels* and other similar writings. Jesus, a divine being, passed through Mary "like water through a pipe," they said. Some of this was the result of an effort to shed the Jewish roots of the new movement. Still, these and similar views were strenuously opposed by those who considered themselves the standard bearers of the true orthodox tradition, people like Tertullian, Irenaeus, Hypolitus, Cyprian, Origen, Justin, Athanasius, Ossius, and others, but the fact is that no single true orthodoxy existed at the time, though it was being created in the interplay of politics and ideologies.

There were other more subtle ways of presenting contrasting interpretations of the life and work of Jesus: letters and accounts were forged representing particular ideologies, and these exercised a great degree of influence, even though we know them to be forgeries. Thus, of the many letters attributed to St. Paul, only Romans, Galatians, First and Second Corinthians, First Thessalonians, Philemon, and Philippians were written by him, and even these have interpolations that obviously were foreign and even contradictory to his thought. But the fact that the other letters continued to carry his name gave them ascendancy and convincing power, and they were the source of many later orthodoxies. All the letters attributed to Paul, however, are valuable in that they expose the variety of views Paul had to deal with and commend or oppose in his ministry.

The Gnostics were, of course, always hovering about the newly minted sect, interpreting old and new teachings in surprisingly novel ways. They resurfaced in the nineteenth century as Theosophists and Anthroposophists as if they had not skipped a beat. Valentinians, Nazareans, Phibionites, Theodotians, Montanists, Manichaeans (who reappeared in the twelfth century as Cathari, Albigensians, and Bogomils), and the later Arians, Monophysites, Nestorians, and Donatists are some of the groups that fought each other, often viciously, for the title of orthodoxy. Matters were complicated when particular emperors adopted one or another of the theological views. The various "creeds" represent some of the compromises that were reached. Their intricate and abstract terminology is part of an ongoing recourse to reason in order to settle disagreements over highly imaginative, metaphorical, and slippery texts whose meaning could not be captured with precision by a single term. Orthodoxy required definition exact enough to exclude unorthodoxy and condemn its supporters as heretics. What emerged, and what remained fixed until the Reformation (and in many cases beyond), was not at all what Jesus had preached but what many interpreted him as having said after much discussion and compromise.

---

It is perhaps worth insisting once more on the fact that the canonical gospels (*Matthew, Mark, Luke,* and *John*) did not come out whole and entire in one book published in the year 100 CE, nor were they the only or the earliest documents. Many other documents can claim equal or earlier ancestry, like the *Sayings Gospel Q* and the *Gospel of Thomas*, and some, like the *Secret Gospel of Mark*, claimed Mark himself as its author, while the *Gospel of Thomas* derived from the teaching of Judas Thomas, the twin brother of Jesus (or of his brothers or sisters). Another early text, *The Shepherd*, by Hermas, was widely read in many churches East and West, and its wide readership commended it for inclusion in the canon, though it was eventually excluded.

No, the four canonical gospels emerged as the only orthodox ones slowly, over a period of two hundred years after their compilation, through a process of weeding out the texts that the hierarchy did not like, and by putting down the churches that used them. This was the case, for example, with the *Secret Gospel of Mark*, which was very much in vogue in Alexandria. A major figure in this march to orthodoxy was Irenaeus (*ca.* 125–202), who was born in Asia Minor but ended up as bishop of Lyons, in France. His *Adversus Haereses* (*ca.* 180), a monumental work of refutation of everything he disagreed with, was extremely influential in this regard, but there were many others who wrote in opposition or in favor of the emerging dogmas. Many of the details of these developments are retold by Hegesippus (*fl.* second century) and by Eusebius of Caesarea (*ca.* 263–339) in his *Ecclesiastical History*, but they can be glimpsed in the writings of Tertullian (*ca.* 160–230), Origen (185–254), Hippolytus (*ca.* 160–235), Cyprian († 258), Epiphanius (*ca.* 315–403), and many, many others.

This brief comment may serve as another warning to those who claim inerrancy for the four gospels they believe come directly from God. Not merely do we *not* have original texts for which we could claim divine authorship, there were dozens of texts as original and as revered as those four, and the latter were excluded from the canon not by divine revelation but by political intrigue that was sometimes devious and nasty.

# From Jewish Man
# to Gentile God

It is difficult to know how and when exactly Jesus "the human being," "the son-of-the-man," became Jesus "the son of God." All Jews, of course, considered themselves to be children of God, and Jesus would at times refer to himself simply as a child of God. But soon after his death, the expression became special and began to denote a transcendental meaning that would have been foreign to the thought of any Jew. The Jews guarded zealously the uniqueness of God, a uniqueness that the First Commandment had emphasized, so it was not likely that any Jew would compromise that very Jewish attitude toward God for which millions of Jews have died since the time of Caligula until the Holocaust. In fact, one of the strongest arguments for the view that the early Jewish followers of Jesus did not see him as divine, as *the* son of God (in the modern theological sense), is that, even today, Jews do not consider Jesus to be divine, and for the same reason, such affirmation would be contrary to Jewish belief. So where did it originate?

The divinization of Jesus was probably due to many factors. One was the way that the new followers of Jesus spoke of him within their communities. Their perceptions do not appear fully formed but developed over time, often in the space of two or three hundred years. And, of course, not all communities developed a view of Jesus as divine: this conception took place mostly among the Hentile converts, while the Jewish one continued to see him as merely human even while using at times the same language that will later character-ize the view of Jesus as the son of God.[1] Another factor was surely the fact that Paul's letters, all addressed to Gentile converts, devel-oped this notion of Jesus as divine for reasons I shall explain later. Paul also insisted on the equality of Jews and Greeks and Christians, thereby eliminating Jewishness as a distinctive mark of Jesus, making it easier to emphasize his divinity. The *Gospel of John*, too, declared from the beginning that Jesus was the divine Word become *human* (*not* Jewish!), making Jewishness secondary and divinity primary, and paving the way for Marcion's views. These were the precursors, as it were, of further elaborations.

It would seem that the divinization of Jesus took place among the Gentile converts to the new sect. This would make sense because divinization of humans was common among the Gentiles, whether in Greece or in Rome. Greco-Roman religion did not conceive of an impassable chasm between gods and humans; in fact, the gods were often described in very human terms, and they often had con-verse and even intimate sexual relations with humans resulting in offspring, which, truly, could be called divine. When Dionysus strut-ted into Thebes as a young and beautiful man, he announced to all (as Euripides tells us at the beginning of *The Bacchae*) that he was "the son of God." And indeed he was, for he was the child of Zeus and Semele, daughter of Cadmus, king of Thebes. Aeneas, too, the legendary founder of Rome, was divine, being the child of the god-dess Aphrodite and the mortal shepherd Anchises, who had been ravished by her (and left crippled!) in the hills surrounding Troy. The great warrior Achilles was even more divine, since he was the son of Zeus and a minor goddess, Thetis. Olympias, the wife of Philip I of Macedonia, tried to claim that her son, Alexander, was not the son of her husband but of the god Zeus—but people laughed at her. The legendary founders of Rome, Romulus and Remus, where twins born

[1] Cf. Bart D. Ehrman, *Jesus, Interrupted* (New York: HarperOne, 2009), pp. 246–254. Also J. Louis Martin, *History and Theology in the Fourth Gospel* (New York: Harper & Row, 1968), and Raymond Brown, SS, *The Community of the Beloved Disciple* (New York: Paulist Press, 1979). Exhaustively, Bart D. Ehrman, *How Jesus Became God* (New York: HarperCollins, 2014).

to Princess Rhea Sylvia and the god Mars. Even the Bible spoke of the Nephilim, great heroes of old, as sons of the gods who had mated with beautiful human maidens (*Genesis* 6:4 and *Numbers* 13:33). So, to claim that Jesus was the son of Mary and the god YHWH would not have seemed outrageous or even much of an exaggeration to the Greeks and Romans hearing the "good news" for the first time.

But Paul? A good Jew proclaiming the divinity of another Jew whose followers he had persecuted? Paul may have come from a Hellenizing family: they had Roman citizenship, they spoke Greek, though they were Jewish enough to send Paul to study in Jerusalem. Moreover, Paul had his own personal problem to solve. As Saul, in his late teens or early twenties, and before his conversion, he had been an accomplice in the stoning to death of Stephen, as he himself tells us (*Acts* 7:58–8:1 and 22:20).[2] He had also approved of the murder of the young man. These were virtuous acts according to the Law, for Stephen (probably a Hellenizer) was considered a blasphemer, and the orthodox had a certain obligation to uphold the traditional religion. So, even after the stoning, Paul could consider himself "blameless," as he avers. But then, suddenly, on the road to Damascus, he experiences a blinding light and hears a voice that claims to be the voice of Jesus, who identifies himself with the dead Stephen and those followers of "the Way" (as the young movement was known at that time) that Saul was then persecuting (*Acts* 9:4–6; 22:6–11; 26:13–18). This experience startles and shocks him, because the stoning of Stephen, which he had interpreted as a good act, was now perceived as an evil one, a murder, a sin. Now, suddenly, from "blameless" he is turned into an accessory to the murder of an innocent man (*Acts* 7:58 and 8:1).

To this overpowering experience of sinfulness, Judaism offered the path of repentance. But regret was not simply a matter of "feeling" sorry, it required an accompanying effort to uproot evil in one's own heart. Repentance required one to change one's ways and to

---

[2]  There are differences, even discrepancies, between what Paul says of himself (or the narrator says of him) in *Acts* and in his letters. This particular acknowledgment, however, though absent from the letters, seems genuine.

walk again in the ways of the Lord. Repentance was *teshuvah*, a return to a life of purity and devotion to the Law. The Torah was the only remedy against the impulse of evil, but Paul must have felt that if the Torah had not been enough to save him from the sin of murder, how could it save him from evil in the future? He must have told himself that if he wanted to be "blameless" (as he had been), he would have to look for a new escape from sin, a new cleansing and forgiveness, and a new and different religious path. This shift would have been easier for him to make because of the Hellenizing background of his family.

Saul was temporarily blinded. His companions heard something like a voice, but did not see the flash of light. They helped him up and took him to Damascus, where he recovered his eyesight. He was then instructed by a disciple named Ananias and by others (*Acts* 9:10), and much later he gave a brief account of what he was taught then (*1 Corinthians* 15:3–10). After this he spent some time, two or three years, by himself in the desert of Arabia and in Damascus (*Galatians* 1:15–17). When he emerged from his own retreat, he was Paul.

Paul was a reasonably well-schooled man. He had grown up in Tarsus, a city that boasted a good school of Stoic philosophy, which Paul may not have attended, but whose teachings show up in the traces of Stoic philosophy in his letters. He grew up in the midst of pagan stories about the gods, which to him must have been commonplace, even though repugnant to his Jewishness. Also, as a Pharisee, he imbibed the apocalyptic expectations of this group, including a belief in the resurrection of the dead at the end of time.

---

Paul never says that he "saw" Jesus, but only that he "heard" a voice, though he often refers to this experience as an "apparition." He interpreted this voice to be that of Jesus's, which seems logical, but he also concluded that this must have been the voice of the *resurrected* Jesus. Why he did this is not entirely clear, for it was not uncommon to have the living hear the voices of the dead without thereby claiming that the dead had come back to life. Both in pagan literature (the ghost of Caesar appearing to and speaking with Brutus) and in Jewish lore (the ghost of Samuel appearing to and speaking to King Saul), similar occurrences had taken place without a claim to resurrection. But this is the way Paul interpreted his own experience, perhaps prompted by the Pharisaic belief that the dead would rise on the final days, and his belief that the final days were beginning just then and there. As he confronted his new experience of sin, Paul may also have come to believe that the righteous Jesus had atoned for the unrighteous Saul (and all other sinners like him) by his death upon the cross and by his resurrection, thus chastening him again and making him acceptable to God. One senses an almost desperate effort to show that if Jesus did not rise from the dead, then our (*his!*) sins are not forgiven (*1 Corinthians* 15:3–8; *1 Thessalonians* 4:13–17), and he peremptorily affirms that only those who affirm the resurrection of Jesus will be saved (*Romans* 10:9). All these thoughts must have wrestled with each other as he spent time in the desert by himself, trying to effect a synthesis and interpretation of his own experiences as a Jew living among pagans in the diaspora of Tarsus, as a Pharisee, as a zealous teenager in Jerusalem, as an apocalypticist, and as a sinner. The theological amalgam he effected in incomparable detail and thoroughness became the blueprint of what was later known as Christianity. It was not accepted by all; James the brother of Jesus, and the Ebionites, for example, disagreed, but the weakening of the traditional Jewish faction and their dispersion with the destruction of the Temple in 70 CE gave ascendancy to Paul's theology, which, after all, was spreading rapidly to the growing numbers of recruits from among the Gentiles. This message, also, would become more palatable to the Gentiles who carried their own religious backgrounds with them when they embraced the new faith. It would also serve to differentiate more clearly the new sect from the traditional Jews surrounding them. Paul would hone this message for the next twenty-something years of preaching and writing until his death in Rome under Emperor Nero, to whose court he had appealed. The struggles among Marcionites, Ebionites, Valentinians, Arians, and Nestorians would still be fought, but in Paul's theology, they all had more to fight about than the simple life and the direct utterances of Jesus, "the human being," "the son-of-the-man." The extent of the progression can be glimpsed in a careful reading of the genuine Pauline letters and in the solemn statements of the Nicene Creed (325).

————— ✦✦ —————

Why was Saul, before his conversion, such a rabid enemy of the followers of Jesus? It is hard to say for sure, but it may be that, after the authorities of the Temple disowned the nascent sect, Saul felt it was his duty to support them against all comers, especially since the high priesthood was securely ensconced in the hands of just one family.[3] Saul, after all, must have expected to share in that authority to teach after his own studies were completed, for that is how he was identified then: a zealous Jew, born in Tarsus but raised in Jerusalem at the feet of Gamaliel, and educated according to the strict manner of the Law (*Acts* 22:3). Some of this was not strictly historical, but it was good public relations.

————— ✦✦ —————

One should not be overcritical of Paul; after all, he may not be responsible for everything that is attributed to him. To begin with, as I mentioned above, about half of the letters assigned to him are forgeries that cleverly used his name to justify opinions quite different from, even contradictory to, his own. *Romans, 1 Corinthians, 2 Corinthians, Galatians, 1 Thessalonians, Philemon, Philippians,* and perhaps *Ephesians,* are generally considered to be authentically Paul's, but even these contain additions and comments that are not his own. And then there are the changes introduced into the texts during the anti-Semitic furor of the second century, where the texts may have been cleansed of many Judaic doctrines deemed offensive. The bitter anti-Semitism discernible in the letters may not be Paul's at all, but the product of Gentile scribes and copyists. Marcion's work would

---

[3]  Crossan, *Birth of Christianity*, p. 464.

have been the model. Later on Paul's views would have been further modified by the Hellenistic theology of the Greek Fathers, and it is this theology that we take today to be Paul's thought. But even if Paul wandered from the Judaism of his upbringing and propounded views that were decidedly un-Jewish, he may not have held opinions that were as extreme in this respect as the ones we discern today in his writings. In other words, we interpret Paul too easily in terms of the theology that was developed centuries after him, and thereby betray the meanings that he most likely had in mind; we rob him of *his* Judaism.[4] Take the hymn from *Philippians* 2:6–11, a hymn that is viewed as parallel to the Prologue of *John* (itself a precursor of the anti-Semitism of Marcion), and which is taken to proclaim a belief in Jesus as God who humbles himself in becoming human, even to the acceptance of death on the cross: this hymn, which was in existence before Paul used it, may refer to the common understanding that all human beings were created in "the image" (*morphe*) of God, as *Genesis* 1:27 has it, a fact that might induce any human being to deem himself/herself special:

> Though he was the image of God
> He did not flaunt this semblance to God
> But humbled himself,
> Acting like a servant,
> Looking like a man
> And behaving like one,
> subject to death
> [even death on a cross].[5]
> Therefore God exalted him
> And gave him a name above all names,
> That in the name of Jesus all knees be bent
> [in heaven, on earth, under the earth],
> And every tongue should intone:
> LORD JESUS CHRIST,
> To the divine honor of the Father.

---

4   James Charlesworth, *Jesus within Judaism*, p. 48.
5   Phrases in square brackets are Paul's (or a scribe's) comments.

In this literal version, the greatness of Jesus is maintained, but his divinity is not emphasized, as it would not have been in a hymn composed by Jews. I should add that the verses that speak of a name given to Jesus, a name above every other name to which all knees should bend, may not be Paul's at all. They do not appear in another version of the hymn found in *The Gospel of Truth* 20, 21:

> Jesus appeared...
> Was nailed to a tree...
> He humbled himself even unto death,
> though clothed in eternal life.
> He stripped off the perishable rags
> and clothed himself in incorruptibility,
> which no one can take from him.

These verses may be additions by a scribe who believed that the name "Jesus" had magical powers. The practice of using Jesus's name as a kind of incantation appears already while Jesus was alive (*Mark* 9:38–41). That it continued after his death can be gleaned from the hilarious incident narrated in *Acts* 19:13–20.[6]

Hymns like these were plentiful around the time of Jesus, to judge by the Thanksgiving Psalms and other hymns of Qumran,[7] the *Sibylline Oracles*, and the later *Odes of Solomon*.[8]

------ ✴ ------

The context of this hymn in *Philippians* 2:6–11 allows us to glimpse another reason Paul was so obsessed with the resurrection of Jesus. The enduring of shame was not a Gentile virtue, for both Greeks and Romans treasured reputation, a good name, and behav-

---

[6] Wayne A. Meeks, *The Origins of Christian Morality* (New Haven, CT: Yale University Press, 1993), p. 114.

[7] See Michael Wise, Martin Abegg, and Edward Cook, eds., *The Dead Sea Scrolls* (San Francisco: HarperSan Francisco, 1996), pp. 84–113.

[8] William Barnstone and Marvin Meyer, eds., *The Gnostic Bible* (Boston: Shanbhala, 2003), pp. 357–385.

ing honorably so that the name of one's family was enhanced in the eyes of all. Yet in the story of Jesus, he had the founder of this new spiritual tradition not merely humiliated in a general way but actually shamed by death upon a cross. What were the followers of Jesus, especially the Gentile ones, to do when confronted with this undeniable fact? One way was to stress the belief that Jesus had not just died on the cross, he had been raised from the dead and crowned in the heavenly glory. The pseudo-Pauline *Letter to the Hebrews* 12:2 stated this explicitly: "Jesus…endured the cross, making light of its disgrace, and has taken his seat at the right hand of God." This message reappears often in the Pauline writings, in the Prologue of *John*, and in other popular materials, including the famous Roman *graffito*. The humiliations of crucifixion are made to seem compensated by the resurrection and glorification of Jesus,[9] and humility and meekness, those virtues that so riled Nietzsche, become acceptable for all Christians to practice. Thus, besides Paul's private psychological reason (mentioned above) for insistence on the resurrection, there is here added a pastoral one, of similar weight, if he is to be successful in his preaching to the Gentiles.

———⋙⋘———

In conclusion, it is still the case that Paul's message was different from the one preached by Jesus and his immediate followers. One may explain why this was so, but it is the case that it *was* so. Jesus, for example, taught that the Law, the Law of Moses, had to be observed in order to enter the Kingdom; Paul, on the other hand, taught that deeds ("works") under the Law were insufficient to effect salvation— only belief in Jesus and his resurrection could do this. As Ehrman puts it, "The historical Jesus taught the Law. Paul taught Jesus."[10]

Further, Paul's view, which the Gentile converts embraced, slowly came to represent the views of the larger number of Christians and of the official hierarchy, especially in the Latin/Roman West.

---

[9]  Meeks, *Origin of Christian Morality*, pp. 86–88.
[10]  Bart Ehrman, *Jesus, Interrupted*, p. 239.

As the Roman presence in the Western world established itself more firmly (if less securely in military terms), Latin grew in importance as the language of the Church. Latin had this advantage over Greek, that it was a more concrete language, less given to abstraction and therefore less liable to misinterpretation. Thus the key theological formulas that Tertullian and Pope Leo the Great had developed in Latin expressed with greater clarity what the Greek formulas of Athanasius and the Alexandrian theologians sought to explain; also, they were much less encumbered by theological and linguistic disputes such as followed the condemnation of Arius. Finally, they were brought into the Nicene Creed by Ossius of Cordoba (256–357),[11] who not only presided at the Council of Nicaea as delegate of the Pope of Rome, but also headed the committee that actually redacted the Creed. Thus the views of the Gentile converts and their theologians came to represent the orthodoxy of the Church, and all other views were thenceforward deemed heretical.[12]

———— ✦ ————

Perhaps the most important factor in the divinization of Jesus was the acceptance and application of the notion of *revelation* to the person of the historical Jesus. Revelation, as Brito explains, "takes place in the dimension of a Word, of a speaking subjectivity whose voice is prolonged in Scripture and is retained in privileged witnesses."[13] More simply put, revelation is "God's speech to us."[14] God was "heard" to speak to us in the person of Jesus, God's son, whose

---

[11] "Ossius the Great" (*hosios ho megas*), as Athanasius calls him (*Apologia contra Arianos* 89). See Isidore of Seville, *De viris illustr.* 5; ML 81, 1086.

[12] Ehrman, *Jesus, Interrupted*, p. 214.

[13] Emilio Brito, *De Dieu. Connaissance et Inconnaissance*, 2 vols. (Leuven, Belgium: Peeters, 2018), II, p. 872.

[14] Michaele Nicolau, SJ, *De Revelatione Christiana* (Biblioteca de Autores Cristianos; Madrid: Editorial Católica, 1958), p. 89. The literature on Revelation is enormous. Most of it concerns the ways in which revelation takes place, and little is said about philosophical difficulties with the concept itself. I believe that revelation is impossible, and I have made my arguments exhaustively elsewhere. See William J. Abraham, "Divine Revelation," in Christopher C. Green and

utterances were therefore deemed infallible. In these utterances, Jesus spoke as God, revealing himself as God's son, and therefore as a divine being.

The adoption of revelation and the hermeneutics that accompanied it were accomplished against the background of a strict biblical belief that God is unknowable in Godself. When Moses asked to see God, YHWH replied: "You cannot see my face, for no one shall see me and live" (*Exodus* 33:20). This tradition continued in Christianity. Gregory of Nazianzus explained: "Whatever we imagined or figured to ourselves, or reason delineated, is not the reality of God."[15] St. Augustine concurred: "If you understand, it is not God [you understand]";[16] and Aquinas, equally explicitly: "One thing about God remains completely unknown in this life, namely, what God is."[17] But the theologians came up with this subterfuge: We can know about God what God Godself reveals about Godself. This is revelation!

But to be valid, any revelation would have to be made by God Godself, and it would have to be made in language that we could understand, which means that it would have to be perceivable as all phenomena are; and this would mean that *ex definitione* it would obfuscate the very God it was trying to reveal; so in effect, it would reveal nothing.

This is the fundamental reason so many so-called revelations all over the world claim uniqueness, yet they cannot substantiate their case, because in fact they are merely phenomenal attestations by people claiming to be the *noumenon*-god, which claim cannot be verified, and therefore their attestations cannot be proved. *But they can be believed*, as long as the believers realize that such an assent on their part is paradoxical; because no phenomenal utterance about the *noumenon* is ever verifiable. For, as Kierkegaard explained, "if a believer

David I. Starling, eds., *Revelation and Reason in Christian Theology* (Bellingham, WA: Lexham Press, 2018), pp. 63–89.

[15] *Oratio* 28. 6 (Brian Matz translation).

[16] *Sermo* 117, 3, 5; ML 38, 663.

[17] *In Rom.*, c. I, *lect* 6.

answer the objection he is *eo ipso* not a believer."[18] This would mean that no dogma is ever provable, and that all faith, really, has nothing to do with dogmas and beliefs, but is merely a person's opening to what ultimately matters.

As a consequence of the acceptance of revelation, the Jewishness of Jesus was thereby lost, obliterated in one fell swoop; for God, obviously, is neither Jew nor Gentile. At the same time, the lowly laborer from Nazareth was imbued with all the attributes of divinity; and even though controversies about his nature would continue through the centuries, his fate was sealed forever.

# A Historical Note

It should be pointed out that the standard Christian version of Israel at the time of Jesus as a decadent and formalistic religious society has no foundation in history. It grew out of a desire to paint Christianity as a new revival of the old faith of the prophets. Casting the temple priesthood in the role of reactionary bigots who rejected the true messiah, Jesus, and the promise of a new resurgence of Israel, was at bottom another form of anti-Semitism. This anti-Semitism is still preserved in the popular naming of the Christian scriptures as the *New* Testament.[19]

---

[18] Søren Kierkagaard, *The Journals* (Oxford: Oxford University Press, 1938), No. 922.

[19] Thompson, *The Mythic Past*, pp. 196–199.

# The Message of Jesus

What was Jesus's message? He preached love of God and love of people (*Matthew* 22:34–40, *Mark* 12:28–31, *Lk* 10:25–28), but there is nothing new here (though Christians have claimed that this is Jesus's special "commandment"); for, after all, such love was already counseled by *Deuteronomy* 6:5 and *Leviticus* 19:18; and Hillel (75–10 BCE), the great Jewish teacher, had already maintained that love was more important than the 613 mandates of the Law. Asked once to expound the Law in the time a man could stand on one foot upon a stone, Hillel said, "Don't do to another what you hate. This is the Law; the rest is commentary." Taking a broader perspective, Mo-tzu (479–381 BCE), in China, had preached an all-embracing benevolence,[1] and even earlier, in India, the Buddha (*ca.* 563–483 BCE) had discovered the doctrine of universal compassion, how he was "to open his whole being to others, and thus transcending the ego in compassion and loving-kindness to all other creatures."[2] Surely there are subtle differences among all of these views, but compassion is not more distinctive of Jesus's message than it is of Buddha's or of Mo-tzu's.

Jesus preached that God is fatherly toward people and suggested that people call God "Father" when they pray (*Matthew* 6:9); and in

---

[1] Fung Yu-lan, *A Short History of Chinese Philosophy* (New York: The Free Press, 1966), pp. 53–55.

[2] Karen Armstrong, *The Great Transformation* (New York: Alfred A. Knopf, 2006), p. 279.

the parable of the kind father (*Luke* 15:11–32), he illustrated the way in which God deals with people.

But perhaps the dominant idea of his message was that God's power is near at hand, that we should pray for the coming of God's presence (*Matthew* 6:10[3]), and that God's presence will be actually felt when we treat all people alike as children of God (especially women). After all, both men and women were created in the image of God. And so he prayed repeatedly that we all should be one (*John* 17:11 and 21), and the *Gospel of Thomas* reports that he said, "When you make the two one...and when you make the male and the female one and the same...then you will enter the kingdom."[4] Another document from the early second century explains:

> The Lord himself, being asked by a certain person when his kingdom would come, said... "When the two shall be one...and the male with the female, neither male nor female."... And by "the male with the female, neither male nor female," he means this, that a brother seeing a sister should have no thought of her as female, and that a sister seeing a brother should have no thought of him as male... "If you do these things," he said, "the kingdom of my Father shall come."[5]

And he did as he preached. Jesus addressed his message largely to women. The imagery he employed appealed to and was drawn

---

[3] "Presence," "rule," "dominion" are better translations of Aramaic *malkuth* (Greek *basileia*) than "kingdom." It is the extension of heaven on earth that we are to pray for. See W. K. Grossouw, *Spirituality of the New Testament* (St. Louis, MO: Herder, 1961), pp. 27 and 31.

[4] *Gospel of Thomas* 22. *The Nag Hammadi Library*, ed. James M. Robinson (San Francisco: Harper & Row, 1971), p. 121.

[5] *2 Clement* 12. The Pauline tradition is full of such sayings. See *Galatians* 3:28; *Romans* 10:12 and 3:22; *1 Corinthians* 12:13; *Ephesians* 2:15; *and Colossians* 3:11.

from local customs and traditions, primarily of women. For example, the images of grain and wheat (*John* 12:24) hearkened to the entire feminine tradition of agriculture and fertility.[6] He did not disdain, as was the custom, to speak to women, even Samaritan women, and women were prominent companions of his walks.

Jesus probably was not a flaming liberal feminist: he was a man of his times. Still, many of Jesus's arguments with the leaders of his day concerned the low status of women and the prerogatives men had granted to themselves and denied to women. For example, the discussion of divorce in *Matthew* 19:3–12 is not about divorce itself as much as about the fact that *men* could divorce their wives, often for trivial reasons, while women were denied the same right even for weighty reasons. Jesus's doctrine, that if a man divorces his wife and marries another woman, he commits adultery, is not so much a repudiation of divorce as of the exclusive male right to it, and the men in the audience understood this well: "If that is the position with husband and wife, it is better not to marry!" they said. That is, "If we cannot divorce our wives, it is better to remain free." Men were not ready to treat women as equals and to grant to them the same rights they abrogated to themselves.

When Jesus was apprehended, the men dispersed, but the women followed from afar. They stood by the cross; they watched as the corpse was lowered from the cross, anointed it hurriedly, and took notice of the provisional burial place; and they were up early on Sunday to go to the tomb and do a better job of anointing the body when Jesus appeared to *them*.[7]

But after Jesus's death, the men found they lacked the courage to implement the equality among the sexes that Jesus had preached. The men did not believe the women's witness, only Peter's; in fact, Paul did not list Mary as a witness at all (*1 Corinthians* 15:5–7). The

---

[6] Anthony J. Gittins, "Grains of wheat: culture, agriculture, and spirituality," *Spirituality Today* 42:3 (Autumn 1990): 196–208.

[7] See *Mark* 16:9–11 and *John* 20:11–18. Also Ferdinand Pratt, *Jesus Christ: His Life, His Teaching, and His Work* (Milwaukee: Bruce Publishing Co., 1950), vol. 2, 420 and 528; and Brown, *Death*, II, 1002 *ff.*

*Gospel of Thomas* 114[8] has Peter asking the risen Jesus, "Let Mary leave us, for women are not worthy of Life"; and in the *Gospel of Mary* 17:10–25,[9] both Andrew and Peter voice their skepticism: "Did he [Jesus] really speak privately with a woman (and) not openly to us? Are we to turn about and all listen to her? Did he prefer her to us?" When Mary defends herself, only Levi comes to her aid, saying: "Peter, you have always been hot-tempered. Now I see you contending against the woman like the adversaries. But if the Savior made her worthy, who are you indeed to reject her? Surely the Savior knows her very well. That is why he loved her more than us" (18:8–15).

———— ⭐ ————

But I would be remiss if I left off without mention of those who claimed that the real message of Jesus was communicated only to a few select disciples. Since the early years following the death of Jesus, his followers began to collect the sayings and explanations that they considered important in terms of his life and his teachings. Thus the collections we know as *Gospels* came into being. But from the very beginning, claims were made that Jesus had not gone public with all the knowledge he possessed relevant to the Kingdom of Heaven. Claims arose that he reserved the real stuff for only a few, the disciples, and even that he singled some among these for special instruction, people like his brother Judas "the Twin" (Thomas), his brother James, Judas Iscariot, and Mary of Magdala. At some point, Jesus told his disciples that he spoke to the general populace in parables, but that with them he could be straightforward and not cryptic: "You have been given the privilege of knowing the secrets of the Kingdom of Heaven, but this privilege has not been granted to anyone else" (*Matthew* 13:11). But even among the privileged ones, some were more privileged than others. In the *Gospel of Mary* 6:2, Peter asks Mary Magdalene, "Tell us the words of the Savior that you know, but which we have not heard." Mary complied, but as was said

---

[8]  "Gospel of Thomas," in *The Nag Hammadi Library*, p. 130.
[9]  "Gospel of Mary," in *The Nag Hammadi Library*, p. 473.

above, Mary's discourse was met with some incredulity (*Gospel of Mary* 10:3–4) because she was a woman; but similar claims are made in the *Secret Book of James* 1:3, and in the *Gospel of Thomas*, which is said to contain "the secret sayings that the living Jesus spoke and which his twin, Judas Thomas, recorded." Again, in the recently discovered *Gospel of Judas* [35], Jesus says to Judas Iscariot, "Step away from the others and I shall tell you the mysteries of the kingdom."

Among the ancient developments of the message of Jesus, the Gnostics claimed to possess a secret knowledge (*gnôsis*) that itself was salvific. This secret knowledge was transmitted only to the initiates in the sect, and there were many sects, followers of Basilides, Valentinus, Carpocrates, Bardesanes, Marcion, and Mani. This secret *gnôsis* was impugned by those who saw themselves as the guardians of orthodoxy, especially Irenaeus (*ca.* 125–202), whose massive *Against Heresies* is our principal source of these reputed aberrations. Irenaeus's main point is that these secret doctrines were not part of the tradition and therefore had no origin in the teachings of Jesus.[10] In other words, Irenaeus denies the existence of an esoteric *gnôsis*, of teachings that Jesus had imparted only to a few and that were contained in documents such as the *Secret Gospel of Mark* and the *Gospel of Judas*. His argument is that there is a direct line from Jesus to the Apostles, and from these to the bishops, of which he was one, and they taught nothing nor knew of anything like the ravings of these heretics. Indeed, if the apostles had known any hidden mysteries that they taught to the perfect apart and in secret, it would have been above all to those to whom they entrusted the churches themselves that they would have transmitted such things.[11]

In other words, if the authorities did not know about them, they did not exist!

With this firm belief in hand, Irenaeus set out to suppress all scriptures that he considered heretical that were circulating in the various churches. He was largely responsible for the exclusion of all but four gospel texts from what became known as the canon. But

---

[10]  See "Letter to Florinus," in Eusebius, *Eccles. Histor.* V, 20, §4–7.
[11]  Irenaeus, *Adversus Haereses* II, 3.

this does not mean that those excluded texts were heretical or unimportant. Simply put, they did not match his criteria of orthodoxy. Many of these documents have now been discovered, and they provide an invaluable glimpse into the early beliefs of the followers of Jesus and into the politics attending the establishment of orthodoxy The message of Jesus, therefore, what we think Jesus taught, will vary depending on the weight we accord to the ancient sources that were excluded from the canon for political reasons.

———————— ✴ ————————

Traditionally we have been taught that the message of Jesus was one of salvation, that Jesus died for the sins of the world and rose for our salvation (*Romans* 4:25), that his death destroyed our death and our sins, and that his resurrection gave us divine life, the life of grace. This is the meaning of the paschal mystery, the mystery of redemption. We say we share in this mystery through baptism, that we die with Christ to sin and are raised with him to a new life, the divine life, a share in the life of God (*2 Peter* 1:4; *1 John* 1:2–4), a life now hidden in God but one day to become manifest and to remain so forever (*Colossians* 3:1–4). In baptism we descend and ascend, repeating the pattern of *The Hero with a Thousand Faces*. We also say that this life of grace, like all forms of life, must be nourished, must be kept strong and healthy through food—not the ordinary type of food that people eat in order to live, but the food of eternal life (*John* 6:27), the food that nourishes now and hereafter; for our life of grace *is* eternal life already present in us. This food of eternal life is the *Eucharist*. It is the "medicine of immortality," as St. Ignatius of Antioch called it,[12] the bread that has come down from heaven and that gives eternal life. This bread is Christ's flesh (*John* 6:49–51).

Jesus himself spoke of this bread when he is reported to have said, "In truth, in very truth I tell you, unless you eat the flesh of the son-of the-man and drink his blood, you can have no life in you. Those who eat my flesh and drink my blood possess eternal life,

---

[12]  Ignatius of Antioch, *Ad Ephes.* 20: 2.

and I will raise them up on the last day… Those who eat my flesh and drink my blood dwell continually in me and I dwell in them… Those who eat this bread shall live for ever" (*John* 6:53–58). These words may have helped the disciples understand what some accounts say Jesus told them later, on a memorable night: "Take this and eat: this is my body!" "Drink from this, all of you: for this is my blood!" (*Matthew* 26:27–28; *Mark* 14:22–25; *Luke* 22:19–20; *1 Corinthians* 11:24–25).

In the words of St. Cyril of Alexandria, "Eating the flesh of Christ the Savior and drinking His blood, we possess life within us!"[13] The reaction of the disciples was understandably joyous: "Give us this bread now and always!" (*John* 6:35); they asked, and Jesus taught them to ask for it daily (*Matthew* 6:11). But he added something startling: *You must work*, he said, *really* work, for this food of eternal life (*John* 6:27).

Actually, this is not a strange advice. All people must work for their daily nourishment; they must earn a living, as we say. But what is the work that Jesus requires? The people asked him, and he replied: "This is the work that God requires: *Believe* in me!" (*John* 6:29). Those who believe in Christ possess eternal life (*John* 6:40, 47; 1:12); it is faith, a deep and sincere faith, that earns us all the Eucharist, the bread of eternal life. As St. Augustine put it, "Those who believe in Christ, precisely because of their faith in Christ, are visited by Christ."[14] This is our work: to believe and to pray that our faith be made stronger! (*Mark* 9:23).

——— ❖ ———

These *Gospel* passages, and the doctrine they enshrine, have been problematic from the time they were first uttered—assuming, of course, that Jesus spoke them exactly as they have been recorded. One must remember that the *Gospel* records bear the imprint of Gentile converts who knew little of the Jewish practices of a Passover

---

[13] Cyril of Alexandria, *Comment. in Lk.*; MG 72, 909–912.
[14] Augustine, *Sermo* 144, 2; ML 38, 790.

*seder* and who were not aware of the profound repugnance Jews felt toward eating meat with the blood in it. The taboo against eating flesh and blood goes back to the Noahide Laws (*Genesis* 9:4), with the prohibition reinforced by *Leviticus* 17:10–11 and *Deuteronomy* 12:16 and 23–25. The taboo was very much in effect in Jesus's time, to judge by the comments in *Acts* 15:20. As popularly understood today, the Eucharist (eating human flesh and drinking human blood) would have made the disciple puke! It was pure anthropophagy.[15] No wonder that when the story was imbued with realism, as retold in *John* 6:60 and 66, some seventy years later, it recorded that the disciples found it repugnant, and many left Jesus forthwith.

It should be noted that the "council" of Jerusalem, which Paul attended (*Acts* 15:20, 29; *Galatians* 2:1–10), agreed to enforce the prohibition against drinking blood even on the Gentile converts. It is unlikely, therefore, that Paul, just seven years after the meeting, would have condoned the very practice he had agreed to forbid. So, when writing to the Corinthians (*1 Corinthians* 11:23*ff.*), he does not enjoin the eating of the body of Jesus and the drinking of his blood, but simply the commemoration of the breaking of his body and the spilling of his blood at the crucifixion. This commemoration is to be like the paschal *seder*, a communal meal in remembrance of the exodus from Egypt.

So how to reconstruct what may have happened historically at the Last Supper?

Joachim Jeremias has painstakingly demonstrated that the words spoken by Jesus during the Last Supper before he died must be understood in the context of traditional Jewish practices during a Passover *seder*. The one person presiding at the *seder*—and Jesus most likely presided—was entitled, even encouraged, to comment at appropriate times during the ritual meal in order to make the celebration relevant to the times. Jesus undoubtedly knew that his fate was sealed and that he would be executed the next day. When he came to the ceremonial breaking of the bread, he added, "Take and eat, this breaking of the bread is like what will happen tomorrow to my

---

[15] Geza Vermes, *The Resurrection*, p. 68.

body;" and when he came to the sharing of the cup, he commented, "Take and drink, for this wine is like the blood which will be shed tomorrow." In a sense, Jesus was enacting what the morrow would bring. We cannot recover the actual words Jesus spoke in Aramaic, but the context of a traditional *seder* leaves no room for doubt.

The occasion was precious, and it was indelibly preserved in the memory of those present, and when it was retold in Greek, the words were taken in a literal sense and ritualized, and the traditional Eucharistic theology began to unfold. *John*'s retelling of Jesus's speech, which presumably was given before the event of the Passover meal, was written chronologically after Jesus's death—in fact, a long time after. It reflects the ongoing theologizing that was necessary to explain the unexplainable, and it cements it very strongly. What is meant by all this? In the words of Walter Wink, "We are invited to live with the Human Being in the most mundane and secular ways, to take it within ourselves, to digest it, to assimilate it into our beings."[16] What Jesus did with his life, what he became, the example of his imitation of the humanity of God, all this we are to "eat" so that it may nourish our own imitation of the humanness of God. In a similar manner, the prophet Ezekiel was told by God: "Son of man, eat what is offered to you; eat this scroll, and go, speak to the house of Israel" (*Ezekiel* 3:1). And Ezekiel ate the scroll, and it was in his mouth as sweet as honey.

Already in ancient times, the *Gospel of Philip* 57 asked, "What is this that Jesus says [in *John* 6:53]?" And it answered, "His flesh is the word, and his blood is the holy spirit. Those who have received these have food and they have drink."

In an imaginative conflation of the wooden cross and the Tree of Knowledge of *Genesis*, *The Gospel of Truth* 18:24–34 depicts Jesus crucified as a fruit hanging on a tree, a fruit imparting salvific knowledge. Those who eat this fruit come alive, and they are found within the savior just as he is found within them.

---

16 Walter Wink, *The Human Being: Jesus and the Enigma of the Son of the Man* (Minneapolis, MN: Fortress Press, 2002), p. 201.

As I said above, a major part of Jesus's message was that the Kingdom of God was at hand. This Kingdom of God was an earthly but spiritual alternative to political Jewish nationalism that was quite active since the time of the Roman occupation of Palestine. Jesus's ministry took place barely sixty years after the demise of the Hasmonean kingdom, and it engendered expectations of a revival of kingship, at least among many, to judge by the proliferation of messianic uprisings culminating in the Great War. According to Mendels, "This short-lived independent Jewish state [the Hasmoneans] sowed the seeds of a stronger nationalistic awareness, which was to come to the fore after 63 BCE."[17] Jesus made very clear repeatedly that he did not wish to be a political king (*John* 18:33–40).[18] In his message he spiritualized the political nationalism, although occasionally he behaved in ways that appeared to confront it head-on. The characteristics of this political kingdom were transferred to the spiritual one, such as that it would be a future event, that it was already present because it did not depend on physical boundaries or armies or language, and that it was opened to all who changed their mind (*metanoia*) and believed in it. Jesus may have been moved toward this earthly but spiritual understanding of the Kingdom of God by the time of the death of John the Baptist, whom he must have respected greatly. If God had not saved John from imprisonment and death, this, perhaps, was a sign that we have to settle our affairs *here*, by ourselves, without waiting to be rescued by some *deus ex machina*. This would make sense since Jesus does not seem to have had any ideas of himself as anything more than a human being.

Jesus's emphasis on the equality of men and women under the fatherhood of God may have been insistent, but the truth is that the apostles could not bring themselves to treat the women as Jesus had instructed and exemplified for them. Jesus's message, that "whoever has the imagination and courage to tackle an entirely new situation

---

[17] Doron Mendels, *The Rise and Fall of Jewish Nationalism* (New York: Doubleday, 1992), p. 26.

[18] Doron Mendels, *The Rise and Fall of Jewish Nationalism*, pp. 7, 200–202, 228–229.

immediately, is fit for the kingdom,"[19] went unheeded. The apostles and disciples could not achieve the "conversion," the change of mind (*metanoia*) needed to usher God's presence on earth (*Mark* 10:15 and *Matthew* 21:31). Maleness prevailed again in the organization of the burgeoning Jesus movement, and women were not even permitted to speak in the assemblies.[20] And to cover up their failure to implement what was clearly Jesus's most distinctive and urgent message (the equality of the sexes, classes, and ethnics), the ideas of resurrection and of a "Second Coming" were introduced:

A proposal of how to live
("Be as merciful as your Father")
which was originally expressed in
an eschatological symbol
("The kingdom of God is among you")
was revised into
an apocalyptic belief
("Jesus will be the Son of Man")
which was further narrowed to
one apocalyptic formula
("Jesus has been raised from the dead")
which was concretized in
a very local legend
(the empty tomb).[21]

The Jesus Movement, which was originally destined to bring an end to patriarchy, and which therefore "should have accepted the fact that Jesus was dead and then gone on from there, ended up trying to hope him out of the grave"[22] in order to cover up its failure

---

[19] Grussouw, *Spirituality of the New Testament*, p. 35.

[20] See *1 Timothy* 2:12, and Rosemary Radford Ruether, *Sexism and God-Talk* (Boston: Beacon Press, 1983), pp. 8–11. Also Patricia H. Labalme, ed., *Beyond their Sex* (New York: New York University Press, 1984), p. 13.

[21] Thomas Sheehan, *The First Coming* (New York: Random House, 1986), pp. 161–162.

[22] Ibid., p. 162.

of nerve. The resurrection and the Second Coming were invented partly to justify the fact that the men were not courageous enough to live as Jesus had lived. What Jesus had preached and been, therefore, became a promise to be fulfilled in a world to come, and things went on pretty much as they had always been, except that now there was a new divinity in the sky.

# The Prayer of Jesus

> Once, in a certain place, Jesus was at prayer.
> When he ceased, one of his disciples said: "Lord,
> teach us to pray, as John taught his disciples."
> (*Luke* 11:1)

Jesus's answer was probably not the precise form we recite today as the *Our Father* or *The Lord's Prayer*, which clearly is arranged as a liturgical prayer fit for ritual recitation, as it is still used today; in fact, we know that this was not the case because the version in *Luke* 11:2–4 is much simpler than the one in *Matthew*, and *The Sayings Gospel Q*, written almost twenty years before *Mark*, contains the briefest of formulas (*Q* 34):

> Father, may your name be honored;
> may your reign begin.
> Grant us the food we need for each day.
> Forgive our failures,
> for we forgive everyone who fails us.
> And do not put us to the test.

But this is more like a model, or a series of pointers for the new spirit of prayer that would belong to the people of the new kingdom;[1] in fact, scholars maintain that the historical Jesus spoke only

---

[1]   Tertullian, *De Orat.* I.

the first two words, *Our* and *Father*;[2] and that the first Christians soon set down the general directives in a liturgical formula that they hoped would forever enshrine the Master's teachings. The following is an explication of what may have been Jesus's instructions that were later codified in the *Our Father* or *The Lord's Prayer* by the first Christians.[3]

> *Our Father*—father of all people, but especially of the new people of God (*Luke* 6:35; *Matthew* 5:9; *John* 1:12–13; *1 John* 3:1–3).
>
> *Who are in heaven*—and also everywhere (*John* 4:21), even in the hearts of people.
>
> *May your name be sanctified*—manifest the sanctity of your name (*Ezekiel* 36:22–27), glorify yourself (*John* 12:28).
>
> *May your dominion come*—may its fullness be granted to us; let your universal reign be established (*Mark* 9:1, *Matthew* 16:28, Luke 22:18); cause that destiny to come toward which we are all journeying.
>
> *May your will come about on earth as in heaven*—you created heaven and earth according to your will (*Genesis* 1:1): let that will be fulfilled (Tertullian, *De Orat.* IV); reconcile heaven and earth to yourself (*Colossians* 1:20) so that we may find you forever on this earth.
>
> *Give us today the bread of the future*[4]—the bread come down from heaven (*Exodus* 16:14; *Psalm* 78:24; *John* 6:38, 50, 51), the bread that gives

---

[2]   See Jack Miles, *GOD: A Biography* (New York: Vintage, 1996), p. 418.

[3]   Raymond E. Brown, SS, "The *Pater Noster* as an eschatological prayer," *Theological Studies*, 22 (1961): 175–208. Also Joachim Jeremias, *The Prayers of Jesus* (Philadelphia, PA: Fortress Press, 1978).

[4]   The meaning of this phrase is uncertain; the words appear only once in Greek, and that is here! Origen thought that the words might have been invented by the writer.

eternal life (*John* 6:35, 48, 50–58): that is like the body and like the blood of Christ (*John* 6:53–58), who will be our ever-living and sustaining example in the never-ending banquet of your kingdom (*Luke* 14:15; *Matthew* 8:11; *1 Corinthians* 11:26). Give us this bread today, hasten your gift to us, give it once and for all, lest we perish on the way (*John* 6:53); for you alone can help us incarnate you as Jesus did, who thus became like real bread to us (*John* 6:32, 49, 57, 65).

*And forgive us our wrongs because we have forgiven those who wronged us*—it is your son who promised that we would be forgiven provided we in turn forgave others (*Luke* 6:37, *Matthew* 18:23–35) so that being generous toward others, we may find you generous toward us (*Matthew* 25:31–46, 5:22; Luke 16:14–31), you who are our father.

*And do not bring us to the test*—"the ordeal that is to fall upon the whole world and test its inhabitants" (*Revelation* 3:10), but at the hour of that battle (*Ephesians* 6:12–13).

*Save us from the Evil One*[5]—"who like a roaring lion prowls around, looking for someone to devour" (*1 Peter* 5:8); do not let him snatch your word from our hearts (*Matthew* 13:19), for we are your sons (*1 John* 5:9). Strengthen us, and guard us from him (*2 Thessalonians* 3:3), for Jesus is our example, your son, as we, too, are your children; for he prayed to you for us, saying, "Keep them from the Evil One!" (*John* 17:15).

---

[5] The Greek text has a definite article in place, which makes "from *the* Evil One" the obligatory translation. The mistake comes from following the Latin, in which language there are no articles at all.

# On Prayer in General

Let me add some general comments on prayer, since its essence is greatly misunderstood today, even by ministers who ought to know better; but since their theological training is greatly deficient, they both misconstrue prayer and mislead the people who are eager to pray. Excellent volumes have been written on this subject; therefore, my comments can only touch briefly on some salient points.

Prayer is a family name, like *Jones*. There are many members in this family, all with the same surname. There is Vocal Prayer, Mental Prayer, Meditative Prayer, Contemplative Prayer, Mystical Prayer, Thanksgiving Prayer, Petition Prayer, Worshipful Prayer, Intercessory Prayer, Sacrificial Prayer, Atonement Prayer, Official Prayer, and Daily Prayer. And there are many grandchildren, like Prayer for Peace, Prayer for the Sick, Prayers of the Community, Prayer for Rain, Prayer for Forgiveness, and many more. Appearing in ancient times, the family pedigree is quite large.

Like members of all other religions, Christians have a tradition of prayer. In some ways they inherit this from Judaism, where prayer was everywhere apparent, as in the Psalms and in the various episodes in the lives of great figures like Moses, David, and the prophets. Being a good Jew, Jesus participated in the religious festivals of his time, in which prayer was an important aspect. More pertinently, as I said above, Jesus himself is reported to have prayed often, and even to have taught his followers how to pray. He also prayed in private and alone (*Mark* 1:35), an example that was imitated by the early anchorites. It would be natural, then, for Christians to pray. Fosdick quotes Samuel Johnson, who was asked what was the strongest argument for prayer. He replied, "Sir, there is no argument for prayer,"[6] meaning, of course, that prayer is not something one has to justify by reason and argument. Prayer is something that comes naturally to all of us.

Many define prayer in general as an ascent or raising of the mind to God (*ascensus mentis ad Deum*). *The Cloud of Unknowing*,

---

[6] Harry Emerson Fosdick, "The Meaning of Prayer," in *The Three Meanings* (New York: Association Press, 1949), p. 1.

chapter XXXIX, says that prayer "is nothing but a devout reaching out directly to God."[7] These definitions place the point of departure of prayer in the individual soul: individuals raise their minds to God, or reach out to him, so the movement toward God begins with the individual. This is an almost instinctive approach to the nature of prayer: *we* pray. On the other hand, von Balthasar stipulates that prayer "is communication, in which God's word has the initiative and we, at first, are simply listeners. Consequently, what we have to do is, first, listen to God's word and then, through that word, learn how to answer."[8] This view is counterintuitive, but nonetheless true, because God's grace first opens up the path through which we walk in answer to his call. The thing is that we do not always hear this call, so we take it for granted that *we* are really the ones taking the initiative. God throws the switch on that empowers our circuits to speak to him; we may not see him do it, but without it, there is no "juice" in the system! This is similar to what happens when lightning strikes: a barely visible "leader" streaks down from the clouds toward earth, and as it approaches the ground, the earth retorts with what we call lightning, the very visible and fiery flash of light. Lightning does not always "fall," it often rises as a response to the imperceptible touch of the clouds.

There is another reason prayer, especially Contemplative Prayer, appears to originate in us. It is that in prayer we answer God *in us*, for God dwells in the innermost sanctuary of our souls. Contemplation, says von Balthasar, "is an inward gaze into the depths of the soul and, for that very reason, beyond the soul to God. The more the soul finds God, the more it forgets itself and yet finds itself in God. It is an unwavering 'gaze,' where 'looking' is always 'hearing'; for what is looked at is the free and infinite Person who, from the depths of his freedom, is able to give himself in a manner ever new, unexpected and unpredictable."[9]

---

[7]   *The Cloud of Unknowing*, trans. and ed. James Walsh, SJ (New York: Paulist Press, 1981), p. 195.

[8]   Hans Urs von Balthasar, *Prayer* (New York: Paulist Press, 1967), p. 12.

[9]   Ibid., p. 20.

What this portends for us is that the call to prayer is a call to answer the "ever new, unexpected and unpredictable" call of God to be what we cannot be without this call and what we cannot become unless we answer this call. Von Balthasar explains:

> The man obedient to his mission fulfils his own being, although he could never find this archetype and ideal of himself by penetrating to the deepest center of his nature, his superego, or his subconscious, or by scrutinizing his own dispositions, aspirations, talents, and potentialities. Simon, the fisherman, before his meeting with Christ, however thoroughly he might have searched within himself, could not possibly have found a trace of Peter. Yet the form "Peter," the particular mission reserved for him alone, which till then lay hid in the secret of Christ's soul and, at the moment of this encounter, was delivered over to him sternly and imperatively—was to be the fulfillment of all that, in Simon, would have sought vainly for a form ultimately valid in the eyes of God for all eternity. In the form "Peter" Simon was made capable of understanding the word of Christ, because the form itself issued from the word and was conjoined with it.[10]

---

"Nowhere in the Christian life is the believer more an individual than in contemplative prayer," wrote von Balthasar.[11] The idea of being alone with God, "alone with the alone," as Gregory of Nazianzus put it,[12] was a legacy of Plotinus and the Hellenistic

---

[10] Ibid., pp. 48–49.
[11] Ibid., p. 68.
[12] Gregory of Nazianzus, *Oratio* 20, 1.

tradition, but it found its way into our recent past, with Kierkegaard being its most ardent advocate.

As far as our salvation is concerned, Kierkegaard asserts, "Every individual must work for himself, each for himself,"[13] because, he argues, God imposes obligations on each single soul, not on a multitude. Commenting on *1 Corinthians* 9:24, he uses the example given by St. Paul: in a race many compete but only one wins. Each one of us must run so as to be the winner: "Every man…should talk only with God and with himself, for only one wins."[14]

All this is true, of course, but what is also true is that Christians at prayer are part of a community, and while they are still singly responsible for their own salvation, they hear God's word addressed to them not only directly but also as members of a community. God speaks to them directly, indeed, but also through the community. Therefore, while they need to learn to listen to God's word spoken directly and singularly to them (as Isaiah did: *Isaiah* chapter 6), they must also learn to discern what God is telling them through the medium of the community; they must learn to be soloists, but equally, they must learn to sing as members of a chorus, to attend to the voices of the other choristers, all of whom respond to the promptings, coaxings, and general direction of the conductor. In a certain sense, the choir is an extension of the conductor, just as the Christian community, the *koinonía*, is an extension of Christ's body. God's call must be picked up in its totality, not just individually, but as it resounds in the hallways of the Christian community.[15]

---

[13] Søren Kierkegaard, *The Present Age* (New York: Harper & Row, 1962), p. 81.

[14] Søren Kierkegaard, "Concerning the Dedication to 'The Individual,'" in *The Point of View of My Work as an Author* (New York" Harper & Row, 1962), p. 111.

[15] Cf. Paul Lehman, *Ethics in a Christian Context* (New York: Harper & Row, 1963), and H. Richard Niebuhr, *The Responsible Self* (New York: Harper & Row, 1963).

It is therefore a misconception of the nature of contemplation to regard the individual as the only hearer of God's word. The people of God also hear God's word, and individuals hear *both* their own word, addressed to them singly and unambiguously, and that word that is addressed to them as members of the community.[16]

———————— ✦ ————————

Now, Jesus did not have any of this in mind while he dwelled in Palestine and taught his followers how to pray. But as people took to praying seriously, they encountered experiences that baffled them and that cried out for an answer. Greek philosophy, with its long tradition of contemplatives and mystics, provided a rich mine that was available to Christian writers for the asking.[17] Thus, slowly, a way of understanding prayer in its various forms came to be developed. Gregory of Nazianzus, St. Augustine, Pseudo-Dionysus, Boëthius, Hildegard von Bingen, Hugh of St. Victor, St. Bonaventure, St. Thomas Aquinas, Meister Eckhart, Juliana of Norwich, St. Ignatius Loyola, St. John of the Cross, St. Teresa of Ávila, Jakob Boehme, Jeremy Taylor, John Bunyan, Emanuel Swedenborg, John Woolman, and many others, left insightful accounts of the ways of prayer, which have provided the foundation for the many treatises on meditation and contemplation. This is a treasure trove of spiritual materials that places Christianity on a par with the traditions of Hinduism, Buddhism, and Islam. In fact, at this level of religiosity and spirituality, the traditions merge into each other with great ease, like many rivers emptying into the same ocean, and they enrich and enhance each other if we only allow them to do so without prejudice.

———————— ✦ ————————

---

[16] Von Balthasar, *Prayer*, p. 71.

[17] Unfortunately, due to the rabid anti-Semitism that developed after the second century, Jewish traditions of prayer were not adopted as readily, if at all. In fact, the anti-Semitic prejudice continued, as is evident, for example, in St. Jerome, who called Jewish prayer "the grunting of a pig and the braying of donkeys" (*In Amos* 5:23).

Prayer of Petition has always presented peculiar problems to the theologians because of the confluence of seemingly contradictory elements resulting in paradoxical situations. Moreover, to the ordinary believer, the question of unanswered prayers presents a problem that turns many people off from prayer altogether. Emily Dickinson's cry, "Of course—I Prayed—/And did God Care?"[18] echoes the sentiments of millions whose orisons have gone unanswered.

But there is more. Given that God is absolutely powerful, absolutely knowing, absolutely good, absolutely provident, what can prayer effect, if anything, at all? How can we influence the will of God by our petitions? If we could, would this not make us more powerful than God? And if we did not, what is the use of praying? Is not God's providence to be fulfilled regardless of our intentions and impetrations?

St. Thomas Aquinas answers that we petition only to obtain from God what God has arranged or planned to happen on condition that we pray.[19] Alonso Rodríguez, a Spanish master of the spiritual life, agrees, writing that "what God, in his divine providence and disposition has determined from all eternity to give to us, he gives in time through the instrumentality of prayer."[20]

But we are free, and God, in his providence, must take into account (through his absolute knowledge) that we may or may not pray for the things he has designed to be obtained by prayer, or that we may pray for their opposite, or not pray at all.[21] But providence must be fulfilled regardless and, as Fosdick explains, often in total disregard of our prayers.[22] So prayer always implies the proviso, "If God has planned for this to be." God's mind is not changed, nor are his plans, and yet prayer is efficacious when it observes the condition of abiding by the absolute will of God. "God," says Fosdick, "*does not*

[18] *Final Harvest: Emily Dickinson's Poems*, selected and introduced by Thomas H. Johnson (Boston: Little, Brown, & Co., 1961), p. 85.
[19] St. Thomas Aquinas, *Summa Theologiae*, 2.2, 83, 2.
[20] Alonso Rodríguez, SJ, *Ejercicios de perfección y virtudes cristianas*, 7th ed. (Madrid: Apostolado de la Prensa, 1950), I, 5, 2, p. 300.
[21] *Summa Theologiae*, 1, 22.
[22] Fosdick, *The Meaning of Prayer*, p. 104.

*remake his world for the asking, not because he cannot, but because he must not.*"[23]

Van Zeller comments: "Dionysus, explaining how the prayers of petition that are answered do not change the mind of God but have all along been elicited from us by grace, compares the soul to a sailor pulling on a rope which is made fast to a rock. To the sailor in his boat the rock looks as if it is coming towards him in answer to his effort. But in fact, the rock, like the will of God, is immovable. We pray, not so as to change the mind of God but so as to obtain from him the good that he wants us to have on condition that we ask for it."[24] Therefore, to quote Fosdick once more, "*To pray about every-thing, in submission to God's will, would be both more human and more Christian than a scrupulous limitation of our prayers to what we might think permissible subjects of petition.*"[25]

But the confluence of the necessity of providence, of human freedom of choice, and of human desires and aspirations remains paradoxical regardless of the many theological efforts to explain it—and there have been many, and very elaborate ones, through the centuries.

---

[23] Fosdick, Ibid., p. 104.

[24] Hubert Van Zeller, OSB, *The Inner Search* (Garden City, NY: Image Books, 1957), chapter 8.

[25] Fosdick, *The Meaning of Prayer*, p. 104.

# 10

# Some Sayings of Jesus I

One of the particulars about Jesus is that he said many things that seemed important to his followers and friends. In the course of a life, one speaks with many people and says many things, and some of them may be memorable, some not. In the case of Jesus, the memorable sayings have been preserved, for the most part (one must assume), though not all in the canonical gospels. In fact, there are "sayings gospels," gospels that contain only sayings of Jesus (such as the *Gospel of Thomas*), and "narrative gospels," that is, gospels that preserve accounts of incidents in the life of Jesus as well as sayings attributed to him. The canonical *Gospel of John* is one example of the latter. But the sayings of Jesus are contained in many other sources, such as the *Acts of the Apostles*, and even in non-Christian sources. Which sayings are considered "authentic" and which not is not an easy question to decide. For example, in *The Infancy Gospel of Thomas*, Jesus is reported to have said to another boy, "Damn you, you irreverent fool!"[1] One would hardly expect such words in the mouth of the young Jesus, so one may legitimately discount this saying. But the case may not be as clear in other situations. Marvin Meyer, in the introduction to his *The Unknown Sayings of Jesus*,[2] details and explains the criteria usually employed by scholars in order to determine authenticity.

---

[1] *Infancy Gospel of Thomas* 3:2.
[2] Marvin Meyer, *The Unknown Sayings of Jesus* (Boston: New Seeds, 2005). Also John P. Meier, *A Marginal Jew*, 3 vols. (New York: Doubleday, 1944), Volume 1.

In this chapter and in the following ones, I have singled out for commentary a few sayings that have had a special importance for me. They may not be the most popular ones, but they have had a strong impact on me, and therefore I have chosen them. I do not discount the others, of course, but these ones I sometimes think were spoken "for me." They may not be the usual ones that Evangelicals write on placards they display at baseball games, but they have as strong a claim to legitimacy as those.

———— ❧ ————

Actually, the text most often displayed in stadiums, *John* 3:16, may not be a saying of Jesus at all. Here are the words: "This is how God loved the world: God gave up an only son, so that every one who believes in him will not be lost but have eternal life."

To begin with, the more reliable and older manuscripts have "*an* only son," while later, less reliable ones, have "*his* only son." The "*his*" may be an interpretation by a copying scribe.

Moreover, it is not completely clear whether or not Jesus actually said these words. The direct quotation of Jesus's words may have ended with verse 13, but then, again, it may have continued to verse 21. In the latter case, the words would indeed belong to Jesus. But this is unlikely to be the case because of what is actually said and the chronology that is implied. In terms of the text alone, it is impossible to be certain where to put the quotation marks. After all, the division of the text into chapters and verses did not appear until 1551.

Many scholars believe that at least part of verses 14–21 is a sermon selected by the writer rather than the words of Jesus himself. It is one of those interpolations added by copyists. They may also reflect some catechetical instruction. Raymond E. Brown feels that the text represents a reworking of some words of Jesus with those of later preachers, so mingled and combined that it is impossible to determine who said what.[3]

---

3  Raymond E. Brown, *The Gospel According to John*, 2 vols. (Garden City, NY: Doubleday & Co., 1966), vol. 1, p. 136.

The preacher may have been trying to draw a parallel between Abraham and God: Abraham was asked to sacrifice his only son, Isaac (*Genesis* 22:2 and 12), the object of God's solemn promise to him, and God has now done the same. In this case, of course, the words would *not* be Jesus's; they would represent an interpretation of Jesus favored by the preacher and/or writer of this account.

Curiously, this passage is not commented on by Herakleon (late second century) in his "Commentary on the Gospel of John," a Valentinian exposition of *John* and the first ever exegetical account of any Gospel.

———※———

Since we are speaking of sayings, I should add that the Gospels also preserve one instance at least of the silence of Jesus. Questioned by Herod, "Jesus did not answer him at all" (*Luke* 23:9). Jesus did not speak! Other of his words are profusely reported in all the Gospels, canonical as well as extracanonical, but in this particular occasion confronting Herod, he spoke not a word. Why?

There is a maxim in law, *qui tacet consentire videtur* ("who is silent is thought to agree"), but this could hardly be applied to Jesus's case: nothing could be gauged from his silence, nor did keeping silent gain anything for him; so it could not have been a ruse, a technique, or a defense ploy, and we misinterpret the situation if we seek an answer along the lines of legal procedure.

For silence is not just the stratagem of last recourse; it is not necessarily a stratagem at all. Neither is silence what we do when we cannot say anything meaningful. Silence may, indeed, be appropriate in such instances, as Wittgenstein observed in the preface to his *Tractatus*: "What we cannot talk about we must pass over in silence."[4] Of course, he was referring to intelligent and meaningful talk, not to talking for the sake of hearing oneself speak. As one of my students quipped once from the back of the class after a heated discussion of

---

[4] Ludwig Wittgenstein, *Tractatus Logico-Philosophicus* (London: Routledge & Kegan Paul, 1961), p. 3.

no consequence, and obviously referring to some of the many statements made in the course of the exchange, "Just because you have nothing to say, it does not mean you should say it." So, if we go ahead and speak, at least it should be with the express knowledge that what we say is not even half of what the truth is.

Silence is a mysterious dimension of human existence. Among other things, it is the matrix of worship, as Gregory of Nazianzus clearly understood when he wrote, "All who know your godhead sing a silent hymn."[5] Gregory probably refers to the whole of nature, which, as St. John of the Cross poetically put it, babbles incoherently in its effort to describe God.[6] Taking nature's lead, says Gregory, *we* should also "worship in silence."[7] The paradox is pregnant and to be dwelled on worshipfully in silence. I should say no more.

---

Finally, there is also a subjective mystery about silence, conveyed perhaps by this saying of "Mr. Blue": "Imagine anyone with anything good to tell keeping it to himself!"[8]

## Born Again

> Jesus said, "In truth, in very truth I tell you,
> no one who has not been born again will enter
> the kingdom of God." (*John* 3:3)

This is one of the most famous sayings of Jesus. John Wesley captured the spirit of this Gospel saying when he wrote, "None can

[5] Gregory of Nazianzus, *Carmen* 29, *Hymn. ad Deum*; MG 37, 507–508.
[6] The untranslatable Spanish reads, "Un no se qué que quedan balbuciendo." See St. John of the Cross, *Spiritual Canticle*, trans. W. Allison Peers (Garden City, NY: Doubleday & Co., 1961), p. 43.
[7] Gregory of Nazianzus, *Oratio* 28, 20.
[8] Myles Connolly, *Mr. Blue* (Chicago: Loyola Press, 2005), p. 32.

be holy, except he be born again."[9] Greven comments: "For every evangelical of whatever denomination, the experience of being reborn was the central event in their lives, indispensable for their salvation and essential for the fulfillment of their innermost needs, desires, and expectations."[10]

This saying has given rise to a whole movement among Evangelical Christians who call themselves "born again." By this they usually mean that they have accepted Jesus as their personal savior. They seem sincere about this and happy with the change that this acceptance has brought to their lives. Little is known, of course, whether or not such changes endure, and how in fact they affect the lives of those who profess to have been "born again." My skepticism arises from the fact that it is hard, or almost impossible, to know how these people have "died," or to what life circumstances they have "died," without which experience it is meaningless to talk about rebirth. I do not believe that dying is easy, physically or metaphorically; in fact, it seems to me that the most important thing is, precisely, this dying that precedes the rebirth, and I take this view from the consideration of stories of exemplary people who have been "born again." My sense is that their dying was extraordinarily difficult and painful, and that most "born-again" Christians would be spooked out of their minds if they had to undergo a true death-and-rebirth experience.

I note that in all the accounts that Greven collects, and in others as well, it is impossible to get a clear and specific sense of what the individuals are dying to. There is no objective account, nothing detailed and specific. Greven says that before they could be born again, Christians had to come to "*feel* that they were totally deserving of nothing more than damnation";[11] but such feelings can be summoned in many different ways irrelevant to a true and genuine conversion, and being merely feelings, even though deeply experienced,

---

[9]  John Wesley, "On the New Birth," in *The Works of the Rev. John Wesley*, 16 vols. (London: 1809–1812), vol. VII, p. 300, quoted in Greven, *The Protestant Temperament*, p. 63.

[10]  Greven, *The Protestant Temperament*, p. 62.

[11]  Greven, *The Protestant Temperament*, p. 75; emphasis added.

they can easily and quickly vanish, leaving the subject committed to rebuilding a life without a solid foundation.

When Jesus talked with Nicodemus about the need to be "born again," he had already undergone his own rebirth experience in the waters of the Jordan River, where he was baptized by John the Baptist. Something extraordinary happened then, for Jesus came out of the water laughing at everything, and his life was changed after that. Even John the Baptist had an inkling into what had happened, as he told his own disciples. But we can only conjecture that what Jesus experienced then had to do with his decision to incarnate God's image in his life even to death upon a cross. Saul, too, after the traumatic experience on the road to Damascus, spent years of self-examination before he could be born again as Paul.

One of the oldest accounts of a death-and-rebirth experience is that retold in the *Hymns of Inanna* contained in cuneiform tablets going back some four thousand years. Inanna, goddess of heaven and earth, decides to visit her sister, Ereshkigal, goddess of the underworld. She decides to go from the Great Above to the Great Below. She begins her journey downward and is met at each stage by guards who slowly strip her of all her regalia. She must enter the throne room completely humbled, and so she does. When she, naked and exposed, finally comes into the presence of Ereshkigal, her sister stares at her with deathly, fierce eyes, and Inanna is obliterated, turned into a nothing, a mere piece of rotting meat hung on a hook in a butcher's shop. This is no picnic, no walking to the front of the nave to the sound of organ music, the peal of bells, and the encouragement of the congregation. This is real death to the self, self-abnegation, the emptying of the self that must precede all replenishing. After three days, Inanna is eventually reborn—her divine parents take care of that—and she regains her place among the gods.

Moses, too, who had killed a man and left the scene of the murder, underwent a horrifying experience of death and rebirth. His journey took long years of compunction, marriage to Zipporah, children, and then the encounter with God amid a burning bush and acceptance of a mission to the Hebrew people back in Egypt, where he was wanted for murder. As he was crossing into Egypt, an angel of the Lord fought with him (*Exodus* 4:24). It was a fierce battle for his own soul and the souls of his family and, eventually, of his people. From this night, he emerged a changed man willing to confront Pharaoh and to lead a people to freedom.

Earlier on, Jacob, too, underwent his own trial. As a heel-grabbing rogue, conniving and deceiving, he was preparing to return to Palestine and to meet with his brother Esau, whom he had cheated out of his inheritance. The night before the meeting, Jacob fought with an angel of the Lord (*Genesis* 32:24–30). The fight was long and frightfully bitter, but at the end of it, Jacob had won the angel's blessing and had been reborn with a new name, Israel. He would also walk with a limp until the end of his days because of an injury suffered at the hands of his foe.

And one must not forget Jonah, who ran away from God rather than undergo the pangs of transformation; but God pursued him even unto the ship in which he was escaping, and when Jonah jumped overboard, he was swallowed up by a big fish, and then spewed up three days later, so that he could be born again and preach salvation to the city of Nineveh.

In other climes, Suddhodana, king of Kapilavastu, a city at the foothills of the Himalayas, had a son, Siddhartha Gautama. Siddhartha's mother, Queen Mâyâ, died a few months later, and the infant was raised by relatives in the palace. As a child he began to express concern for the pain and suffering he saw around him, both in the animal world as well as among the inhabitants of the city. His father tried to assuage his unrest by arranging a marriage to Princess Yasodhara. Siddhartha was sixteen, and he and his wife would not be graced with offspring until thirteen years later. But not even the birth of Râhula, his son, could dispel his ennui. At twenty-nine he left both palace and family and undertook six years of meditation, ascetical practices, and prolonged fasts that almost resulted in his death. Finally, after many days of meditation, he was reborn as the Buddha, "the enlightened one."

I do not sense any of this wrenching of the self from the inadequacies of the past in the lives of the millions who call themselves "born-again" Christians. What I observe is a cheapening of the experience of death and rebirth, a devaluation of the struggle to recreate the self, so that without much effort, anyone can be "born again." It seems as if all one has to do to be "born again" is show up, walk up, be counted, and be done.

---

Christianity is not the only religious tradition in which there are "born-again" people. Hinduism, centuries before Christianity ever appeared on the historical scene, spoke of the "twice-born" (*dvijâtis*), men of the brahmin, kshatriya, and vaishya castes, who were purified by the sacrament (*samskâra*) of *upanayana*.[12] This sacrament was part of a ceremony that marked the initiation of the boy into manhood and life in the religious and social community in which his orbit was cast. It involved the shaving of the boy's head (*cuddâkara*) except for a tuft at the back (*shika*), the girdling with a grass belt (*mauñja bandhan*), and the recitation of the *gâyatrî mantra* for the first time, which would become one of life's favorite daily prayers: "May we attain that excellent glory of Savitar the god: so may he stimulate our prayers!"[13] The boy would then be fitted with a cord woven of three single threads, about two yards long (*janëu*), that would be worn day and night from then forward, hung from the left shoulder and across his chest and back.

After the ceremony, in ancient times, the boy would proceed to the forest to begin his intellectual apprenticeship under the guidance of a guru. This was the beginning of the first stage of life, *brahmacariya*, to last some twelve or more years. During this time, the young man was to remain chaste in every respect. He had been reborn to the Hindu way of life; he was one of the "twice born."

---

[12] *Manusmṛi* II, 26.
[13] *Rigveda* III, 62, 10.

The rebirth of which we are speaking here is spiritual, no question about it. But this was not always understood, either then or now. Today, thousands of people are involved in efforts to rejuvenate themselves through the elimination of facial wrinkles or breast augmentation (or diminution, as the case may be), hair transplants or hair coloring, all without the slightest understanding of or interest in the inner, spiritual transformation, which should support such physical changes, and without which, the latter remain an empty show. An old Spanish proverb states, "A monkey dressed in silk is still a monkey." Without the inner rebirth, all rejuvenations are a mere dressing up.

Centuries ago and more, Gilgamesh, the great king of Uruk, in ancient Mesopotamia, had watched Enkidu, his friend and combat-at-arms comrade, die a slow and painful death, and had stayed by his friend's corpse until it began to stink. Shaken by his encounter with mortality at such close quarters, Gilgamesh embarked on a quest of immortality, a way to beat death. Legend had it that Utnapishtim, the Sumerian Noah, had been granted such a boon by the gods, and Gilgamesh wanted to learn from him the secret of never having to die. Following many trials, Gilgamesh arrived at the shores of the Persian Gulf. There he embarked to the island wherein Utnapishtim dwelled with his wife. It took many entreaties, but finally Gilgamesh managed to wrest from Utnapishtim the story of a plant named "Your Old Men Shall Be Young Again"—that is, they will be "reborn"— which was to be found in the depths of the sea. After much travail, Gilgamesh plucked the plant from the bottom of the sea, resurfaced, and, instead of consuming it there and then, decided that his people back in Uruk would benefit from its rebirthing powers as much as he, so he decided to take it back with him. The journey back took many days, and already in sight of the city, exhausted from the journey, Gilgamesh stopped to rest at an oasis and fell asleep by a pool of water. Out of the water a snake crawled up to the plant, ate it, and sloughed its skin (was "reborn") as it went back to the water. When Gilgamesh awoke, he discovered that the boon he was bringing to his people had disappeared, and with it the hope of eternal youth. It was only then that Gilgamesh came to understand that the rejuvenation he was seeking was to be spiritual, not physical. The gods explained this to him: "Eternal life is not your fate," they told him. But we have no gods to explain to us this profound understanding of rebirth.

⸻ ❧ ⸻

If it is difficult for individuals to die and be reborn, it is even harder for entire nations and peoples, but the idea of death and rebirth applies to them as much as to individuals. The Bible story of the Hebrews' flight from Egypt illustrates this point: a disorganized, servile, and enslaved people escaped from the dominion of Pharaoh, crossed the Reed Sea, and emerged on the far shore as a new, reborn people with a strong and distinct identity. As Tertullian put it, "The people of Israel bent the power of Pharaoh and went free, passing through the waters of the Sea."[14]

After World War I, many Europeans felt that the paroxysms of violence and carnage they had witnessed could only be a presage of a better world, the death throes before the rebirth of peace and renewed culture. In his novel, *Demian* (1925), Hermann Hesse described a vision of collective death and rebirth:

> A huge city could be seen in the clouds out of which millions of people streamed in a host over vast landscapes. Into their midst stepped a mighty, godlike figure, as huge as a mountain range, with sparkling stars in her hair... The ranks of the people were swallowed up into her as into a giant cave and vanished from sight. The goddess cowered on the ground, the mark luminous on her forehead. A dream seemed to hold sway over her: she closed her eyes and her coun-

---

[14] Tertullian, *De Baptismo* IX. By using this simile, I do not mean to suggest that the story of *Exodus* is historical—we have no independent records that it ever occurred—or that the Hebrews crossed the "Red Sea," a mistranslation of the text's *jam suf*, "Sea of Reeds."

tenance became twisted with pain. Suddenly she cried out and from her forehead sprang stars, many thousands of shining stars that leaped in marvelous arches and semicircles across the black sky.[15]

This vision, unfortunately, did not materialize for Europe, as World War II soon followed, but some nations, like Japan and China (after the Cultural Revolution) have been able to die to their old, dysfunctional collective selves and have emerged reborn and vibrant into the present. As with individuals, it is not easy for nations to stamp out the myriad selfish interests that divide us as a people in order to become a new and wholesome organism.

## The World Is a Bridge

Jesus said, "This world is a bridge. Pass over it, but do not build your dwelling there." (Inscription from a mosque at Fatehpur Sikri, India)

It may seem strange that such a saying attributed to Jesus should be found in a Muslim mosque, but Fatehpur Sikri, Akbar's famous capital city, built during his reign (1556–1605), was a great center of learning, and Christian scholars, including Jesuits, lived within its walls. We often forget that by conquering Egypt, the entire Middle East, Syria, and Persia, Islam became the repository of ancient documents from the old Grecian and newer Christian traditions.

Bridges connect masses of land separated by a chasm. The chasm may or may not be deep, but it separates places people desire to have united, and therefore they build bridges. The town of Ronda, in the province of Málaga, in Spain, built itself a bridge to connect both parts of the city split by a deep and steep precipice. As in Ronda

---

[15] Hermann Hesse, *Demian* (New York: Harper & Row, 1989), pp. 169–170.

and other places, there is often a body of water, river or lake, at the bottom of the chasm. Jesus says we should use bridges to get where we want to go but should not dwell on them; still, regardless of this advice, people in Florence built the Ponte Vecchio with dwellings on it.

Bridges need not be physical structures. Jesus seems to be saying that the entire world should be used as a bridge to heaven, or to the kingdom of God, but heaven is not a physical place in the same way as Europe and Asia are, which are connected by the International Bridge in Istanbul. Using this world as a bridge is a metaphorical way of saying that we should not consider this world as our final abode. In another metaphorical use, Martin Buber says that "independence is a foot-bridge, not a dwelling place,"[16] which means that we need a certain amount of individuality in order to be able to deal with others, but that the goal is not simply to be an individual, but to relate to others in the community, to form a crisscrossing network of bridges. This is a hard saying for Americans to stomach, bent as we all are on becoming "individuals" even at the expense of others.

Bridges can be seen also not merely as means of going from one place to another but as places for climbing, for ascending from one level to another, whether in a metaphorical sense or in a physical sense. Footbridges often do this, as the points they connect are not always at the same level. Bridges can also be used for descending. Aqueducts, which carry water over long distances through valleys and hills, must dip slightly in order to maintain the requisite flow of water. The Panama Canal also functions as a watery bridge, its locks raising or lowering the ships they carry between the Pacific and the Atlantic oceans, whose levels differ considerably.

In the prologue to the first part of his *Thus Spoke Zarathustra*, Nietzsche had the Prophet Zarathustra walk into a village fair in which various stalls were selling different kinds of wares, and a tight-rope walker was performing his feat. Looking at the people with a sort of quizzical smile on his face, Zarathustra spoke to them:

---

[16] Martin Buber, "Education," in *Between Man and Man* (New York: Macmillan, 1965), p. 91.

"Man is a rope, tied between beast and overman [*Übermensch*]—a rope over an abyss. A dangerous across, a dangerous on-the-way, a dangerous looking-back, a dangerous shuddering and stopping.

"What is great in man is that he is a bridge and not an end: what can be loved in man is that he is an *overture* and a *going under*."[17]

Here we have the use of bridge as a stepping stone to something higher, not necessarily a heaven, but something better and more fulfilling than what we have been able to create. The point, says Nietzsche, is to use ourselves as bridges to something higher, not to something on the same level, much less to something lower. The point is to use bridges to grow, not to become stagnant.

Adin Steinsaltz wrote:

I like bridges because bridges are almost always beautiful. And they are beautiful because they have to be functional and the function itself creates the beauty. So I am saying about tools, and other things. It's a beautiful bridge, very nice. Now, the second question is, where does it lead? And if it doesn't lead anywhere, then there is a question about the bridge. What good is it?[18]

[17] Friedrich Nietzsche, *Thus Spoke Zarathustra* (New York: The Viking Press, 1966), prologue, 4, pp. 14–15.

[18] Adin Steinsaltz, "What is the right way to make a cake?" *Parabola* 31:1 (Spring 2006), p. 35.

People, too, are bridges; they take others over the rough terrains that they often encounter at certain crucial periods of their lives. Thousands of teachers perform this thankless task for their students, and the fact that their role is not acknowledged does not mean it is not fulfilled. Among many examples, in antiquity, Mentor, Odysseus's trusted friend (whose visage the goddess Athena had assumed), guided young Telemachus in his search for his father, who was presumed dead because he had not returned to Ithaca so many years after the fall of Troy. Conrad, also, tells the story of a young sea captain, unsure of himself, who grows to maturity in his first command by sheltering an escaped convict, a "Secret Sharer," whom he hides in his own cabin. In the same way, Demian becomes Emil Sinclair's bridge to himself, and Hermine serves the same function in the case of Harry Haller, as does the ferryman Vasudeva with regard to Siddhartha.

Nietzsche asserts that he used Schopenhauer as a bridge to himself, just as young Plato employed Socrates to the same effect.[19] It goes without saying that Plato, too, was a bridge to the young Aristotle, that Ambrose was a mentor to Augustine, Hypatia to Synesius of Cyrene, and Bonaventure to Aquinas.

Being a bridge for others requires infinite patience, for the crossing is often delayed by the many vicissitudes of life; it requires courage, because bridging a chasm for others poses a danger to oneself: many bridges have collapsed under a heavy weight or when buffeted by strong crosswinds; and, finally, humility, for the important thing is to help others cross the gap, not to take glory in one's own utility.

The *midrash* of the astrologers who paid their respects to Jesus at his birth (*Matthew* 2:1–2) contains a pertinent lesson: the star that guided them dropped out of the story once its task was accomplished. It was a guide, a bridge to a place, nothing more.

---

[19] Friedrich Nietzsche, *Ecce Homo*, "Why I write such Good Books," on "The Untimely Ones," Section 3, in *On the Genealogy of Morals* and *Ecce Homo*, trans. Walter Kaufmann (New York: Vintage, 1967), pp. 280–281.

# The Dancer

*And he sang: "He who does not dance*
*does not know what happens."*
—*Acts of John* 95–97[20]

The *Acts of John* narrate the following episode: after the Last Supper, Jesus went out with his disciples. They gathered in a clearing, and Jesus asked them to form a circle. He then invited them to dance with him and to respond "Amen!" as he led them in the dance. He told them that by dancing they would appropriate his Passion as if they were eating the bread and drinking the wine that symbolized his body to be broken and his blood to be spilled. In other words, by being caught up and ruled by the rhythm of the dance, they would commune with him, who thus would become the Jewish "Lord of the Dance" (just as Shiva Natarājā is the Hindu equivalent).

If I may paraphrase Arthur Nock, ancient religion was not just believed, it was danced.[21] King David danced ecstatically in front of the Arc of the Covenant (*2 Samuel* 6:14), and Christian ministers still dance their highly choreographed ceremonial dances around the altar of God.

In the same way as Christians are invited to partake in the Eucharistic meal, so too they are still invited to join in the sacred dance. For unless we join in the dance, we will not know what is happening.

Why should we have to dance to know what happens? Because in the dance, we discover the rhythm of the motions that surround us, and we invent a response using our own bodies to articulate it.[22]

Movement is all around us; after all, God moved over the face of the nothing, and while he moved, he spoke, and the universe was set in motion. By his side, at that moment when time began, was

---

[20]  In *New Testament Apocrypha*, ed. Edgar Hennecke and Wilhelm Schneermelcher (Philadelphia, PA: The Westminster Press, 1964), pp. 227–232.

[21]  Quoted in Sam Keen, *To a Dancing God* (New York: Harper & Row, 1970), p. 51.

[22]  Gerardus Van Der Leeuw, *Sacred and Profane Beauty: The Holy in Art* (New York: Holt, Rinehart and Winston, 1963), p. 14.

Wisdom, and she too moved, she danced, constantly making merry in his presence and delighting in the human world that was coming to be (*Proverbs* 8:30–31).

As astronomers tell us, the planets and the stars still dance their ponderous rhythms in the immensity of the heavens, and Lucian of Samosata (*fl.* second century) sees in this whirling the origin of dance: "In the dance of the heavenly bodies, in the complicated movements by which the planets are brought into harmonious relation with the fixed stars, you see an example of this art in its infancy."[23] Dante considered this measured movement to be powered by God's glory,[24] and the Dutch poet Joost van den Vondel (1587–1679) has Adam sing:

> *Learn to dance the festive measure*
> *Which the Lord*
> *God invented in his leisure;*
> *Imitate with knowing pleasure*
> *Heaven's chord.*
> *If you'd change to form supernal*
> *Fields of earth,*
> *Follow heaven's course diurnal:*
> *Stars obey the role eternal*
> *Of their birth.*
> *Some stand fixed; yet always spinning*
> *Seven dance,*
> *Dancers who the prize are winning,*
> *Ringing in since time's beginning*
> *Sky's expanse.*
> *Bride, begin! For I am taking*
> *Every day*
> *The journey which the suns are making.*
> *Thou, like moonlight fresh awaking,*
> *Lead the way!*[25]

---

[23] Quoted in Van Der Leeuw, *Sacred and Profane Beauty*, p. 22.
[24] Dante, *La Commedia*, "Paradiso," Canto i.
[25] In Van Der Leeuw, p. 23.

Van Der Leeuw quotes the words of an old man from Halmahera, the largest of the Moluccas islands, to the missionary who wanted him to reform his ways: "My dancing, drinking, and singing weave me the mat on which my soul will sleep in the world of the spirits."[26] And this is why Jesus danced, too, the day before he died, moving like the shuttle and the woof through the warp of his life's destiny, weaving the shroud on which his fame would rest.

The writer of the *Acts of John* concludes his narrative of Jesus's dance with these words: "After the Lord had so danced with us, my beloved, he went out. And we were like men amazed or fast asleep."[27]

According to a Chinese maxim, one may judge a king by the state of dancing during his reign. If this is so, then Jesus gets high marks!

## Disowning One's Kin

> Jesus said, "Those who do not hate their own father and mother, cannot be my disciples."
> (*Q Gospel* 14:26, *Gospel of Thomas* 55:1–2, *Luke* 14:25–26, *Matthew* 10:37)

This statement of Jesus is striking for its virulence.[28] It seems to demand that one hate one's parents as the price of admission to the Kingdom of Heaven. This is the way I took it when I was a fourteen-year-old adolescent full of "up-vistaed" hopes.

From my thirteenth year, I had decided to enter the Society of Jesus—really, the Jesuit Army, since the word "Compañía" (the name chosen by St. Ignatius Loyola for his religious confraternity) referred to a battalion of soldiers. My intent was no secret, and I found no real opposition at home. My stepmother would occasionally push me

---

[26] Ibid., p. 17.
[27] "Acts of John 97," in *New Testament Aprocrypha*, Edgar Hennecke and Wilhelm Schneermelcher, p. 232.
[28] Crossan, *Birth of Christianity*, p. 323.

to do things by quipping, if I showed some reluctance, that in the monastery, I would not have the freedom to refuse. My father, on the other hand, was more subtle.

One weekend we had gone to La Guaira, the seaport, to embark on a trip in my uncle's cruiser, a beautiful yacht named *Lily May*, which featured crewmen's quarters, galley, bedrooms, showers and toilet, and boasted two Hudson engines packing 240 hp each. Besides our family and my uncle and aunt, there were two crewmen from Trinidad, where my uncle had bought the boat. There was another family with us, and they had two children—a somewhat handicapped boy about my age or younger, and a beautiful and very attractive girl about a year older than I. The three of us were the only teenagers on board.

We sailed up and down the western coast of Venezuela, dropping in on coves with rustic villages and anchoring off beyond the surf for meals and in order to spend the night. We had a wonderful time, even though my father was constantly popping out of portholes and the like to snap photos of the girl and myself engaged in conversation. It was obvious that he was placing before me the lure of happiness in marriage, not necessarily to this particular girl, but as a general alternative to a life of celibacy in the priesthood.

I did not particularly relish my father's antics, but I had a great time in spite of them. By the end of the trip, when we were returning to port, the wind rose and whipped up the sea a bit, which made for a rougher sailing. The young woman and I were standing on the prow, our hands firm on the railing, braving the lurching of the boat as it plunged into the rising waves, and enjoying the sprays of ocean foam as it did.

It was there, silently, with the coastal mountains to my right and the immense ocean to my left, that the question arose, Should I choose her, and all women in her, or the monk's life? The choice presented itself with great simplicity, without fanfare or fireworks, but clearly and distinctly, and demanding assent. I remember choosing Christ without great difficulty, and repeating to myself in summary the words I believe Voltaire uttered on his deathbed, "Thou didst triumph, Galilean!"

---

I said above that my intentions were not secret, and although my mother was not particularly happy about it, I had no indication that she would in any way try to stop me from joining the Jesuits. Thus, it was with some surprise that I heard my father tell my stepmother one day after work that he had been subpoenaed to appear in court in the matter of my joining the Jesuits.

After the divorce of my parents, my father had retained custody of the two children, my bother Eduardo and myself. We were allowed to visit my mother, but this was solely due to my father's willingness to honor my mother's requests. Legally, my mother had no rights in the matter, but over the years, we had been allowed to visit her, sometimes twice a week for one hour at a time, sometimes once a week for two hours, and by the time I was fourteen, once a week for five hours at a time, a situation that permitted us to do some sightseeing together or to visit relatives who lived at some distance from the city.

When I heard my father say that he had been ordered to appear in court, I volunteered to go with him. I believe he was happy about this, though he simply acquiesced to my wishes. And so it came to pass that one afternoon, I found myself sitting in a dark courtroom waiting to be called in by the judge. My father was there, but I could not see my mother, though it is possible she was following the proceedings from some sequestered place.

The judge was pleasant but firm. He asked me why I wanted to join the Jesuits, and I answered that I wanted to lead a religious life at a higher level of perfection. He asked if I had been coerced or brainwashed into choosing this state of life, and I replied that I had not, that, on the contrary, my confessor had tried to dissuade me, an action I construed as his way of testing my resolve. The judge then argued that what I was proposing to do was contrary to the biblical command to honor father and mother. It was then that I replied, "Jesus said that those who love father and mother more than him cannot be his disciples." The judge acknowledged that this was so, and after asking my father what he thought of the matter, he adjourned the hearing and we all left.

I felt very proud of myself at the time. I felt I had acquitted myself effectively and that my answers mirrored the religious feelings I harbored then. It is only over the years that I have come to realize that Jesus could not have been preaching the dissolution of family ties for the sake of his Kingdom. This would have been utterly unethical, as the judge had tried to point out to me. Jesus was not preaching a rupture with the commandments of old, much less with the injunction to respect and honor one's parents. But he would have surely counseled the abandonment of decadent social organizations for the sake of the Kingdom, and the family under Herod Antipas and the Romans had become dysfunctional in many places, due partly to economics and partly to the overwhelming male chauvinism of the family unit and the enslaving of women within it. Jesus may have been suggesting an alternative, a new familial organization made up of his followers, such as existed already among the Essenes at Qumran and in other charitable confraternities throughout the Roman Empire.

Jesus's words made sense in my case because my immediate family had become dysfunctional after the divorce. But I was wrong in interpreting his words universally, even though that was what I had been taught. And what I had been taught was only partial, for in *Gospel of Thomas* 101, Jesus affirms that those who love father and mother *as he does* are welcome as his disciples![29]

## Happiness and Giving

> Happiness lies more in giving than in receiving. (*Acts* 20:35)

Of Jesus's many sayings, this is the favorite one of development officers and preachers who live off of the contributions of their sub-

---

[29] See James Charlesworth, *Jesus within Judaism*, pp. 84–89.

scribers and congregations. Christian fund-raising is almost totally based on this encomium of generosity. It is also a very male statement, since it emphasizes what is typically masculine, this intrusion by giving into the world of others.

It is difficult to argue against the obvious goodness of this saying, yet giving and receiving cry out for a more definite balance, such as exists between male and female, high and low, man and woman. Receiving may make one as happy as giving does, so long as one understands the nature and the importance of it.

———— ⋙⋘ ————

*Once I heard a Master say:*
*"The greatest gift is to receive."*
*I queried:*
*"Master, explain!"*
*And he said:*
*"Blessed the hands that deliver a woman's child.*
*"Blessed the winds that carry a song.*
*"Blessed the heart that relieves another's woe.*
*"Blessed the sands that soak the rising tide.*
*"Blessed the mouth that stems the overflow.*
*"Blessed the eyes that get dazzled,*
*"the lungs that breathe the abundant air,*
*"the firmament that cradles a myriad worlds,*
*"the bosom that shelters a tired head.*
*"Blessed the one who receives."*
*I insisted:*
*"Master, why is it more blessed to receive?"*
*And he said:*
*"The greatest gift is to receive because the greatest need is to give."*

———— ⋙⋘ ————

The *Didache*, or *The Teaching of the Apostles*, 1, carries a curse on those who receive: "Woe to those who receive," but the text clearly specifies that this refers to those who accept gifts they do not need or deserve. The same statement appears in *The Shepherd* of Hermas, Mandate 2, 4–7: "Those who receive by false pretense shall pay the penalty." Obviously, Jesus encouraged generosity and wanted giving to take place without hope of return, as we read in the gospel *Q* 6:30: "Give to everyone who begs from you; and when someone takes your things, don't ask for them back." But it is clear that generosity was to be tempered with prudence and caution lest some take advantage of it.

I believe there is another warning implicit here, and this is against giving with the expectation of return, not so much from other people, but from God. Many people serve God because they expect God to reward them for their service with eternal life in heaven or paradise. The story is told about Rabi'a (d. 801), the saintly woman of Basra, in Iraq, that one day people saw her running along with fire in one hand and water in the other. They asked her, "Where are you going? What does this mean?"

Rabi'a replied: "I am going to burn paradise and douse hell-fire, so that both veils may be lifted from those on the quest and they will become sincere of purpose. God's servants will learn to see him without hope for reward or fear of punishment. As it is now, if you took away hope for reward or fear of punishment, no one would worship or obey."[30] And 'Attâr, in his *Tadhkirat al-'Awliyâ*, repeats her sentiments in the form of a prayer: "O Lord, if I worship you out of fear of hell, burn me in hell. If I worship you in the hope of paradise, forbid it to me. And if I worship you for your own sake, do not deprive me of your eternal beauty."[31] The thing is to engage in the service of God for its own sake, simply because one desires to be with

---

[30] Shams ad-Dîn Ahmad Aflâkî, *Manâqib al-'Ârifîn* (Tehran: Duniyâ-yi Kitâb, 1983), vol. 1, p. 396. Cited in *Early Islamic Mysticism*, ed. Michael A. Sells (New York: Paulist Press, 1996), p. 151.

[31] Cited in Sells, *Early Islamic Mysticism*, p. 169, #53.

him. One should be able to express most truthfully the sentiments Newman voiced in his *Dream of Gerontius*:

> I would have nothing but to speak with Thee
> For speaking's sake.[32]

There is a sixteenth-century Spanish poem popularly attributed to Saint Teresa of Ávila but probably anonymous, which expresses the same sentiments, though here, it is Jesus who is addressed:

> 'Tis not the heaven Thou hast promised me
> that moves me, dear Lord, to so love Thee,
> and it is not threat of hell, how terrible it be,
> that keeps me from offending Thee.
> Thou movest me, my Lord; it doth move me
> to see Thee crucified and taunted by the mob;
> to see Thy body wounded doth move me;
> Thy death and Thy affronts move me to sob.
> Lastly, I am so moved, Lord, by Thy love,
> that though there were no heaven I would
> love Thee,
> and though there were no hell I would still
> fear Thee.
> For this my love, Lord, Thou must not
> pay me,
> for even if I hoped naught from above,
> so would, as now, for e'er remain my love.

---

[32] John Henry Newman, *Dream of Gerontius* (New York: Schwartz, Kirwin & Fauss, 1916), III.

# Some Sayings
# of Jesus II

I grew up in the kind of Christianity that saw itself as totally apolit-
ical. It interpreted the so-called Sermon on the Mount—which was
not delivered on a mount, or even a hill, and was only a collection
of utterances delivered at sundry times—in a purely spiritual way.
In fact, it preached—and this was a selling point for Christianity
at the beginning—that being poor on this earth was to be endured
for the sake of the riches that would be distributed in the Kingdom
of Heaven (*Matthew* 5:3). And not just poverty: slavery, too, was to
be accepted for the sake of the Kingdom, and modern "liberation
theologians" who disagreed were publicly reprimanded and silenced.
In other words, the acceptance of Christianity did not entail revolt
against the unjust, even cruel *status quo*, but meek acquiescence for
the sake of the promised guerdon. This Christianity shook hands
with kings, despots, tyrants, corrupt governments, and millionaires,
not with the poor and the oppressed, to whom it simply promised
redress in a world to come; and sometimes even in *this* world: in
America, Christian compliance and silence is bought by tax exemp-
tions amounting to billions of dollars. The ease with which prelates
of all ranks cozy up to power bothered me, but I figured I did not
fully understand these things, so I should let them be; and I did.

And there was precedent for this. As Meeks points out, the early
Christian movement was often dependent on the support and pro-

tection of people with greater wealth and influence than the poor.[1] Rich converts made their homes available for meetings and often offered protection when this was needed. The Gospels themselves paint Nicodemus as a man of means and influence (*John* 3:1–2; 19, 39), and the same applies to Lazarus (*John* 12:1–2) and Zacchaeus (*Luke* 19:1–10). Among Paul's many influential friends was Philemon, whom Fitzmeyer calls "a young, well-to-do Christian."[2]

However, over the years, I have become convinced that the easy union of Christianity and power betrays, even today, the example and the teachings of Jesus. I have come to agree with Borg that "the way of Jesus was [is] both personal and political. It was [is] about personal transformation. And it was [is] political, a path of resistance to the domination system and advocacy of an alternative vision of life together under God."[3] In other words, discipleship may cost one one's life, as it did to Thomas à Becket (1117–1170), to Thomas More (1478–1535), and to Dietrich Bonhoeffer (1906–1945).

## Laughing and the Kingdom

The Lord said: "Some have entered the kingdom of heaven laughing, but they have come out." (*Gospel of Philip* 74:26)

The narrator explains that some came back out because they were not Christians, or because they really had not thought through what they were doing, so they regretted their entrance. But all one has to do is follow the example of Jesus, who, when he went down into the waters of the River Jordan to be baptized by John the Baptist, "came out laughing at everything." Jesus did not laugh because he did not take "the world" seriously, but because he understood the transitory nature of this world. In fact, the *Apocalypse of Peter* 83:1–4 says

---

[1]   Meeks, *The Origin of Christian Morality*, p. 129.
[2]   Joseph Fitzmeyer, *The Letter to Philemon* (New York: Doubleday, 2000), p. 12.
[3]   Borg, *Jesus*, p. 226.

that Jesus laughed at those who lacked this elementary perception. On the other hand, those who scorn "the world" after the example of Jesus will also "come out laughing." This, too, was the realization of the Buddha, which is the reason all his statues depict him with an almost imperceptible smile, as if he were saying, "Yes, I *know!*"

I like this saying very much because it is one of the few ones in which Jesus commends laughter. In fact, the narrator describes him as laughing, and there are not many places, if any, in the canonical gospels where this is the case. Of course, it would have been impossible for Jesus to have lived his life without laughing; after all, he was a human being like any of us, and we laugh a lot. But the strange thing is that those who recorded the stories of his life left out the jokes, the funny situations, the hearty laughter, the "festive celebrations" (as Bruce Chilton calls them[4]). The result has been a Christianity devoid of fun and mirth and full, instead, of the spirit of gravity, which, as Nietzsche quipped, makes all things fall! St. John Chrysostom insisted that Jesus never laughed or smiled, "even a little."[5] And he added:

> That is why Christ says so much to us about mourning, and blesses those who mourn, and calls those who laugh wretched. For this is not the theater of laughter, neither did we come together for this intent, that we may give way to immoderate mirth, but that we may groan, and by this groaning inherit the kingdom.[6]

And St. Augustine, aware of what was going on around him and trying to oppose it, could preach in a sermon, "People laugh and weep, and it is a matter for weeping that they laugh."[7]

---

[4]  Bruce Chilton, *Rabbi Jesus: An Intimate Biography* (New York: Doubleday, 2000), p. 75.

[5]  St. John Chrysostom, *Homilies on the Gospel of Matthew* (New York: Catholic University of America Press, 1998), VI, 6.

[6]  Ibid., VI, 5.

[7]  St. Augustine, *Sermo 31.* "Opera Omnia," in *Patrologiae Cursus Completus,* Series Latina, ed. J. P. Migne (Paris: Garnier, 1844–1855), vol. 38, col. 194.

I am convinced that Jesus did not promise heaven to the sad alone. I like the image of Jesus coming out of the water, stark naked, shaking his head, and laughing at the insight he had just obtained. I also like the picture of Jesus laughing at the seriousness with which his disciples performed their rituals, a picture preserved for us in the *Gospel of Judas* 34:10–13. If Jesus laughed at the misunderstandings and misrepresentations that had crept into the faith and religious observances of his followers so close to the time when he had actually lived among them, how would he laugh at the rituals that have been developed through the centuries purporting to represent and commemorate his life and his teachings?

Like the Buddha, Jesus should always be depicted as laughing quietly at our misunderstandings of his life and death, simple events whose import is profound precisely because it is so simple, while our theologies conflate and complicate it *in excelsis*.

To all the feast days already in the liturgical calendar, we should add one dedicated to the laughter of Jesus, as the people in medieval times celebrated a Feast of Fools. Much though I like Mozart's music, we should not sing of a *Dies irae* but of a *Dies risus*, a "day of laughter."

———————

Saint Teresa of Ávila warned about mistaking melancholy for holiness.[8] She is said to have prayed, "God deliver us from gloomy saints!"

## Sexual Equality

*Jesus said to them: "When you make the two*
*into one, and when you make the outer like the*

---

[8] Letter 96, 11, in Santa Teresa de Jesús, *Obras Completas*, ed. Efrén de la Madre de Dios, OCD, and Otger Steggink, O. Carm. (Madrid: Biblioteca de Autores Cristianos, 1967), p. 749.

*inner, and the upper like the lower, and when*
*you make male and female into a single one, so*
*that the male will not be male nor the female*
*female...then you will enter the Kingdom."*
—*Gospel of Thomas* 22:4–7

The sense that the Kingdom of God will be available for entry only when oneness and unity prevail among Jesus's followers is a recurring theme both in Gospels and letters.[9] The *Gospel of the Egyptians* has Jesus answering a query from Salome (probably his sister) and saying, "When you have trampled the garment of shame, and when the two become one, and the male with the female is neither male nor female," then the things that he has spoken about will become known.[10] It is not merely a matter of establishing a heavenly androgyny here on earth, but the implication is also that one must strive for justice in the treatment of men and women. Some of the Pauline texts refer explicitly to equality between Jews, Greeks, and Gentiles, and this social justice must extend equally to the sexes.

The early Jerusalem community seems to have understood well the meaning of social equality, at least in some respects. They had difficulty with equality between men and women, and initially also between Jew and Gentile. But in terms of social justice and equality, they seem to have been quite successful. The *Acts of the Apostles* describes the organization of the Jerusalem community as follows:

> The whole body of believers was united in
> heart and soul. None of them claimed any of
> their possessions as their own, but everything was
> held in common... They were all held in high

---

[9] See, for example, *Matthew* 19:4 and 22:30; *John* 17:11 and 21; *Galatians* 3:28; *Romans* 3:22; and 10:12; *1 Corinthians* 12:13; *Colossians* 3:11; and *Ephesians* 2:15.

[10] *Gospel of the Egyptians* 3, in Clement of Alexandria, *Miscellanies* 3, 13, 92. The consistency of the theme in all these sayings bears witness to an ancient source kept in many traditions. The statements also have a Gnostic meaning, which is not necessarily primary.

> esteem; for they had never a needy person among
> them, because all who had property in land or
> houses sold it, brought the proceeds of the sale,
> and laid the money at the feet of the apostles; it
> was then distributed to any who stood in need
> (*Acts* 4:32–35).

From each, the community received what each could give, and to each one was given according to each one's need. Those who cheated, as happened with Ananias and his wife Sapphira, were struck dead by God (*Acts* 5:1–12).

It never ceases to amaze me how people who parade themselves as Christians, as "born again," and so forth, want to eliminate the social programs that precisely seek to implement this provision proclaimed by Jesus and observed by the first Christians. It is about people like these that God spoke through the prophet Amos:

> I detest, I loath your festivals,
> I have no satisfaction in your solemn
> gatherings.
> Whatever you sacrifice to me
> —your burnt offerings and gifts—
> I cannot accept
> —your peace offerings and fat cattle—
> I cannot approve.
> Take your loud songs away from me!
> I won't listen to your instrumental music.
> But let justice roll on like the ocean,
> And equity like a perennial stream (*Amos*
> 5:21–24).

The sacrifices and religious festivals Amos referred to had been instituted by God himself, and the people felt that, as long as they celebrated these, God would be pleased. They did not look beyond, to the social conditions that they had created. They had become sanctimonious, and therefore they had difficulty seeing the emptiness of their worship. Amos sought to awaken them from their dreams and delusions, and perhaps we need a new Amos to wake people up today to the superficiality of their Christianity, and to practice more resolutely what Jesus called "the weightier demands of the Law, justice, mercy, and good faith" (*Matthew* 23:23).

In a well-known passage in *Matthew* 15:14, a young man asked Jesus what to do in order to be a good Jew, and Jesus replied, "Follow the Law and the prophets." The young man replied, "I have already done that. What next?" Jesus replied, "Sell everything you have, give the proceeds to the poor, and follow me." The young man showed his disappointment and walked away because, as the *Matthew* gospel says, he was very rich. The *Gospel of the Nazoreans* 6:3–4 adds a twist that is pertinent here. Jesus restarts the conversation by calling after him and saying, "How can you say, 'I have done what is in the Law and the prophets'? For it is written in the Law, 'Love your neighbor as yourself.' And look, many of your brothers, sons of Abraham, are covered with filth and dying of hunger, but your house is full of many good things, and not a single thing comes out of it for them."[11]

We would do well to remember that not all those who call themselves "born again" will enter the Kingdom (as Jesus himself averred), but those who do the will of God (*Matthew* 7:21). Clement also preserved this same saying of Jesus: "Not everyone who says to me, 'Master, master,' will be saved, but whoever does righteous-ness."[12]

---

To return to equality between the sexes: Paul was not a traveling companion of the living Jesus. If he knew how Jesus felt about the equality of men and women, he did because he had been told, and not from personal experience. Yet his writings show a remarkable concern for this equality, as is very clear from the care with which

---

[11]  *Gospel of the Nazoreans* 6:3–4, quoted in Origen, *Commentary on Matthew* 15:14. See Marvin Meyer, *The Unknown Sayings of Jesus* (Boston: New Seeds, 2005), pp. 28–29.

[12]  *2 Clement* 4:2, in Marvin Meyer, *Unknown Sayings of Jesus*, p. 93.

he words texts like *1 Corinthians* 7:1–7. But obviously not everyone agreed with him on this point, for there are letters pretending to be from Paul that present views about women entirely different from the ones expressed in *1 Corinthians* and in *Romans*. The passages from *Ephesians* 5:21–33 (often read at weddings), *1 Timothy* 2:8–15, and *Colossians* 3:18–19, which sound so male chauvinistic to us today, come from letters that Paul did not write, so they cannot be taken as representative of his views. The same goes for the passage in *1 Corinthians* 14:33b–36, an anonymous addition inserted in an authentic Pauline letter in order to modify its meaning. It does not represent Paul's thinking.

I should add that when pseudo-Paul states in *Ephesians* that man is the head of woman, he is referring to *Genesis* 2:21–25, a text that speaks poetically of the creation of Eve from Adam's rib. On the other hand, man is born *from* woman, so the derivations are equalized. Whatever the symbolism that is being sketched in these passages, the overriding principle is equality.[13]

---

It should be noted that the equality of men and women was anathema to Evangelicals in England and in this country from the time of the colony to this day. In England, John Wesley insisted that a wife must

> know herself the inferior, and behave as such… When the woman counts herself equal with her husband, (much more if she counts

---

[13] William F. Orr and James Arthur Walther, *1 Corinthians* (Garden City, NY: Doubleday & Co., Inc., 1976), p. 263. The analogy of God-Christ-Church to Christ-man-woman does not fully work because Paul omits mention of *Genesis* 1:26–27, in which there is no derivation of woman from man. The omission may have been unintentional, though it may have been made with the knowledge that the Gentiles he was writing to in Corinth would not know the difference, since they were not as well versed in the Hebrew Scriptures as he was. See also John Dominic Crossan, *God and Empire*, pp. 172–183.

herself better,) the root of all good marriage is
withered, the fountainhead dried up... Whoever,
therefore, would be a good wife, let this sink into
her inmost soul, "My husband is my superior, my
better: he has the right to rule over me. God has
given it him, and I will not strive against God.
He is my superior, my better."[14]

In America, Jonathan Edwards agreed, "It's against nature for a
man to love a woman as wife that is rugged, daring and presumptu-
ous, and trusts herself, and thinks she is able to protect herself and
needs none of her husband's defense or guidance. And it is impossible a woman should love a man as her husband, except she can
confide in him, and sweetly rest in him as a safeguard."[15]

One might excuse the male chauvinism of these old preachers
because they did not possess the critical knowledge of the Scriptures
we have today. But to construct, on the basis of spurious letters and
texts (as some Fundamentalists and Evangelicals still do), an argument for the subordination of women to men within the family unit
and in society at large, is totally unwarranted, and rather a sign of an
*outré* patriarchalism that speaks more to the insecurity of the claim-
ants than to the truthfulness of the claims.

## Clever Money Changers

*Be ye careful money changers.*
*—Kerygmata Petrou 5*

Among the many sayings attributed to Jesus, this one has always
held a particular interest for me: "Be ye careful [or expert] money

---

[14] John Wesley, "The Duties of Husbands and Wives," in *Works*, Vol. IX, pp.
74–75, quoted in Greven, *The Protestant Temperament*, p. 127.
[15] Jonathan Edwards, "Miscellanies," No. 37 on "Faith," typed Ms., pp. 169–171
(The Beinecke Rare Books and Manuscript Library, Yale University), quoted in
Greven, *The Protestant Temperament*, p. 128.

changers."[16] To be in business, money changers must know how to distinguish good coinage from the counterfeit; otherwise, they are ruined. In point of fact, in many countries throughout the ancient world, people would bite gold coins given to them in order to ascertain whether they were truly gold or shining copper.

This skill of discernment was applied to the spiritual life by the early Fathers of the Church and remained a simile repeated through the centuries. St. Ignatius of Antioch († *ca.* 110) used it in his *Letter to the Magnesians*, 5, and so did Clement of Alexandria,[17] Origen,[18] and Cassian. Gerson (1363–1429), the chancellor of the University of Paris, remarked, "Counterfeit and genuine coins are being circulated. God's money and the devil's money are being passed around; and what is most needed at the present time is, according to our Lord's word, 'expert money changers.'"[19] St. Ignatius Loyola (1491–1556), in his *Spiritual Exercises*, included two sets of "Rules for the Discernment of Spirits," which operationalized this need for discernment.[20]

Ignatius Loyola (or Iñigo, as his original name was) had been a courtier and military man. He was injured in the battle of Pamplona (1521) and was brought on a stretcher to his ancestral castle at Loyola. During his convalescence, his life was transformed by reading the lives of the saints, with whom he compared himself and found himself wanting. After his recovery, he traveled to the little town of Manresa, northwest of Barcelona, and put himself through several weeks of intensive self-scrutiny and prayer. He kept notes of what he felt and experienced during these weeks, and these notes became

---

[16] This saying is found in the *Kerigmata Petrou*, 5, in *New Testament Apocrypha*, ed. Edgar Hennecke and Wilhelm Schneemelcher (Philadelphia, PA: The Westminster Press, 1964), vol. 2, p. 102. See also *1 Thessalonians* 5:22: "Test everything."

[17] Clement of Alexandria, *Miscellanies* 1, 28, 177.

[18] Origen, *Commentary on John* 19, 7, 2.

[19] Gerson, "De distinctione verarum visionum a falsis," in *Opera Omnia* (Antwerp, 1706), vol. 1, pp. 44–45.

[20] Louis J. Puhl, SJ, trans., *The Spiritual Exercises of Saint Ignatius* (Allahabad, India: St. Paul Publication, 1962), Nos. 313 *ff.*; Hugo Rahner, *The Spirituality of St. Ignatius Loyola* (Westminster, MD: The Newman Press, 1953), pp. 79–80.

the core of what he later developed as the "spiritual exercises," that is, meditations on the life of Jesus and of the principal truths of the Christian faith, with the aim of rearranging one's life for the better. The two sets of "Rules for the Discernment of Spirits" constitute a set of guidelines or rules of thumb designed to help one interpret what suggestions or inspirations or insights are conducive to a reformed life and which are not; in the language of the time, which promptings come from the "good" spirit and which come from the "evil" spirit, namely, Satan.

The third suggestion in Rule 9 (No. 322) lays down clearly the purpose of these self-examinations: "to give us true knowledge and understanding of ourselves." As a commentator says, this means two things: to be aware of the stirrings within ourselves and to understand them—that is, "to be perfectly aware of what is going on in one's soul, and to realize the difference between the different types of promptings. Both things are necessary for the spiritual life."[21] In all of this, one may need the help of an experienced counselor who has traveled the road before. And the reason is given in Rule 13 (No. 326): "When the enemy of our human nature tempts a just soul with his wiles and seductions, he earnestly desires that they be received secretly and kept secret. But if one manifests them to a confessor, or to some other spiritual person who understands his deceits and malicious designs, the evil one is very much vexed. For he knows that he cannot succeed in his evil undertaking, once his evident deceits have been revealed." This very thing is the subtext of C. S. Lewis's sagacious analysis of temptations in *The Screwtape Letters* and *Screwtape Proposes a Toast*:[22] under all circumstances, the young tempter, Wormwood, is to make sure that the tempted person *never* suspects a tempter. "Our policy," Screwtape writes to Wormwood, "is to conceal ourselves."[23]

---

[21] Ignacio Casanovas, SJ, *Comentario y explanación de los Ejercisios Espirituales de San Ignacio de Loyola* (Barcelona: Balmes, 1945), vol. 2, p. 150.

[22] C. S. Lewis, *The Screwtape Letters & Screwtape Proposes a Toast* (New York: Macmillan, 1962).

[23] Ibid., p. 32.

Guidance is especially needed also because, as St. Ignatius says in Rule 4 (No. 332) of the second set, "it is a mark of the evil spirit to assume the appearance of an angel of light. He begins by suggesting thoughts that are suited to a devout soul, and ends by suggesting his own." How to tell the good inspirations from the bad ones? St. Ignatius says insightfully that "the action of the good angel is delicate, gentle, delightful. It may be compared to a drop of water penetrating a sponge." On the other hand, "the action of the evil spirit… is violent, noisy, and disturbing. It may be compared to a drop of water falling upon a stone."

Again, with great sagacity, St. Ignatius suggests in Rule 5 (No. 318) of the first set that "in time of desolation ['a sort of spiritual crisis'[24]] we should never make any change, but remain firm and constant in the resolution and decision which guided us the day before the desolation." When one is upset or bewildered, one should make no change. I have found this advice most important, both in my life and in the counseling of countless young people.

Now, as Jesus's saying implies, discernment has been a part of Christian spirituality from the beginning. The church fathers added their own advice, at times very explicit, as in the works of St. Augustine and Dionysus, and later during the Renaissance in those of St. Teresa of Ávila, St. John of the Cross, Jeremy Taylor, and in the many excellent commentaries that followed them. Nor was Christianity alone in this quest for discernment: the *Yoga Sûtra* of Patañjali, the various classical *sûtras* of the Buddhist tradition, the *Tao-Te Ching* of Lao-tzu, the *Chuang-tzu*, Nasafi's *The Book of the Perfect Man*, and many other priceless documents bear witness to the need for discernment and the efforts to fill this need among those who have traveled the path. For in our own days, as much as in any other age, counterfeit Christian, Hindu, Buddhist, and Islamic coins are being circulated, and we need to know how to pick out the true from the false.

———※———

---

[24] Hervé Coathalem, SJ, *Ignatian Insights* (Taichung, Taiwan: Kuangchi Press, 1961), p. 262.

Unfortunately, counterfeiting does not take place only in the realm of the spirit. It occurs also whenever people obliterate reality by their own interpretations of it, as happens when people misconstruc texts, historical facts and events, and scientific data. Claiming that God created the world four thousand years ago is counterfeiting. Asserting that humans and dinosaurs coexisted in Eden is counterfeiting. Rushing into war under false pretenses is counterfeiting. And while some forms of counterfeiting may not do much harm to others, some result in death and destruction, as the circle of young counterfeiters in Gide's *The Counterfeiters* discovered only too late.

————⊰✸⊱————

It is also counterfeiting to create and pander a false image of oneself as righteous and virtuous when in fact one is an adulterer, an alcoholic, a swindler, a liar, a trafficker in bribes. We all play roles, but some roles are better than others—certainly, more beautiful. At any rate, the trick lies in being able to relinquish playacting when our integrity is at stake.

————⊰✸⊱————

One final word: in our own days, psychology has thrown a different and welcome light on the workings of our souls in the pursuit of perfection. In a sense, discernment has put on a psychological garb. Though psychologists often think they have invented the wheel in this respect, they have merely added a new—though important—way to look into the inner processes of self-development. Bartering is as old as humanity; modern business practices merely refine what has existed before. Similarly, psychology has only added novel ways of figuring out, in the spiritual life, who is cheating whom, how, where, and why.

# Passersby

Jesus said: "Be ye passersby." (*Gospel of Thomas* 42)

This is a strange saying. According to the Gnostics, Jesus counseled us to go through this life without becoming entangled in it, especially in the material aspects of life such as money, riches, drugs, and sexuality. Others read into this saying a call not to make permanent dwellings for ourselves here on earth, for heaven is our final destination.

According to the *Genesis* story, humans were expelled from their original abode in Eden and plunged into exile. Exile, thus, became a condition attendant upon human existence itself, a kind of cosmic condition that transcended actual exiles experienced throughout thousands of years by various peoples in their earthly pilgrimages. Historically, we humans have been nomads for much longer than we have been settlers. We have spent more time passing by than staying put.

The point here is not to recommend the life that Aristotle termed a foreigner's life (*bios xenikos*),[25] unattached to (and therefore unharnessed by) any political society or state, such as the gypsies have led and continue to lead—this is hardly possible in today's world, where foreigners (and *a fortiori* "stateless" people) arouse suspicion because of the threat of terrorism and contraband; the point is the possession of an inner centeredness, an inner direction (as Riesman might have termed it) that holds one to one's course like a gyroscope whether in exile or in the Promised Land.

I find it interesting that this *logion* of Jesus is preserved in the *Gospel of Thomas*. This gospel is attributed to Judas Thomas, the twin brother (*didymos*) of Jesus (or of one of the other brothers or sisters). The gospel was treasured by "Thomas Christians," probably followers of Thomas in Syria, from where he went to India and founded there a Christian community extant to this day. He, too, exiled from

---

[25] Aristotle, *Politics* 7. 2 [1324ᵃ 16].

the Galilee and become a passerby as his brother Jesus had counseled, kept in focus the message and died in witness to it.

In the words of Walter Wink, such people had "the realization that we can live out of an interior center, secure yet flexible, capable of enduring tension, with a tolerance for ambiguity, anxiety, and conflict, traveling like turtles with our homes on our backs."[26] Al-Hallâj, if I remember correctly, said of the Prophet's vision, "He blinked beyond the where." His mystical insight carried him beyond the confines of time and place into the only realm the human spirit can call its own. We too, apprentices though we may be, need to learn to blink beyond the wheres of nationalities and property ownership.

Being a passerby means one is a pilgrim. Christianity has understood this well, and John Bunyan's *Pilgrim's Progress* is a beautiful example of such belief. In the tradition of Islam, considering life a pilgrimage has also been *de rigoeur*. Nasafi's *Manâzil al-sâ'irîn* I (*Book of the Stages of the Pilgrims*) illustrates this endeavor. He writes the following:

> You must learn that the destiny and the supreme and final end of all those on the way is the knowledge of God. This knowledge is the product of God's light...therefore the task of the pilgrims is to give themselves to work and striving under the direction of a wise person, with the objective of reaching God's light and of knowing Him... "Which is the way?"... If you ask about the stages on the way to God you must know that there are absolutely none—what did I say? there isn't even a way.[27] Whether you speak in terms

---

[26] Walter Wink, *The Human Being: Jesus and the Enigma of the Son of the Man* (Minneapolis: Fortress Press, 2002), p. 82.

[27] In the *Tao-Te Ching* I, we read: "The Tao [Way] that can be 'tao-ed' cannot be the infinite Tao. It is the same with the name of things: if things are explicable, the names we give them cannot be the original Name." Similarly, when Faust (*Faust*, line 6222) asks Mephistopheles for the way to "the Mothers," he answers:
> No path! Unto untrodden way,

of longitude or latitude, there is no way from you to God. There is only a point. To the one prepared, God's knowledge is granted by a single word from a wise guide, and that concludes the entire journey to God.

There is no way from you to God, and if there were one, it would be you yourself. You must therefore erase your self so as to abolish any distance between you and God. You must know with certainty that being comes only from God.

*Put one foot on your ego and another on the alley where your Friend dwells; see your Friend in everything, do not concern yourself with this or that!*

Those who reach God and know Him have finished their journey, and they are at peace with all the creatures of the world. For those who, having the knowledge of God, see and understand the essence of all things and the wisdom of this essence, the journey has ended. They know everything, and there is nothing that eludes their knowledge. The Prophet certainly has reached such a stage, and therefore he prays, "Lord, show the world to us as it is."

Of a hundred thousand pilgrims who begin the journey, one reaches God and knows Him. Of a hundred thousand pilgrims who reach God

---

Not to be trodden, a path to the unseekable, nay,
not to be sought. Are you in mood?
There are no locks, no bolts to push aside.
By loneliness will you be driven far and wide.
Have you a concept of the void and solitude?
Hermas, at the beginning of *The Shepherd* (Vision 1.1), writes how the Spirit took him "away through a pathless tract, through which no one could pass."

and know Him, one attains the point wherein he sees and understands the essence of things and the wisdom of this essence. The rest remain on the road.

You must have great spiritual strength, and you must strive always while in this life, for the knowledge and wisdom of God are limitless.[28]

———⟶×⟵———

The Way. This is the name the early Christian movement was given at the beginning (*Acts* 9:2, 19:9). This name was given also to the Tao, the Chinese path that could not be walked, as the *Tao Te Ching* 1 says; and by Hesse to "the East," which is "everywhere and nowhere, it was the union of all times."[29]

Of this path Ephrem the Syrian (*ca.* 306–373) wrote that "smooth is the way for the simple, that way which is faith,"[30] and he blessed those who on this voyage become pilots of their own souls.[31] But all these names were mere indications of a mystery—that is, a truth that is only known to the initiated, the *mystes*—namely, that the path is undefinable, unspecifiable, the kind that suddenly disappears, as happened to Dante when, in the middle of life, he found himself lost.[32] Preachers and divines often think they know precisely what this way is, where it starts, where it leads, and they therefore presume to lead others on this path, until they falter, suddenly bereft of a sure sense of direction, lost.

---

[28] Azizodin Nasafi, *El Libro del Hombre Perfecto*, trans. Isabelle de Gastines (Málaga: Editorial Sirio, 1984). My own translation into English.

[29] Hermann Hesse, *Journey to the East* (New York: Bantam, 1970), p. 27. See note 27, above.

[30] Ephrem the Syrian, *Hymns against Heresies* 22, 8, in Murray, *Symbols of Church and Kingdom*, p. 246.

[31] Ephrem the Syrian, *Hymns on Virginity* 31, 15, in Murray, *Symbols of Church and Kingdom*, p. 251.

[32] Dante, *La Commedia*, "Inferno" 1, 1.

For the imagery that describes the Way is only metaphor, whether or not it be called theology; and one should always be able to go beyond the metaphor to the things themselves to which the metaphor directs, because this is precisely what metaphor means, a *carrying-beyond*, there, where one cannot be sure. For, to paraphrase Dante, it would be a disgrace if someone invented a metaphor, or a simile, or some other figure of speech or ornament, and then, on being asked, could not divest his/her words of such covering so as to reveal the true meaning;[33] it would be a shame if one claimed one was on the Way but could not explain what the Way is, and where it leads, and how.

For the Way, like the Kingdom, is metaphor for something undefinable and indescribable, and therefore being a passerby is metaphor for a state or situation that the soul knows only when it is involved in it. The Buddha understood this when he claimed that the Path could not be walked because there is no Path; nor can one cross to the Other Shore because there is no Other Shore nor the crossing to it; nor can Wisdom be attained because there is no way to attain it.[34] Jesus also knew this when he reportedly said in answer to his brother Thomas's question (who wanted to know how they could follow him if they did not know where he was going!), "I am the Way" (*John* 14:6)—a strange answer, for a man is not a road. But this is the point: he could just as easily have answered, "Oi vey!" or "Come on!" or "Look at the sparrows, how busily they fly about (though they do not know what it means to fly!)." For the point is not to know the destination and the way thereto, but to set out trusting in God's providence and one's sense of direction; because the Way, as Paul says, is untraceable (*Romans* 11:33). *This* is the mystery.

God, wrote Augustine, created us to tend toward himself, and our hearts are restless until they rest in him.[35] Like heat-seeking missiles, we plough along through space after the heat source, to merge

[33] Dante, *La Vita Nuova* XXV, 80 (New York: Penguin Books, 1980), p. 75.
[34] *Astasâhasrikâ Prajñâpâramitâ* 8; *Vajracchedikâ* 21–22.
[35] Augustine, *Confessions*, Book I, 1.

with it in a paroxysm of love; and in this journey, as Hesse put it, we have no other guide but our homesickness.

## On the Poor 1

Jesus said: "There will always be poor around." (*Matthew* 26:11)

This saying has been interpreted traditionally to mean that Jesus acknowledged the fact that there would always be poor people around on whom the generosity of people could be exercised. He would not always be with them (the disciples), but *they*, the poor, would always be around. It is almost as if Jesus were saying that his followers would always have opportunities to be "do-gooders," giving alms to the poor and feeling good about having shown their generosity.

When I was a kid, I lived with the extended family of one of my aunts. There were many of us in the house, my aunt and uncle, my father, my grandmother, and my younger brother, and then there were the many servants—the cook, the nanny, the maid, and the washerwoman. We lived toward the front of the house; the servants had their quarters toward the back. And I was not supposed to go there, and I never did.

Every year, on Christmas Day, the family would wake up early and go to the formal living room where the beautiful *crèche*, with its expensive figures of shepherds and angels and Mary, Joseph, and the Child Jesus, was exhibited, and where our presents were stacked and arranged with identifying labels. It was a joyous occasion, and I thoroughly enjoyed it. Then, in the evening, at dusk, we would all gather in the space outside the formal living room, which opened toward the patio, family members and servants, and my aunt and my grandmother would give the servants their presents—woolen blankets: gray, coarse, heavy woolen blankets. To this day, I remember the sullen expression on the faces of all the servants. There were no smiles; there was no joy, no laughter, just a formal and half-muttered "thank you." I felt uncomfortable, though I really didn't know why, and I felt that the servants themselves were ill at ease in the situation. The truth was that this occasion was there for my family to exercise their charity, to show generosity to "the poor who were always with us"; it was not an opportunity for the servants to enjoy themselves and be happy with the rest of us.

I think Jesus's saying has nothing to do with the fact that poor people still live around us after so many centuries of fake charity. Just look at the situation: the expensive perfume with which a woman cleansed his feet, and some of Jesus's followers noticed this, and they commented, "Geez, what a waste. It would have been better to sell that perfume and give the proceeds to the poor!" But Jesus *knew* that they were just being sanctimonious, that they did not care about the poor, really, as much as about *appearing* to care for them. His comment was sarcastic, then—something like, "Yeah, you will make sure that there are always poor people around for you to show off." Or, perhaps more pertinently, "You will always have the poor around because you won't eliminate poverty!"

One of Christianity's major selling points at the beginning, one reason it spread so quickly, was because it was preached to the poor, to the destitute, to those whom high society had forgotten; and what Christianity offered them was not, really, a change in their condition here on earth, but a future Kingdom in heaven where their grievances would be redressed. In fact, as Jesus told them, "Congratulations, you poor in spirit! The Kingdom [of heaven] already belongs to you!" *(Matthew* 5:3). And in this way, Christianity became complicitous with the rich and powerful of this world in their neglect and deprivation of the poor. Christianity helped keep the poor appeased. Napoleon is reputed to have said that we have religion so that the poor will not murder the rich!

And this is one major reason Christians resent communists and socialists, because they expose Christianity's pompous self-righteousness in the face of poverty *and* because they point an accusing finger at the conspiracy to preserve poverty in the world, a conspiracy in which Christians are major players.

Many in America today worry about the demise of "the West," which they attribute to the rise of socialism around the world and the introduction of social welfare programs like Social Security, Medicare, and Medicaid, into the economic fabric of American society. They think this has weakened our country. They call themselves Christian, but their Christianity fails at its root, which is the concern for and love of everyone, especially of those less fortunate. As John wrote, "Only those who love their brothers dwelling light: nothing can make them stumble" (*1 John* 2:10).

## A Historical Note

Following St. Francis's death in 1226, the Friars Minor (as they were called) saw their Rule relaxed somewhat so that it could be accessible to more people. By 1280, there were two hundred thousand Franciscan monks in eight thousand monasteries. But not all the followers of St. Francis accepted the relaxation of the Rule. Many protested, and writes Durant,

> As "Spirituals" or "Zealots" they lived in hermitages or small convents in the Apennines, while the great majority of Franciscans preferred spacious monasteries. The Spirituals argued that Christ and His apostles had possessed no property; St. Bonaventura agreed; Pope Nicolas III approved the proposition in 1279; Pope John XXII pronounced it false in 1323; and thereafter those Spirituals who persisted in preaching it were suppressed as heretics. A century after the death of St. Francis his most loyal followers were burned at the stake by the Inquisition.[36]

---

[36] Will Durant, *The Age of Faith* (Simon and Schuster, 1950), p. 802.

## On the Poor 2

Jesus said, "Happy are the poor, for yours is
the Kingdom of Heaven." (*Gospel of Thomas* 54,
*Luke* 6:20)

This saying has been interpreted through the centuries as a praise
of poverty, whether incurred by accident or deliberately sought, as
in the case of ancient eremites and present-day monks who take a
vow of poverty. But, as Crossan indicates, "The term poor denoted
the vast majority of the world."[37] Most people at the time of Jesus
were poor in some way or another, there being very few rich who,
however, had the power and control over the poor that riches tend
to give. But while the destitute are so economical, monks and ascetics vowed to poverty assume a destitution that is primarily spiritual
and only secondarily economical. Saint Francis of Assisi is reported
to have said that he needed very little, and that even the little he
needed, he needed very little. This is the case with voluntary poverty:
monks vow to desire very little, even the few things they are allowed
to use. They vow to divest themselves of attachment to things, a very
difficult thing to achieve. All religious orders in the East and the
West have insisted on this spiritual dimension of poverty as the most
essential one, the one that would imbue actual poverty with sanctity
and merit, the one lacking, which all renunciation would be mere
show. Of course, as Crossan remarks, "Temporary hunger from what
is there is never the same as permanent hunger from what is not
there,"[38] and this applies even with all the detachment in the world.
Ascetics always know that they could have it all at the flip of a switch,
as it were, while the poor know they could never have it here and
now. And who knows about the morrow?

Further proof of the difference between the voluntary poverty
and real poverty is the fact that monks and nuns generally live long

---

[37] Crossan, *The Birth of Christianity*, p. 321.
[38] Ibid., p. 421.

lives in poverty and eventually die peacefully in their nunneries and monasteries. On the other hand, as Gutiérrez put it,

> In the final analysis, poverty means death: lack of food and housing, the inability to attend properly to health and education needs, the exploitation of workers, permanent unemployment, the lack of respect for one's human dignity, and unjust limitations placed on personal freedom in the areas of self-expression, politics, and religion. Poverty is a situation that destroys peoples, families, and individuals.[39]

No monk or nun is ever buried in a "Potter's Field"!

But, as I explained before, given the fact that most people in the world were poor, this blessing of Jesus, this praise of poverty, helped sell the new religion of Christianity. The message seemed to say, "Even if you are poor here on earth, you should count yourself happy because you will inherit the Kingdom of Heaven." Thus the status of the slave, of the handmaid, of the servant, was validated when seen *sub specie aeternitatis*.

And yet, at the same time, the *status quo* that favored the rich and the powerful was equally validated, at least in the present age, in the time that the poor and the rich, both, have to live their lives on earth. Christianity, thus, became the endorser and preserver of the *status quo*, the sustainer of the powers that be, at least by way of not opposing them, at least by keeping the poor quiet with the promise of a Kingdom to come. Christianity became the supporter of systemic poverty, the poverty created by the system, whether of kings or of dictators, whether of feudalism or of democracy.

Seen from this perspective, the happiness of the poor becomes rather suspect. It is still romanticized and given lip service by the rich, but its reality can be seen in more concrete terms as deprivation,

---

[39] Gustavo Gutiérrez, *A Theology of Liberation*, rev. ed. (New York: Orbis Books, 1988), p. xxi.

as destitution, as misery, as the uncaring exploitation of the many by the few.[40] It is this kind of praise of poverty that so enervated Nietzsche, who saw Christianity as the preserver of the weakness of people by praising their poverty as something holy and worth enduring. For Nietzsche, embracing systemic poverty was tantamount to accepting injustice, and he saw this fate as a renunciation to having a full human life. Singing the happiness of poverty was, for Nietzsche, equivalent to praising one's diminution, one's obliteration from the social sphere. This is why he quipped sarcastically, "Blessed the poor in spirit, because they shall soon drop off."[41]

But surely, Jesus did not mean to bestow praise on systemic injustice and cruelty. He was not so deluded that he would have stood for such oppression as existed in his own time in Palestine. Surely he did not romanticize destitution and poverty. But he *did* set up a contrast between those who suffer here and now and their oppressors, no matter how rich and powerful. In this he was but echoing the long tradition of concern for the poor that characterized Israel from time immemorial. He was making sure that everybody, rich and poor alike, understood that poverty, the poverty created by unjust economic and social systems, would not be tolerated in the coming Kingdom of God, and conversely, that systemic injustice would not be tolerated there either. As Crossan puts it, "God is for the destitute and powerless not because they are individually good but because their situation is structurally unjust. God is against the rich and powerful not because they are individually evil but because they are systemically evil. The Jewish God has no preferential option for the poor; rather, the Jewish God has a preferential option for justice."[42]

---

[40] Crossan, *The Birth of Christianity*, p. 322.
[41] Nietzsche, *Thus Spoke Zarathustra*, Part I, "On the Teachers of Virtue," p. 30.
[42] Crossan, *Birth of Christianity*, p. 322.

After I joined the Jesuit Order as a young man, I took a vow of poverty that placed me among the favored of God. This suited me fine, for having lived for three years in a Jesuit boarding school, I was used to that ordered life and was accustomed to living within restricted means. Joining the Jesuits did not introduce any great change. I still had three meals provided me, I still had a roof over my head, I still had clothes and shoes to wear, and I still had the necessaries for the novice's life: paper and pencil and books were all there for my use. That none of this was "mine" made no difference, really.

Of course, I tried to work on "detachment," on not being attached to the things I used, and on not being attached to the places I lived in. Hence I had no difficulty at all being sent to live in Europe and then to India: the same arrangements applied everywhere.

But as the years passed, I began to realize that even poor Jesuits had access to things that the "real" poor could not even dream of using. Jesuits traveled by air, rode in cars, lived in school buildings that were often palatial. Moreover, I myself had access to things and opportunities that were not available to most of my coreligionists. This happened because my mother would supply whatever I asked her—always with permission from the superior, of course. If we needed to hire a cricket coach for the students in the school, my mother would pay the salary. If we needed to engage the services of the best choreographer in town to train the students for a pageant, my mother would provide the fee. Thus I began to realize that, vow of poverty or no vow of poverty, my life was not very different from that of rich people outside the monastery.

When I realized this, I began to deal in earnest with the questions of inner detachment and actual poverty. Taking the vow of poverty involved renunciation, but in fact I was living *as if* I had not renounced anything. Inner detachment did not seem to be sufficient, and I agonized over this matter at length and over many years.

Two things came to my help. The first was the discovery of the doctrine of *karma yoga* in the *Bhagavadgîtâ*. According to this teaching of Krishna, one must act without becoming attached to the results or fruits of one's actions. Beyond inner detachment, which is a condition of the individual soul, this doctrine demanded that one become "indifferent" (as the Stoics had preached and St. Ignatius Loyola recommended in his *Exercises*) to what happened in the world around us: "An agent who is free from attachment, whose speech is free from 'I'-talk, who has a strong resolve and zeal and yet is unmoved by failure or success, possesses an authentic quality," said the *Bhagavadgîtâ*.[43] The thing was to remove the ego from the picture, to act as if actions took place by themselves, so that success or failure was not appropriated by the self. For St. Ignatius, "indifference," as he called it, arose from the fact that everything on earth was created to help us attain our primary goal, to serve God and save our souls. Consequently, he wrote, "We should not prefer health to sickness, riches to poverty, honor to dishonor, a long life to a short life. The same holds for all other things."[44]

The second thing that affected me was my reading of Teilhard de Chardin's *The Divine Milieu*. This book confirmed what I had learned from the *Bhagavadgîtâ* and placed it all in a Christian context. What I learned was that there are two types of asceticism, one of detachment (to which I was used) and one of "right use." This was the new discovery. One does not need to give up things in order to be poor; it is as hard, and even harder, to use things correctly, without attachment to the fruits of the action or to the things themselves, and for the good purposes to which such things can be used. It is easier to give up eating bread for Lent than to eat bread only in the amount absolutely necessary. It is easier not to watch TV at all than to watch only certain programs at certain times.

Teilhard placed his views in the context of the letters attributed to St. Paul, for whom it was essential that Christians *not* renounce the world, but rather that they act in it in order to Christianize it. St. Paul, in fact, described the world as clamoring for such Christianizing activity, for only then would the whole world belong to God in Christ. Later on I also came to understand the Taoist notion of *wu-wei*, "act without acting," and found much resonance in it. I learned from it

---

[43] *Bhagavadgîtâ* 18:26.
[44] St. Ignatius Loyola, *The Spiritual Exercises of Saint Ignatius* (Allahabad: St Paul Publications, 1962), No. 23, p. 21.

to let the world be and not to act in it precipitately as if its very existence depended on me. In other words, I learned not to place myself at the center of my world.

My point is that achieving detachment, being "poor in spirit," is easier said than done, especially for people like myself who aspire to be active in the world in order to spread God's power throughout it.

# 12

# Some Sayings
# of Jesus III

There are sayings of Jesus that cannot be subjected to the criteria referred to in chapter 10. In some ways they belong to history because they were reported by historical individuals, but in other ways they escape history because they were uttered to individuals in the privacy of their own souls. There were no witnesses. They are mystical sayings, and some were addressed exclusively to those reporting them while some carry messages to be made public in some way or another.

St. Paul, for example, on his way to Damascus, heard Jesus say to him, "I am Jesus whom you are persecuting" (*Acts* 9:5). Paul was the only hearer of this saying, and if he had not shared it with others, we would not know about it. The saying is significant because Jesus seems to say that he is alive in his followers, a meaning that obviously did not escape Paul's attention, but which Paul chose to ignore, fascinated as he was by the idea that Jesus might have been truly raised from the dead. Interpreting the words of Jesus this way rather than the former and obvious one was decisive for the view of the resurrection that Paul would eventually develop.

For another example, one might turn to St. Teresa of Ávila (1515–1582), who, in one of her private accounts of conscience, reports that Jesus told her, "Do not strive to lock me up within you, but rather to lock yourself up in me."[1] On another occasion she reported that Jesus had assured her, "Do not fear, daughter, for no one will separate you from me."[2]

These sayings are edifying or not depending on one's credulity and the degree of honesty one attributes to those reporting them. They do not carry the same weight as those sayings contained in the Scriptures.

## On Seeing God

Jesus said to Philip, "He who has seen me
has seen the Father." (*John* 14:9)

Traditionally, this saying of Jesus has been interpreted to mean that Jesus is affirming his oneness with God the Father, the oneness that the Council of Nicaea defined as "consubstantiality," or "being of one substance" with God the Father. The assumption, of course, was that Jesus was divine; he was the son of God become man, and being God's son, he had to be of the same substance as his Father—not just divine by adoption, as it were, but of the same substance.

There is, of course, a very different interpretation of this saying. Jesus seems to have understood that the divine substance included humanness, since humans had been created "in God's image." God's substance contains the fullness of humanness, an infinite fullness that is not exhausted by the diversity of the billions of humans who have populated the earth since the beginning. The human image in God is still capable of further actualizations. Jesus may have decided to strive to his utmost to actualize as much of the perfection of humanness in God as he could, so that anyone who saw him could see the image of God realized in him. To know Jesus, therefore, would be to know

---

[1]   Account of June 30, 1571, "Cuentas de conciencia," 15ª 3, *Obras completas de Santa Teresa de Jesús*, ed. Efrén de la Madre de Dios, OCD, and Otger Steggink, O. Carm. 2nd ed. (Madrid: Biblioteca de autores cristianos, 1967), p. 463.

[2]   Account of November 18, 1572, "Cuentas de conciencia," 25ª, *Obras*, p. 465.

God. *A fortiori*, also, to imitate Jesus would be to imitate God. The gist of the Christian life, according to Thomas à Kempis, consists in striving to form our whole life after the pattern of the life of Jesus.[3]

————— ❧ —————

There is more. Statements like "He who has seen me has seen the Father" had for Jesus, probably, a *functional* meaning, not a *substantive* one. The substantive interpretation, which most traditional Christians accept today, was developed over two or three hundred years by the Cappadocian theologians who, with their Greek philosophy backgrounds, had a tendency to interpret such things in substantive terms.

Jesus probably intended to say that his actions were in accord with the will of God, the Father of all, so that those who saw him act could readily discern the will of God; how he *functioned* or lived his life manifested the will of God. But the theologians fastened on being, on what the statement said about the nature of Jesus and God. If to see Jesus was to see God, this meant that they both were of the same *substance*, just as to see a clay pot is to see clay, and to see a nestling is to see the parent birds. Thus interpreted, the statement became a confirmation in the lips of Jesus himself that he was divine, "of the same nature as God the Father" ("consubstantial with the Father," as the Nicene Creed has it).

## On Violence

"The Kingdom of God has been subjected to violence and the violent are seizing it." (*Matthew* 11:12, Luke 16:1)

This saying attributed to Jesus has presented a challenge to me for many years. In some ways it is uncharacteristic—certainly in terms of the domesticated view of Jesus, Christians have been fed for years—for

_____
[3] Thomas à Kempis, *De imitatione Christi*, Lib. I, cap. 1, 2.

it implies that the violent alone capture the Kingdom, and this despite the many utterances of Jesus regarding peace and meekness. And yet this saying must have seemed important enough to remember and to transmit to future generations. Albright/Mann reconstructed the likely original text as follows: "From the time of the Law all the prophets prophesied...until John the Baptist. From that time the Kingdom of heaven is violently attacked and violent men lay hands on it."[4] In other words, until the time of the Baptist, things went on pretty much as expected, but since John's death, everything is a struggle, and only those who struggle gain entrance to the Kingdom.

Inspired by this text, I wrote the following sonnet sometime around 1955:

## XXIX

March on abreast, ye clouds, the mountain
peak
    In siege to conquer. From 'cross yonder vale
    Its swollen pride doth beckon ye to seek
    The friendly wind's unfriendly help, the gale.
    Rush on and storm its battlements! Destroy
    The proud dominion of its crownèd head,
    And reign instead in majesty, with joy,
    Stamping the skies with your imperial lead.
    Take up the challenge, die a thousand deaths,
    Traverse the seas with full unfurlèd sails:
    To live one life one heaves uncounted breaths,
    To conquer once is worth a thousand fails.
    March on! Rush on! Take all that life can give!
    Who has no will to fight should no more live.[5]

---

4  W. F. Albright and C. S. Mann, *Matthew* (Garden City, NY: Doubleday & Co., 1971), p. 138.

5  The imagery arises from childhood memories of afternoon clouds climbing toward the tops of the Andean Sierra Nevada until they had conquered the heights.

My ancestors would have been proud of me, I feel sure, for on the coat of arms of the Römers, my mother's family, the following words are emblazoned: "To do and to endure behooves strong Romans" (*et agere et pati fortium Romanorum est*).[6]

This is not meant to condemn the peaceful, only the passive. An enormous amount of willpower and spiritual strength is needed just to be, as Milton intuited when, blind and infirm, he wrote in 1655, "They also serve who only stand and wait." Waiting expends as much will as seeking; it is not just a state of inertia and passivity. Similarly, to receive requires as much effort as to give, though giving always seems to capture the limelight. If being peaceful were an easy thing, there would be no wars! And so, to enter the Kingdom, one must *overcome*—oneself, especially, but often also the obstacles that arise to thwart one's quest.

---

It is understandable that preachers should avoid sermonizing on this saying of Jesus: it is much easier to shepherd souls who have lost their fighting spirit and have become docile to all the promptings and coaxings of the leaders. Asceticism and obedience have stilled the human passions, the insistence on rigid dogmas has silenced any questioning voices, and the threats of anathemas have stifled the urgings of the indomitable human spirit. As a result, Christians have become a bleating flock of sheep. This is how, according to Nietzsche, Christianity has become for all practical purposes a herd of "tame animals."

---

The thing is that Jesus did not advocate violence, but he was much more of a sociopolitical revolutionary than preachers give him

---

[6]  The words of the motto are Mucius Scaevola's retort to Etruscan king Lars Porsena, whom he had tried to assassinate. The episode is narrated in Livy's *History of Rome* 12, 12.

credit for. Most of them practice a kind of political Docetism, as Hendricks calls it,[7] meaning that they divest Jesus's message of any earthly connotation, as if his messages were totally and uniquely spiritual. But this view is far from the truth.

Whether Jesus could read or not—he probably could not, but the passage would have been read aloud at the synagogue gathering anyway—Jesus appropriated to himself the words of *Trito Isaiah* 61:1–2 (*Luke* 4:18–19):

> The spirit of the Sovereign Lord YHVH is upon me,
>> because YHVH has anointed me.
>
> He has sent me to announce good news to the poor,
>> to bind up the wounds of those broken in spirit,
>> to proclaim freedom to captives,
>> release to those in prison;
>> to proclaim…
>> a day of vindication for our God;
>> to comfort all those who mourn.

Obviously, it is not just spiritual consolation that he envisaged as his task, but the establishment of God's reign *here on earth* (as it already *is* in heaven: *Matthew* 6:9–13). In this reign, equality will be emphasized (*Matthew* 20:25–28), and the rich and privileged, whether Romans or the priestly aristocracy of Jerusalem, will be eliminated, as he very explicitly and very publicly proclaimed throughout his ministerial life. In fact, this is one very important reason for Jesus's invectives against priests and Pharisees.

By adopting this task for himself, Jesus was simply carrying on the powerful traditions of social justice, which had been legislated

---

[7] Obery M. Hendricks Jr., *The Politics of Jesus* (New York: Doubleday, 2006), pp. 77–80. See also John Dominic Crossan, *God and Empire* (San Francisco, CA: HarperSanFrancisco, 2007), *passim*.

and practiced in Israel in ancient times. Jews were forbidden to charge interest to poor borrowers; they were required to be consistent in the use of measures of weight and quantity; creditors were not allowed to importune debtors in their homes; outstanding balances were to be written off every seven years; employers had to pay employees the wages earned at the end of each day; bribes, especially in legal matters, were forbidden; the giving of false testimony was punishable; the amount of tithing was adjusted according to the financial ability of the giver; and every fifty years, a Jubilee Year was to be held in which all lands were to return to their original owners and all bond servants were to be released.[8]

According to Hendricks, this uncompromising example of Jesus

> places upon every Christian minister the responsibility to withstand the temptation to align oneself with the secular ruling powers. It is true that it is part of every minister's calling to be a pastor to his or her parishioners, to be a spiritual leader and teacher and a comforter of the sick at heart and those afflicted in mind, soul, spirit, or body. Ministers of the Gospel must comfort the afflicted, but they also have the prophet's duty to afflict the comfortable. It is every shepherd's charge to stand against anything that would harm his or her flocks, be it by direct assaults on their well-being or by willful neglect. Every minister's prophetic duty as a servant of the God of Exodus is to bring good news to the poor and deliverance to the oppressed, not to bow to the desires of those in power simply because they are in power.[9]

---

[8] Ibid., pp. 45–46, where all the biblical sources are specifically detailed.
[9] Ibid., p. 33.

On the other hand, there has crept into Christianity, from Augustine and the Crusades up to the present crop of Evangelicals, a sense that Jesus will come again as a military commander, vicious in his extermination of all dissenters, and will thus reinstate the Kingdom of God through a military victory. But this vision arises from vengeful people who departed from the original nonviolent vision of Jesus. Crossan summarizes:

> It is the radicality of God's justice and not the normalcy of civilization's injustice that, as a Christian, I find incarnate in Jesus of Nazareth. Thereafter, within the Christian Bible's New Testament, first Paul of Tarsus lives and proclaims that same radical God until his vision is deradicalized by the pseudo-Pauline letters, and finally, John of Patmos deradicalizes the nonviolent Jesus on a donkey by transforming him into the violent Jesus on a battle stallion [of the *Apocaplypse*].[10]

---

Once, at a dinner party hosted by mutual friends, Norman Vincent Peale told me that he feared that, in his writings and his preaching, he had made Christianity seem too easy, as if all you needed to do in order to be a good Christian was to think positively. I was surprised and also edified by his confession, for it is a mark of a good man to be able to acknowledge whatever shortcomings might have been incurred in the course of a public life.

Then I remembered Bonhoeffer, both the man who wrote and preached and the man who practiced what he preached even though it cost him his life at the hands of the Gestapo. In one of his books,

---

[10] John Dominic Crossan, *God and Empire* (San Francisco: HarperSanFrancisco, 2007), p. 238.

Bonhoeffer wrote of a distinction between "cheap grace" and "costly grace." He said:

> Cheap grace is the deadly enemy of our Church. We are fighting today for costly grace.
>
> Cheap grace means grace sold on the market like cheapjacks' wares. The sacraments, the forgiveness of sin, and the consolation of religion are thrown away at cut prices. Grace is represented as the Church's inexhaustible treasure, from which she showers blessings with generous hands, without asking questions or fixing limits. Grace without price; grace without cost! The essence of grace, we suppose, is that the account has been paid in advance; and, because it has been paid, everything can be had for nothing. Since the cost was infinite, the possibilities of using and spending it are infinite. What would grace be if it were not cheap?
>
> Costly grace is the treasure hidden in the field; for the sake of it a man will gladly go and sell all that he has. It is the pearl of great price to buy which the merchant will sell all his goods. It is the kingly rule of Christ, for whose sake a man will pluck out the eye which causes him to stumble, it is the call of Jesus Christ at which the disciple leaves his nets and follows him.
>
> Costly grace is the gospel which must be *sought* again and again, the gift which must be *asked* for, the door at which a man must *knock*.
>
> Such grace is *costly*...because it costs a man his life, and it is *grace* because it gives a man the only true life.[11]

---

[11] Dietrich Bonhoeffer, *The Cost of Discipleship* (New York: Macmillan, 1968), pp. 45 and 47.

I guess Reverend Peale was acknowledging that perhaps he had been preaching too much "cheap grace" and not enough "costly grace," and he regretted the lack of balance.

Today I wonder at the millions of Christians who crowd so-called megachurches where all they get is "cheap grace," without even the slightest indication that there is a costlier merchandise around, one that is not bought with monetary contributions. I wonder, too, at the words of Jesus, that we must *strive* to enter the Kingdom, and that the Kingdom must be *fought* for.

Again, this does not mean that Jesus advocated violence, he certainly did not; in fact, he offered himself as an example of counter-violence and absolute power when he entered Jerusalem sitting on a donkey while the Roman procurator entered by an opposite gate sitting on a horse and with all his military retinue; but he did preach nonviolent *resistance* to the injurious dominance of Rome and its local associates. Anyone who wants to be an imitator of Jesus must understand this and put it in practice.

———— ✶ ————

An example of forceful resistance may perhaps be found in the injunction of *Matthew* 5:39 (and parallel passages in *Luke* 6:29 and Q 5:39): "Don't react violently against the one who is evil: when someone slaps you on the right cheek, turn the other to him as well."

For too long, this and similar statements have been interpreted to mean that response to violence should be meek humility and self-abasement before the powerful; but this view does not reflect the posture Jesus himself adopted when confronting his accusers and those in power over him.

The most insulting of all physical blows was that of striking the right cheek with the back of one's hand;[12] it implied disdain, the kind of blow a master would give a slave. Jesus's counsel, "Turn the other cheek as well," is not a mere invitation to repeat the slap, but a

---

[12] Albright and Mann, *Matthew*, p. 68.

way of standing up to power, as if to say, "Don't hit me as if I were a slave, but as an equal; after all, I *am* a human being!"

Camus has argued that the very act of resistance, however small it be, affirms *ipso facto* a solidarity with the striker, with the abuser or master, the solidarity of all humans. Resistance is not just negative, a "no!" uttered or implied. Rather, it is the recognition in oneself of a human value, shared by all, that must be affirmed and promulgated at all costs.[13]

Christians are not less human because they are Christians, even though thousands of preachers have led their congregations to believe so, and that only in heaven will their ills be healed and their wrongs redressed. On the contrary, to be a Christian is to be passionate about God's justice *in this world, on this earth*, even as it is in heaven.

## Lazy Seekers

"You lazy rascal!" said the master. "You ought to have deposited my money in the bank, so that on my return I should have got it back with interest." (*Matthew* 25:26–27)

These words come from a well-known story attributed to Jesus. A master goes away on a long journey. Before leaving, he distributes his assets among three of his servants for safekeeping. Each of the three receives an amount in proportion to his business abilities. The first two invest the money wisely and return a profit. The third one simply digs a hole in the ground and buries the money, because, as he explains, he is afraid to take any risks with his master's money. Upon his return, the master praises the first two servants and castigates the third one with the harsh words quoted above.

When I was younger, I thought that Jesus, speaking through the master, was being unnecessarily rough with the third employee; after all, the master *knew* he did not have a good business sense (that is

13 Albert Camus, *The Rebel* (New York: Vintage, 1956), pp. 13–22.

why he was given a smaller portion of the estate), and no money was lost, though none was added. So what was all the fuss about? But I learned later that this servant's fault was one of *omission*, the kind of thing we often do *not* do without even noticing—like not stopping to smell the roses, or failing to utter a kind word to one in need—and that omissions may be just as bad as commissions; in fact, millions of Christians every Sunday ask God's forgiveness for those things left undone that they ought to have done, as well as for those things done that they ought not to have done! This may have been one point Jesus was trying to make.

Omissions are strange things. They are negatives, and it is difficult to deal with negatives. It is like dealing with minus numbers, or with deficits; but all of us fall into this negative kind of behavior, often without even realizing it. We fail to yield the right of way, to offer our seat in the bus or train to an older person or a pregnant woman, to say "Please!" or "Thank you!", to avoid hurting someone's feelings, to encourage where encouragement is needed. We bow down to the pressure of unenlightened laws and narrow down the curriculum of our schools to the point we no longer appreciate science, poetry, literature, or art. And we lapse into these negative modes without realizing it, simply by not giving our full attention to what we do as we course through our daily routines. We become so used to driving a fully automatic automobile that, when we drive a stick shift, we no longer know when to shift gears by the mere sound of the revving motor. Similarly, we grow so deaf to the sounds of living things around us and so blind to the colors of the environment in which we live that we no longer notice, much less appreciate, their extraordinary diversity and beauty.

———※———

One of the things we omit often in our daily lives is wonder. Wonder is a form of receptivity, which means that one of the things we often omit in life is receptivity and acceptance. This is because we live in a very masculine society, one that seeks continually to intrude into the world, to raise skyscrapers, to pilot shining airplanes, to wield guns and pistols, to swing baseball bats, and to inquire deeply into our world. Wonder is the opposite of all these things.

There are different modes of wonder. One can wonder *whether or not* something happened, *what* happened, *why* and *how* it happened, *where* it happened, and *who* made it happen. All these modes are rooted in curiosity, which is a form of intrusion into the world. In them one seeks to satisfy an urge to know, to wrest answers from the world by probing rather than wait until the world unveils itself, of its own volition, to our expectant eyes. These modes are inquisitive and masculine.

There is, however, a mode of looking that merely wonders *at* things or events. One may wonder at the way things are while pondering the fact that they need not be so. Curiosity may be involved in this mode only peripherally and distantly, but the *why* is not pursued at all. One does not get a rise out of it.

There is something feminine about this mode of wondering, and it is difficult to engage in it because the cultures the Christian West has created are very masculine, even phallic. Patriarchal Christianity's fight against the feminine and the receptive has succeeded in turning the former into sugary pietism or devilish temptation, and the latter into dispirited humility. The frenetic pace at which we live our lives is another major obstacle. On the other hand, there is this dreamy sort of wondering, relaxed, open-ended, and profoundly satisfying.

It is worth noting that as we grow from childhood into adulthood and beyond, we stop dreaming and imagining, and start thinking. Bachelard quotes Ernest La Jeunesse to the effect that humans began to think when they were no longer able to dream,[14] and *we* think that this move to thinking is what marks us as human! But in truth, humans came to be humans when they first raised their faces toward heaven to dream. Ovid implied as much,[15] and so did Loren Eiseley.[16]

---

[14] Gaston Bachelard, *The Poetics of Reverie* (Boston: Beacon Press, 1971), p. 176.
[15] Ovid, *Metamorphoses*, Book I, 81–82.
[16] Loren Eiseley, *The Immense Journey* (New York: Vintage, 1957), pp. 107 *ff*.

It should be added that the return to the femininity of wonder and reverie can be traumatic, for it opens our minds to so many more things than we were accustomed to before, and this may be overwhelming; but in the end, such wonder is the way to go. Oedipus, having plucked out his eyes—the masculine eyes of reason that inquire and penetrate, and which uncovered his ruin—gave himself up to the guidance of the feminine, his daughters, who led him to the acceptance of his fate. Similarly, it was not Virgil, but Beatrice, who alone could lead Dante to the heights of the divine vision. It was Marguerite, too, who saved Faust from eternal damnation.

Those who have ears to hear, let them hear!

———— ✦ ————

To return to omission: there is also a certain gentleness that we often omit in our daily exchanges with other people and with the world at large. The tone of contemporary living, especially in the big cities, is jarring, strident, cacophonous, enervating. On the other hand, gentleness, good manners, never inflicting unnecessary pain— something that Newman considered a characteristic of the educated person, the *gentle*man, the *gentle*woman[17]—adds a distinctive flavor to a full human life. Adrian van Kaam describes this gentleness:

> When I am gentle, I have time to listen. I have time to be quiet, to think without strain, to work without pressure. There is time to look at birds and flowers and blooming trees. Time to enjoy music, to see friends, to laugh and talk, to be silent and alone. Above all there is time to pray, time for many moments of prayerful presence to the Divine. Gentleness finds time to listen to the goodness and truth of the persons and

---

[17] John Henry Newman, *The Idea of a University* (Garden City, NY: Doubleday & Co., 1959), Discourse VIII, 10, p. 217.

things I meet and time for presence to the Divine Origin that is in and beyond them.[18]

"Be still and know that I am God," sang the psalmist (*Psalm* 46:10 [11]). And the writer of the *Book of Kings* has kept the words God spoke to Elijah in the cave in which he had sought refuge: "Go out and stand on the mountain before YHWH. Lo, YHWH is passing by, and a great and mighty wind, rending mountains and shattering rocks goes before YHWH. But YHWH is not in the wind. And after the wind, an earthquake. But YHWH is not in the earthquake. And after the earthquake, fire. But YHWH is not in the fire. And after the fire, the sound of sheer silence" (*1 Kings* 19:11–12). And Elijah understood that in this silence dwelled the Divine Presence, so he covered his face with his cloak and went out and stood at the entrance to the cave, where he heard again the voice of the Lord.

———※———

There are many omissions, and one of them is the refusal to confront one's own obscurity by questioning what has been handed down, the beliefs and traditions in which we have grown up and with which we feel comfortable. When confronted with such questions, says Walter Kaufmann, we have three basic options: to avoid making a decision; to stack the cards so that one alternative appears to be clearly the right one; and to decline responsibility.[19] And he discusses ten strategies we unwittingly employ to achieve this insulation from decision-making, one of which is belonging to a religious or political group. For once in a group, groupthink takes over, and one does not need to make any decision anymore. In fact, very often one does not even have to make a decision to join, because one is born into a religious community or into the political party of one's parents.

---

[18] Adrian van Kaam, C. S. Sp., *Spirituality and the Gentle Life* (Denville, NJ: Dimension Books, Inc., 1974), p. 31.

[19] Walter Kaufmann, *Without Guilt and Justice* (New York: Dell Publishing Co., Inc., 1973), p. 4.

So, what are we to say of people who are afraid to take risks with the message Jesus entrusted to all of us? I think it is pertinent to ask if all of us have made a serious effort to understand his words and his teachings "according to our capacities"; or perhaps we have been satisfied with doing nothing, digging a hole in the ground, as it were, and burying his treasure. We do this when we take someone else's word instead of his, when we accept another's authority without question, and when we fail to stand up for what we have devised after a critical, rational examination of *all* the pertinent data.

Now, some people call this stance a liberal one, and they are right if by liberal they mean liberating, empowering, which is what Jesus claimed he had come to give us, "a more abundant life" (*John* 10:10). According to Gary Dorrien,

> Liberal theology is the idea of a Christian perspective based on reason and experience, not external authority, that reconceptualizes the meaning of Christianity in the light of modern knowledge and ethical values. It is reformist in spirit and substance, not revolutionary. Specifically it is defined by its openness to the verdicts of modern intellectual inquiry, especially historical criticism and the natural sciences; its commitment to the authority of individual reason and experience; its conception of Christianity as an ethical way of life; its advocacy of moral concepts of atonement or reconciliation; and its commitment to make Christianity credible and socially relevant to contemporary people.[20]

This obligation to take risks with an investment of our Christian lives is more strictly placed on those of us who "teach." Jesus himself asked Nicodemus in disbelief, "You are a teacher and you don't

---

[20] Gary Dorrien, "American Liberal Theology," *Cross Currents* 55, 4 (Winter 2006), p. 458.

understand this?" (*John* 3:9). The implication is that it is *especially* incumbent upon teachers to be open to the risks that faith presents and to encourage all learners to shoulder their own responsibility according to their capacities.

# Truth

*Jesus said: "If you adhere to my teaching…you will*
*know the truth, and the truth will set you free."*
—John 8:31–32

In another place, Jesus said, "Blessed are those who sought after the truth, and when they found it, they rested upon it forever and were unafraid of those who wanted to disturb them" (*The Book of Thomas the Contender* 140:40–141:2). It is clear that Jesus believed that those who accepted his teachings as true, and meditated on them—"rested upon them"—would be set free by that knowledge. He did not explain what he meant by "free," but one can surmise that he included freedom from attachments, freedom from undue concerns, freedom from perils both spiritual and physical, and freedom from the unnecessary constraints of the Mosaic law. Most Christian denominations, however, by means of their dogmas and restrictions, by means of their orthodoxies and *ex cathedra* pronouncements, by means of their stubborn refusal to inquire into what Jesus *really* might have said, have changed Jesus's saying to, "The truth shall make you bound." They use the very teachings that Jesus thought would make us free in order to hold people bound—to themselves, really, not to Jesus. They hold it to be of greater importance that people "belong" to this or that sect, that they dub themselves followers of this or that preacher, than that they proclaim themselves followers *of Jesus*. St. Paul ran into this problem already in Corinth, where he had established a community that had grown fractious, some claiming Paul as their teacher, others Apollos (a preacher who had consolidated the faith that Paul had planted) (*1 Corinthians* 3:1–9). St. Paul's solution? It is God who holds us in his hand; in him we move and have our life and our being.

Now, John interprets Jesus as saying that he is the truth (*John* 14:6). Therefore he is the one who sets us free. Actually, it is knowledge of him, knowledge of his truth, that sets us free. So, anything that prevents us from knowing Jesus, from knowing the truth that he is, enslaves us, whether it is a preacher's preaching or a theologian's theologizing or a government's governing. *Anything* that hides from us the truth of Jesus is a shackle and a bond.

In our time, Heidegger wrote that "the essence of truth is the truth of essence,"[21] by which he meant that the essence of truth is the revelation or uncovering of what reality is essentially. In this sense, the essence of the truth that is Jesus is the uncovering, the revelation of what Jesus *is*. Consequently, *anything* that stands in the way of this disclosure and revelation must be shaken off as resolutely as we would any other shackle. Not that this is easy to do; in fact, it is a heavy burden, but it is the price we must pay if we wish to have the truth of Jesus set us free.

———— ✦ ————

This is precisely what the Grand Inquisitor, the protagonist of Ivan Karamazov's prose poem, understands when one day he suddenly spies Jesus moving among the people following a splendid and magnificent *auto da fé* in which many wicked heretics were burned at the stake. The people recognize Jesus immediately, and they flock around him with eagerness and admiration. The commotion generated by his presence does not go unnoticed by the Inquisitor.

> He knits his thick grey brows and his eyes
> gleam with a sinister fire. He holds out his finger
> and bids the guards take Him. And such is his
> power, so completely are the people cowed into

---

[21] Martin Heidegger, *Vom Wesen*, 26, in *Basic Writings* (New York: Harper & Row, 1977), p. 140. In Greek, "truth" is *aletheia* (*a*[un-]-*letheia* [covering]).

submission and trembling obedience to him, that the crowd immediately makes way for the guards and in the midst of deathlike silence they lay hands on Him and lead Him away.[22]

That evening the Grand Inquisitor visits the Prisoner in jail. There he asks Him: "Why art Thou come to hinder us? For Thou hast come to hinder us, and Thou knowest that." "What does the Inquisitor mean by this?" the befuddled Alyosha Karamazov asks. The Inquisitor himself explains:

> For fifteen centuries we have been wrestling with Thy freedom, but now it is ended and over for good... Today, people are more persuaded than ever that they have perfect freedom, yet they have brought their freedom to us and laid it humbly at our feet... We have corrected Thy work and have founded it upon *miracle, mystery* and *authority*. And men rejoiced that they were again led like sheep, so that the terrible gift that had brought them such suffering was, at last, lifted from their hearts... They will be convinced that we are right, for they will remember the horrors of slavery and confusion to which Thy freedom brought them. Freedom, free thought, and science will lead them into such straits and will bring them face to face with such marvels and insoluble mysteries, that some of them, the fierce and rebellious, will destroy themselves, others rebellious but weak, will destroy one another, while the rest, weak and unhappy, will crawl fawning to our feet and whine to us: "Yes, you were right, you alone possess His mystery, and

---

[22] Fyodor Dostoevsky, *The Brothers Karamazov* (Chicago: Encyclopaedia Britannica, 1952), pp. 129–135.

we come back to you, save us from ourselves!"…
So, tomorrow Thou shall see that obedient flock
who at a sign from me will hasten to heap up hot
cinders about the pile on which I shall burn Thee
for coming to hinder us. For if anyone has ever
deserved our fires, it is Thou. Tomorrow I shall
burn Thee. *Dixi*!

Almost a century after Dostoyevsky wrote these words, Nikos
Kazantzakis gave us the story of the life and death of a modern Jesus,
Manolios, assassinated because he took the sins of his people upon
himself. His priest lamented:

> In vain, my Christ, in vain… Two thou-
> sand years have gone by and men crucify You
> still. When will You be born, my Christ, and
> not be crucified any more, but live among us for
> eternity?[23]

## The Son of God

> The High Priest questioned him: "Are you
> the anointed one, the son of the Blessed One?"
> Jesus said: "I am, indeed, and you all will see the
> son of the man sitting at the right hand of the
> power, coming with the heavenly clouds." (*Mark*
> 14:61–62)

This saying of Jesus has always puzzled me, and it obviously has
puzzled many others. The purpose here is to ascertain, not what the
readers read or the writers wrote after the death of Jesus, but what

---

[23] Nikos Kazantzakis, *Christ Recrucified* (London: Faber and Faber, 1954), p.
467. Kazantzakis wrote this novel after being excommunicated by the Greek
Orthodox Church for writing *The Last Temptation of Christ*.

the protagonists might have said at the time. This is a very complex question, and thousands of articles and books have been written to elucidate it. I can only touch on some of the relevant issues.[24]

The gospels of *Matthew* and *Luke* have slightly different versions of this episode. For one thing, Jesus's answer is more evasive there: "The words are yours" (*Matthew* 26:64), and "It is you who say I am" (*Luke* 22:71). In fact, several manuscripts of *Mark* have the same evasive words rather than the categorical assertion we quoted above, which anyway could also be translated as a question, "Am I?"[25] since the original manuscripts have no punctuation marks. Some scholars even claim that there is a slight possibility that *Mark* 14:61b–62 is a later Christian insertion made by a scribe with anti-adoptionist concerns. We know that many such changes were made in the texts, so this would not have been totally unheard-of.[26] The reference to "the son of the man sitting at the right hand of the power and coming with the heavenly clouds" is a mixture of the vision of *Daniel* 7:13[27] and *Psalm* 110:1,[28] all against the background of Ezekiel's vision in *Ezekiel* 1, especially verse 26.[29] "The son-of-the-man" is, as we have seen, Jesus's favorite way of referring to himself.

The later non-Jewish Church saw in these statements of *Mark* an affirmation of the divinity of Jesus and of his messiahship, but such an interpretation does not fit the facts as we know them. For example, we know that Jesus remained a good Jew to his death. Given this fact, it would have been totally uncharacteristic of him to make himself divine, to speak of himself as "the son of God" *sensu transcendente* ("with a transcendent meaning," as the theologians say), or even to claim for himself the title of "messiah," especially since the

[24] See Raymond E. Brown, SS, *The Death of the Messiah*, 2 vols. (New York: Doubleday, 1994), especially, with regard to this saying, vol. 1, pp. 461 *ff.*
[25] Marcus J. Borg, *Jesus* (San Francisco, CA: HarperSanFrancisco, 2006), p. 263.
[26] See Ehrman, *Misquoting Jesus*, pp. 157 *ff.*
[27] *Daniel* 7:13: "In a vision I had at night I saw that with the clouds of heaven there came one like a son of man."
[28] *Psalm* 110:1: "YHWH said to my lord: 'Sit on a throne at my right hand.'"
[29] *Ezekiel* 1:26: "Above the dome...was something that looked like a throne made of sapphire, and above this throne was one like a human being."

understanding of the messiah in Judaism at the time was not fixed at all. Moreover, it would have been unthinkable for the High Priest to ask Jesus (or anybody else, for that matter) if he was "God" or "the son of God"!

Moreover, to see these words as the self-revelation of God in Jesus is subject to all the strictures we have made above about *any* "revelation" of God or of any *noumenon*.

Finally, to use these words, and other similar texts, as a proof of the divine sonship of Jesus is to confuse stories with historical evidence.[30] Let me give an example. In the nineteenth century, Parson Weems told the story how little George Washington, when asked by his father if he had felled his precious cherry tree, replied, "I cannot tell a lie, Father, you know I cannot tell a lie! I did cut it with my little hatchet";[31] but no one would take the words of this story as proof that in his whole life, George Washington never told a lie. This is a cute story, not a historical précis. Similarly, we cannot, from Shakespeare's *Hamlet*, reconstruct the historical figure of the Danish prince.[32] So, even after we apply all the pertinent criteria of historical research and writing, the Gospels remain accounts, not of what Jesus said and did, but of what was thought to be meaningful interpretations of his life and sayings by the Gospel writers and their audiences.[33] So how are we to interpret this saying?

To begin with, the High Priest's question is derisive and sarcastic in the extreme. Picture this: people are claiming that Jesus said this or did that, but it is hard for him to believe that this marginal Jew from the Galilee could be so important. His question, therefore, would have sounded like, "Are *YOU* the anointed one, the son of the Blessed One?" "Anointed one" (*xrestos*, in Greek; Christ) and "son of the Blessed One" were expressions by which the kings of Israel were

---

[30] Thomas L. Thompson, *The Mythic Past* (New York: Basic Books, 1999), p. 34.
[31] Mason Locke Weems, *The Life of George Washington the Great*, reprint (Augusta, GA: G. F. Randolph, 1806).
[32] Thompson, p. 15.
[33] Ibid., p. 68.

known.[34] They were metaphor for the sense that the king represented God's presence among his people; they were a way of signifying God's immanence in the world.[35] Looking at the poor laborer in front of him, the High Priest wonders how such a poor chap could claim to be the expected ruler of Israel, or even to be the vehicle of God's presence.[36] Jesus's answer, then, could have been, "Yes, I am, but this should not seem such an outrageous claim considering that Daniel and Ezekiel saw a mere human being sitting at the right hand of the power and coming upon the clouds." No claim of divinity here. The question has nothing to do with divinity, only with kingship.

Furthermore, Jesus's peremptory affirmation is ambiguous. That is, Jesus refuses to accept the role of regal messiah, but he is not able in good conscience to deny that, in Wink's words, "God is working messianically through him."[37] Jesus is not interested in being *the* messiah, but he is, instead, committed to being "the human being," "the-son-of-the-man," the incarnation of God's humanness in the world.

The High Priest, of course, jumps on what he takes to be the ambiguous acceptance of messiahship (*not* divinity!)—"We have heard the bragging!" he exclaims—and uses it as *the* argument to be

---

34   See, for example, *Psalm* 2:2 and 7, and *2 Samuel* 7:14. Also *Wisdom of Solomon* 2:13–18, *4 Ezra* 7:28. Karen Armstrong, in *The Great Transformation* (New York: Alfred A. Knopf, 2006), p. 47, writes: "This was a typical Canaanite monarchy. The cult centered on the person of the Davidic king, the earthly counterpart of the divine warrior and a sacred figure because of his cultic relationship with Yahweh. At his coronation, he became one of the holy ones, a son of God. He was adopted by Yahweh, who declared: 'You are my son; today I have become your Father' [Psalm 2:7]. As Yahweh's special servant, he sat on the divine assembly with the other sons of God." See Mitchell Dahood, SJ, *Psalms I* (Garden City, NY: Doubleday & Co., Inc., 1966), pp. 11–12, commenting on *Psalm* 2:7. Also James Charlesworth, *Jesus within Judaism*, pp. 150–153.

35   Thompson, *The Mythic Past*, p. 337.

36   Ibid., p. 359. It should be remembered that the angel told Joseph that Jesus's name would mean "Immanu-el" or "God with us" *(Matthew* 1:23). See also *Exodus* 3:12. This does not have to mean that God is incarnate in Jesus, but simply that he is a metaphor for God's presence among us.

37   Wink, *The Human Being*, p. 124.

presented to Pontius Pilate; for to the Romans, *any* claim of kingship was a capital offense.[38]

———⋙⋘———

We should add that there is no reference in Jesus's words to an apocalypse, a *parousia*, a future "Second Coming," as was claimed later by the non-Jewish Church. The reference is to the present; *Matthew* 26:63–64 even says clearly, "From now on you will see." What will you see? The Kingdom of God, not in the hands of kings and high priests, but in those of the people.

There is need to dwell on this. The words "you will see the son of the man sitting at the right hand of the power of God, coming with the heavenly clouds" (*Mark* 14:62) have been taken to mean a reference to the triumphal "Second Coming" of Jesus. A whole mythology, and many works of fiction, have been built on this statement, which, in fact, may not refer to Jesus at all.

Daniel's vision of the four beasts emerging from the sea was interpreted for him at that time as representing four kingdoms that would hold power until the Ancient One arrived and eventually vanquished them. After the beasts arose, Daniel saw a being in human likeness (*kᵉ bar 'ĕnāš*) coming with the heavenly clouds. To it, all power was given (*Daniel* 7:13–14), signifying that the power would, from then on, be in ordinary human hands. The text is explicit: "The Kingship and the dominion and the grandeur of all the kingdoms under the heavens will be given *to the people*" (*Daniel* 7:27; emphasis added). In other words, while the earthly powers are symbolized by beasts, the final power is symbolized by "one like a human being." *Daniel* 7, writes Borg, is "an anti-imperial vision and an anti-imperial

---

[38] Other charismatic leaders assumed messianic dimensions and were saluted as "kings of the Jews." Simon bar Giora, for example, was put to death as king of the Jews in 70 CE during the victory celebrations of Vespasian and Titus in Rome. See Josephus, *Jewish War* 7, 29–155, and Horsley and Hanson, *Bandits, Prophets, and Messiahs*, pp. 126–127.

text."[39] Earthly empires are symbolized by beasts, but the Kingdom of God is symbolized by a human figure.

In quoting *Daniel* 7, therefore (if he actually did!), Jesus is not projecting himself into a future apocalyptic Second Coming, but telling the High Priest that the Roman Empire, with which the Temple priests had allied themselves, like all such empires, will be eventually superseded by God's Kingdom, in which ordinary human beings will be free to be themselves.

---

Putting all the emphasis on the supposed divinity of Jesus robs this passage of its implication *for us*. Jesus eventually became known as "Jesus Christ," that is "Jesus the-anointed-one" (this is what Christ means!), but the usage, liturgical and otherwise, downplayed the human Jesus in favor of the divine Christ. By making Jesus divine, the Church basically robbed Jesus of the identity that he had striven so hard to build for himself and which he defended against the High Priest by insisting that he was, really, "the son-of-the-man." As Marcus Borg puts it, by emphasizing the divinity of Jesus, "we lose track of the utterly remarkable human being that he was."[40]

And in a similar manner, every time the Catholic Church beatifies or canonizes people, it robs them of the human identity they strove to achieve for themselves here on earth. But the canonized cannot complain, as Jesus did, because they are dead!

---

[39] Marcus J. Borg and John Dominic Crossan, *The Last Week* (San Francisco, CA: HarperSanFrancisco, 2006), p. 132. See also John Dominic Crossan, *God and Empire* (San Francisco, CA: HarperSanFrancisco, 2007), p. 4 *ff.*

Some scholars argue that the reference in *Mark* 14:62 is *not* to Jesus himself but to a future "Son of the Man," as Daniel saw him, who will come to right things up. In other words, Jesus puts himself in the place of Daniel and forecasts a future messiah, *not* himself.

[40] Marcus J. Borg, *Jesus* (San Francisco, CA: HarperSanFrancisco, 2006), p. 49.

Against the background of *Daniel* 7:13 and *Ezekiel* 1:26, Jesus, as the son-of-the-man, becomes a model for us. As Wink puts it,

> To say that Jesus is at the right hand of God is to make Jesus a *criterion* of humanness. In Jesus's life it becomes clear what it means to be human—and this is so even though he was not perfect. As the emergent possibility of our humanness, Jesus is not just the lure of the future or the desire to be more, but also the standard by which humanness is known. Against that standard, the ultimate question unavoidably thrusts itself upon us: What have I done with my life?—but in such a way that it takes on immediate urgency: What am I doing, right now, with my life?[41]

Elie Wiesel tells the story of Rabbi Zusia (d. 1800), who said, before he died, "When I shall face the celestial tribunal, I shall not be asked why I was not Abraham, Jacob, or Moses. I shall be asked why I was not Zusia."[42]

———— ✴ ————

Let us *re*visit the question, Who *was* Jesus? by means of a story. "Do you believe God can do anything?" That was the question thirteen-year-old Ozzie Freedman asked his teacher, Rabbi Marvin Binder, in a short story by Philip Roth.[43] The question had to do with the divinity of Jesus and the virgin birth. Rephrased, the question is, could God have become a man—or a woman, for that matter; for once the question of "becoming" is answered, it would be truly immaterial whether God became a man or a woman (had a

---

[41] 41 Wink, *The Human Being*, p. 167.
[42] Elie Wiesel, *Souls on Fire* (New York: Random House, 1972), p. 120.
[43] Philip Roth, "The Conversion of the Jews," in *Goodbye, Columbus* (New York: The Modern Library, 1959), p. 157.

son or a daughter). In fact, Mother Ann "the Christ," founder of the Shakers, claimed to be such an incarnation.

Tertullian, one of the first ones to answer the question, stated simply that "nothing is impossible for God but what he does not will."[44] St. Augustine took essentially the same position—"[God] does what he wills"[45]—and in the late Middle Ages, Duns Scotus, a Scotch professor of theology at Oxford, Paris, and Cologne, defended the same view.[46] The only limit to God's omnipotence is his own will. *We* may have difficulty understanding this, but that is *our* problem.

A different position was staked out by St. Thomas Aquinas. He distinguished between God's absolute power and his relative power. God is absolutely all-powerful, so theoretically, God can do anything he wills. But God is not just power, he is also reason; his power must be understood in relation to his reason. Therefore, there are certain "things" it would not be possible for God to do because they are "unreasonable" or "self-contradictory"[47] or at least paradoxical, like "a red flavor, or a bitter sound, or an aromatic color…or a love-stricken triangle, or an enraged ellipse."[48] Could God, for example, create an absolutely perfect world, one in which there were no hurricanes, no earthquakes, no pestilences, and in which the principle of entropy did not hold sway? Well, no, says Aquinas,[49] because to create such a world would be to create something absolutely perfect, and this would be to create another God, and this is not possible; if absoluteness is taken seriously, there cannot be two absolutes!

The question, then, is whether or not God, the absolute, the all, the supreme being, can "become" anything. Can being become?

---

[44] Tertullian, *De carne Christi* III, 1.

[45] Augustine, *De symbol. ad catech.* I, 2. Also *De civ. Dei*, XXI, 7, 1; *Enchir.* 95; *Confess.* VII, 4.

[46] See *Report.* 1, 45, 2 no. 7; *Opus Oxon.* 1, 17, 3 no. 18.

[47] St. Thomas Aquinas, *Summa theol.* 1, 25, 1, *ad* 4. It is not so much that Aquinas disagrees with Scotus (as is clear from *Summa theol.* 1, 25, 5, *ad* 1), as that he emphasizes reasonableness over will.

[48] Miguel de Unamuno, *The Tragic Sense of Life* (New York: Dover Publications, Inc., 1954), pp. 234–235.

[49] *Summa theol.* 1, 25, 6 *ad* 1 and 1, 7, 2. Also *De pot.* 1, 2.

Can the Rock of Ages rock? Can the absolute be particularized? Theoretically, one could answer yes, but reasonably, there seems to be a contradiction in terms here, and one that theologians have sought to explain for two thousand years; and they are still trying. Because the truth is that such things cannot be explained, that such questions cannot be answered. Theologians often forget this when they assert their answers as if they were really responding to questions beyond the shadow of a doubt, but the fact is that this is impossible. Theoretically one could answer Ozzie's question by saying that it *is* possible for God to become human, but in reality, this does not seem possible—at least not *reasonably* possible.

Is there room for faith here? Is it here where faith must make its entrance? Yes and no. Faith may make no claim to elucidate what the will of God keeps shrouded in mystery. It may try in order to achieve some understanding, as Anselm explained,[50] but such an understanding will always be deficient. Faith, on the other hand, may simply leap into the darkness (or brightness!) of the mystery and allow itself to be sucked into the abyss. Theological faith wants too much definition, too much explanation, but faith itself is a simple openness to the mystery that makes no claim to know anything, much less to know anything with certainty.

———— ✦ ————

So, was Jesus *the* son of God? Was he divine? Obviously not. At any rate, it is impossible for us to know more because the divinity was imputed to him *after* his death by Greek and Roman converts for whom being divine meant something very different from what it means to us. This view was then systematized by the theologians of the first four centuries and refined in the subsequent millennia. As I said above, Jesus the Jew was made God after his death in the same way as Roman Catholics make saints of good, ordinary people after their deaths! Moreover, the question is irrelevant because the important thing is to imitate the earthly Jesus, a burden we escape when we make him divine.

---

[50] Anselm of Canterbury, *Proslogium*, chapter 1.

What is important is that he was a very good human being who was put to death because of his passionate opposition to injustice.

## Life

> Jesus said: "Life belongs to you! Rejoice and exult as children of God. Keep his will, so that you may be saved." (*Secret Book of James* 6:38–39)

I do not know what meaning my spirit finds in these words, but I can hardly keep them out of my mind. There is some resonance I find in them, something that appeals to me very intimately, like an echo from some long forgotten utterance. If I believed in such things, I would say that here is a memory of words spoken by the spirit at my birth.

Also, these words (among many other reasons) help us understand why there was a rejection of the Hebrew God, YHWH/Elohim, among many of the early followers of Jesus seeking to shed all connections with Judaism. Here we have Jesus offering life to us while the Hebrew God, angered by Adam and Eve's transgression, took the source of life, the Tree of Life, from them, and condemned them to hardship and death (*Genesis* 3:22–24).

———❊———

Many decades ago, I participated in a weekend retreat designed to train the young people who were to work in a crisis center at the University. There were probably about a hundred of us, divided into groups of twenty-five or so. The first evening, we met in different rooms, large enough to accommodate all of us squatting around in a circle with our backs toward the walls. The exercise consisted in personal narratives, retold in the present tense, of two episodes from our childhood and youth.

Retelling events in the present tense was extremely involving for storytellers and listeners alike. Many speakers broke down and sobbed and were then nurtured by the group. After my turn came, I ended up in tears. The leader asked me quietly, almost in a murmur, "What do you feel now?" Almost fiercely, and without hesitation, I answered resolutely, "I *love* life!"

————❊————

Some time ago I tried to tame these strong feelings for life into three composite propositions, each of which, after the first one, entailed by the preceding one:

First Proposition:

> *I am alive!*
> *I have been living these many years!*
> *Oh! It's nice to be alive!*
> *I must think so, since I have continued living*
> *this long.*

Second Proposition:

> *Those around me must feel and think the way*
> *I do—they tell me so, or seem to act the way I do.*
> *To be alive must be the greatest and most irre-*
> *ducible human value.*
> *Human life must have value in itself.*
> *Oh, the beauty of human life!*
> *I love living!*

Third Proposition:

> *What enhances human life is good.*
> *The good of humankind is the criterion of*
> *human good.*
> *All humans are worthy of respect*[51]

---

[51] Ignacio L. Götz, *Manners and Violence* (Westport, CT: Praeger, 2000), p. 70.

The words do not, and cannot, comprehend, much less exhaust, the exhilaration of being alive, what Kant, in a marvelous phrase, called "the feeling for the beauty and dignity of human nature."[52] The words merely articulate in an inchoate manner what is essentially inexpressible except by a kiss or a hug or a shout.

———✻———

In one of his philosophical fictions, Nietzsche once imagined that an all-powerful demon appeared to him while he was writing, and said to him, "Do you know what? Everything you are doing now, your writing, this little spider that is weaving a web between the wall and the lamp's electrical cord; everything you have been and done; everything you have suffered both physically and emotionally; everything will come to pass again, and again, and again, eternally!" If such an apparition came to you, asks Nietzsche, would you cry out in despair, "Curse you! You could not have foretold a more despicable fate!" Or would you exclaim from the bottom of your heart, "Bless you! You are a god!"[53]

For Nietzsche understood this: if we have enjoyed life to the point of wanting to live it again in order to relive the joys of being alive and the joys that come from being alive, then we have wished the pains too, "for all things are entangled, ensnared, enamored; if ever you wanted one thing twice, if ever you said 'You please me, happiness! Abide, moment!' then you wanted *all* back. All anew, all eternally, all entangled, ensnared, enamored—oh, then you *loved* the world. Eternal ones, love it eternally and evermore; and to woe too, you say: go, but return! *For all joy wants—eternity!*"[54]

[52] Immanuel Kant, *Beobachtungen über das Gefühl des Schönen und Erhabenen* [1764], in *Immanuel Kants Werke*, ed. Ernst Cassirer (Berlin: Bruno Cassirer, 1922–1923), vol. 2, pp. 256–257.
[53] Friedrich Nietzsche, *The Gay Science*, trans. Walter Kaufmann (New York: Vintage, 1974), No. 341, pp. 273–274.
[54] Friedrich Nietzsche, *Thus Spoke Zarathustra*, trans. Walter Kaufmann (New York: The Viking Press, 1966), Part IV, 10, p. 323.

I hear Jesus saying all this, and more, when he says, "All life belongs to you!"

———❊———

Kathleen Norris tells the story of how she went once to visit an elderly monk she had known for many years. He, in turn, suggested they both go to see another monk, recently retired, who had taken a bad fall the day before. When they arrived at the monk's cell, a nurse was leaving his room. She explained that the monk had been napping off and on all morning, waiting to be taken to a nearby hospital for a CAT scan. Norris writes:

> I was nervous about disturbing a man who might be sleeping or in great pain, not wanting company. Nothing could have prepared me for what happened. Another nurse entered the room and called out, "You have a visitor. Two visitors." We heard a weak voice respond, "Ah…it's a sweet life." As we entered the room, and he got a look at us, he said again, "It's a sweet life."[55]

———❊———

Shortly before his death, Moses spoke to the Israelites at length, and among many memorable things, he told them: "I have put life and death before you, the blessing and the curse; therefore choose life" (*Deuteronomy* 30:19). This is a ringing affirmation of life,[56]

---

[55] Kathleen Norris, *The Cloister Walk* (New York: Riverhead Books, 1996), pp. 365–366.

[56] There are similar ones in other ancient literatures: the Egyptian, forty-five hundred years ago, choosing *this* life with all its pains rather than death and the peaceably beyond (T. W. Thacker, "A dispute over suicide," *sub fine*, in D. Winton Thomas, ed., *Documents from Old Testament Times* [New York: Harper Torch-books, 1958], p. 166); and Ulysses choosing Ithaca and Penelope—

and equally of choice, but Moses himself had chosen to slaughter those who worshiped the Golden Calf (*Exodus* 32:27–29), Elijah put the prophets of Baal to the sword (*1 Kings* 18:40), and David ordered the death of Uriah to cover up his tryst with Bathsheba (*2 Samuel* 11:15–27); and in 313 CE, Constantine the Great massacred the forces of Licinius assured of victory by a vision of the cross with the words "You will win in this sign!" (*en toutô níka*).

St. Augustine did not choose life when, around 414, he ordered the imperial troops to eliminate the Donatists; and St. Cyril of Alexandria stood by the side of death as his deacons led a rabble of Christian monks in the torture and murder of Hypatia in 415. Later, the Crusaders, the Conquistadores, the Inquisitors, the people of Salem, the Nazis who carried out the Holocaust, the Americans who atom-bombed Hiroshima and Nagasaki—all chose death; and I am barely skimming history. Moreover, these were crimes of commission, but in numberless occasions, we have stood callously by as millions were starved to death or massacred. In far too many instances many of us have acted as if the gift of Jesus to his followers had been in vain!

———➤✄———

This is as good a place as any to add a brief note on the hypocritical slogan, "Pro-Life," common among opponents of abortion, hypocritical because most adherents of the Pro-Life position are also "pro war" and "pro capital punishment," both of which destroy life. Surely, one can argue that the case of the innocent unborn is differ-

---

and eventual death—rather than immortality with Calypso (*Odyssey* V, 214 *ff*.).There is also, of course, Gilgamesh, who spent the last years of his life looking for immortality; but it is his friend Enkidu who is addressed as "You who love life."

In our own times, J. R. R. Tolkien, in *The Lord of the Rings*, part 3, *The Return of the King*, 2nd ed. (Boston: Houghton Mifflin Co., 1965), chapter 6, p. 252, has told the story of Arwen Undómiel, the Elf who gave up eternal life in the West in order to live with half-mortal Aragorn.

ent from that of the aggressor in war and the convicted criminal, but the fact is that war and capital punishment inflict death, not life. If consistency in moral judgment is a virtue, the Pro-Life position is inconsistent and fallacious, and therefore it is morally suspect.

The Pro-Life position is morally suspect also because it is *for* the life of the fetus but *against* the life of the mother; it favors an unborn human life over a fully grown human life, the life *of a woman*. In this it is guilty of male chauvinism.

Moreover, it is based on a moral reasoning called Natural Law morality, developed in Christian theological circles in the Middle Ages and based on the philosophy of Aristotle (384–322 BCE). This moral point of view argues that actions are objectively right or wrong depending on whether or not the objective goals of actions are achieved or thwarted, regardless of the intention of the agent. Thus, the argument goes, sexual intercourse between humans aims naturally at the production of human life; consequently any action (such as contraception or abortion) that impedes the fulfillment of this aim is wrong.

But Natural Law morality, while widely accepted among Christians, is not the only valid system of morality that could be applicable to a consideration of abortion. In the eighteenth century, Kant (1724–1804) developed a different system for determining the morality of an action and its consequences. This system, unlike the one based on Aristotle, assigned priority to the subject making any moral decision. Morality, therefore, could not be determined by a nearly automatic consideration of actions and their consequences regardless of intention; on the contrary, intention was paramount. As long as the person making a decision never used other people for a selfish purpose, and as long as the action itself could be reasonably generalized so that one could claim that anyone in similar circumstances should act likewise, the action was morally justified regardless of the consequences or other extraneous considerations. Here the inviolability of the person making a decision is safeguarded, as behooves any system of morality that applies to persons.[57] In the case of abortion, if a pregnant woman should consider herself as a person first with ultimate and inviolable worth as a chooser, and judge that any reasonable woman in similar circumstances would decide as she is about to decide, her action is morally justified regardless of the consequences.

Further, proponents of the Pro-Life opposition to abortion do not grant the woman's life the same value that they attribute to the fetus. This is morally reprehensible. This inconsistency has a long history in Christianity in which women have been subordinated to men and to their judgments; actually, women were not deemed capable of making moral judgments at all. Otto Weininger, only a century ago, could write that woman "is as non-moral as she is non-logical. But all existence is moral and logical existence. So woman has no existence."[58] The Pro-Life position considers men only to be worthy of a moral life. This is wrong. It violates everything Jesus taught about life.

There is a deuterocanonical story of great antiquity that is often inserted in the gospel of *John* (*John* 7:53–8:1–11), though it is a clear addition. A married or betrothed woman is caught by several men in the act of adultery. Nothing is said about her male lover because only married or betrothed women could be guilty of adultery, not single or married men (*Deuteronomy* 22:21). The crowd wants to stone her to death, and they ask Jesus's opinion. Jesus, who is squatting on the ground, doodles on the sand at his feet, biding his time. The woman's accusers leave, one by one. When he is left alone with the woman, Jesus tells her, "I do not condemn you" (*John* 8:11). Even

---

[57] It should be pointed out that Aristotle made allowance for subjective considerations through the notion of *epieikeia* (reasonableness, fairness, equity), but this is hardly ever applied in moral deliberations based on his system. See Aristotle *Topics* VI.3 [141ᵃ 16–19], *Nicomachean Ethics* V.10 [1137ᵃ 31–1138ᵃ 3], VI.11 [1143ᵃ 20], *Magna Moralia* II.1 [1198ᵇ 25–35], *Rhetoric* I.12 [1372ᵇ 18], I.13 [1374ᵃ 25–1374ᵇ 23], and I.15 [1375ᵃ 30].

[58] Otto Weininger, *Sex and Character* (New York: A. L. Burt Co., *ca.* 1906), p. 286.

though Jesus judged her action morally wrong (he *did* add, "Don't do it again!"), he respected her choice.

Human choice is as much a moral good as human life. Is this not why we fight wars against tyrants? And are we willing to sacrifice the lives of thousands of soldiers in the pursuit of this freedom of choice for others, and are not ready to grant the same freedom of choice to the women among us?

CHAPTER

# 13

# Christianity

That Christianity is connected with the message and the life of Jesus is hardly worthy of mention, but this does not mean that Jesus founded Christianity or that Christianity is a faithful elaboration of the message of Jesus or even an imitation of his life. As the Minorites argued in the Middle Ages, if Jesus was a poor Jew, how could the pope and the bishops, luxuriant in their rich robes and sumptuous palaces, claim to be *imitatores Christi*? Moreover, after Jesus's death, his followers dispersed and many returned to their communities, uncertain about the future and about the direction of the new movement—the Way, as it was called. And those who were in the leadership were at odds among themselves, both about the implementation of Jesus's message of social equality and about the inclusion of non-Jews in their membership. The recently discovered documents from the period reveal how diverse the views of the movement were, and how orthodoxy appeared over a period of several hundred years. Nothing augured success for the new movement.

The early followers of Jesus were not particularly discerning people. They were peasants, fishermen, laborers. Josephus intimates that they were gullible or easily convinced, as would happen with simple folk.[1] This is not surprising, since the Jewish population in Palestine at the time of Jesus was between 95 and 97 percent illiterate. Therefore the traditions that developed about Jesus were, of necessity, oral. There was no written record at all until some forty years after

---

[1] Josephus, *Antiquities* 18. 63–64.

his death, and then it was written in "kitchen" Greek (*koine*), and it shows unmistakably that the traditions were being elaborated partly by non-Jews who had little understanding of Judaism. No originals are extant from this period.[2]

It is hard to speculate what would have happened to the nascent group had it not been for James (Jesus's younger brother), Peter, and the man Saul, later called Paul. The immediate family of Jesus was intimately connected with his work. His four brothers—James, Joses (or Joseph), Judas "the Twin" (Thomas), and Simon—were among the Twelve Apostles. Before his death, Jesus was asked about a successor, and he is reputed to have said, "No matter where you are, you are to go to James the Just" (*Gospel of Thomas* 12). James, Jesus's younger brother, secured the governance of the community in Jerusalem and became a respected figure there, known for righteousness and piety. He was eventually accused of sedition and prosecuted by Annas, son of the High Priest who had presided over Jesus's trial. He was stoned to death in 62 CE.[3] He was succeeded by his (and Jesus's) brother Simon, who in turn was crucified in 106 CE by order of Emperor Trajan. It was under the leadership of Simon that the disciples who survived the sack of Jerusalem in 70 CE escaped to Pella in the hills of Gilead.

Jesus's family became the repository of his teachings, and thus a Christianity grew that was at odds with the one that was being developed by Paul, as is clear from the conflicts that arose in Galatia, where Paul's teachings were challenged by teachers from Jerusalem. Calling them Judaizers, as is often done, reflects the bias of those who won the day! While Paul saw Christianity as a way beyond the Jewish faith, James and the rest saw it as a fulfilment of Judaism. Paul

---

[2]  James L. Crenshaw, *Education in Ancient Israel* (New York: Doubleday, 1998); Bart D. Ehrman, *Misquoting Jesus* (San Francisco, CA: HarperSan Francisco, 2005), chapter 1.

[3]  Josephus, *Antiquit.* 20. 200–201. It is said that James the Just, or the Elder, evangelized Spain before dying in Jerusalem, but there is no evidence for this, though the Spanish claim to have his relics (brought there centuries later—if they are *his* relics) and with characteristic Eurocentric naivete call Spain "the eldest daughter of the Church."

relied on his own mystical experience of Jesus (*Galatians* 1:1–21) while James, who had grown up with Jesus in the same household and in the same family, was more intimately conversant with Jesus's thoughts and expectations.[4] Paul emphasized the power of faith to achieve salvation by itself, while James insisted that faith without works is dead (*James* 2:17). Also, for James, the Kingdom was to come *on earth*, while Paul may have shifted the advent of the Kingdom to heaven, the "Jerusalem above" (*Galatians* 4:26). Again, while Jesus was for Paul the transcendent Son of God, the Savior, there is no evidence that James ever considered his older brother, Jesus, divine, though he continued to support and propagate his teachings.[5] Yet, this version of the person of Jesus and of his teachings preserved by his own immediate family was definitively superseded by that contrived by Paul, who thus gave Christianity the character it still possesses.

This new breed of Hellenistic Christians had grown up without the tradition of Passover, so the incipient celebration of the Eucharist was deprived of a context, and there were disputes even about the words themselves, as is clear from the gospel narratives; in fact, it would be centuries before Christians realized that their typical "meal" had been a *seder*. Similarly, the new converts, most of them adults, had grown up in a context in which emperors and major legendary figures had been sons of God. Jesus would have had no chance of succeeding as the focal point of the new movement if his followers had not been able to claim for him divine sonship. The more Christianity took root among Greeks, Romans, and Hellenized Jews, the more it departed from the traditional faith of the early Jewish followers, including Jesus's own family; but at the same time, the more it became non-Jewish, the better chances of survival it gave itself. What is important to realize is that the ideological characteristics of Christianity to which we are used today did not come from the closest followers of Jesus, but were devised by those, like Paul, who had never met Jesus in the flesh, and others who had no knowledge

---

[4]  James D. Tabor, *The Jesus Dynasty*, p. 272.
[5]  Ibid., p. 282.

of the traditional Judaism in which Jesus had lived and from which his message had come.

Besides James and Jesus's family, Peter took up the leadership in gathering together the believers, first in Jerusalem, then in Syria and Antioch, where he "ordained" Evodius (who succeeded him) and Ignatius (who succeeded Evodius), and later in Rome, where the *Gospel of John* was forbidden because it spoke ill of Peter. In Jerusalem they all lived in community, sharing their goods, expecting from each according to their capacity, and apportioning to each according to their need[6]—an expression later sloganized by Karl Marx. Their faith bolstered, members of the community spread far and wide carrying their version of Jesus's message. But to understand fully the early beginnings of the Christian community, one has to look more steadily toward the East, something that most scholars have not done.

Tradition has it that Philip and Bartholomew were martyred in India, east of Mumbai (Bombay) and on the way to Pune leaving no known followers, but there is no historical evidence to support this claim. On the other hand, Judas "Thomas," Jesus's twin brother (or twin to some of the other brothers and sisters), is said to have arrived in Kodungalloor, Kerala, probably around 52 CE (the date of Paul's first letter to the Thessalonians), though solid historical evidence is lacking. He is said to have established seven churches there. He may have visited Mylapore, but was put to death in southeast India by order of King Vasudeva; or he may have been murdered by a brahmin. His tomb was shown in Mylapore when the Portuguese arrived there in 1498. He left there a strong community of believers known to this day as Thomas Christians. His relics were removed to Edessa (modern Urfa, in Turkey), in the fourth century.[7]

Thomas may not have reached south India; at least there is no serious evidence to this effect. But the *Acts of Thomas* 17 has him

---

[6] *Acts* 2:42–47 and 4:32–37.

[7] *If* Thomas's and James's bones are extant, and *if* DNA can be extracted from them, and *if* the record that makes them Jesus's brothers is true, then we would have Jesus's DNA. The results could be correlated with DNA from the Syrian Christian community of Jerusalem, which claims ancestry to the times of Jesus and Thomas. Lots of *ifs*, but also, certainly, tantalizing possibilities.

arriving in north India during the reign of King Gundaphorus (alias Vindpharna, or Gūdnaphar in Syriac, Hindopheres in Greek), a real historical personage.[8] Gundaphorus was king of Parthia in the northwest of India from 16 to 45 CE. His kingdom, occupying part of modern Afghanistan and Iran, as well as northwest India, was very cosmopolitan due to the extensive trade with Mesopotamia and the Persian Gulf region. It is very likely that there were small Christian communities there, and they would almost certainly have brought with them the Thomas tradition—if Thomas was not in fact their founder.[9] From there Christianity could have spread southward even if Thomas himself never set foot in Kerala. The Christian communities of South India remained under the official jurisdiction of the Syrian church; and Syrian/Aramaic was the liturgical language, and it continues to be so among some monastic communities, like the Carmelites, as I myself witnessed many years ago. The development of Christianity in Syria and in India was concurrent with the preaching of Paul to the Gentiles, yet it remains largely unexplored.

And then there was Saul. Born around 10 CE in Tarsus, Cilicia (southern Turkey)—the city where Antony first met the seductive Cleopatra in 41 BCE—Saul was by birth a Roman citizen, which would indicate that his family, though Jewish, had either distinguished itself enough to have earned citizenship as freemen, or had bought it—for as little as five hundred drachmae—a not uncommon practice at the time. While Jewish, they may have been Roman sympathizers.

Young Saul was a Pharisee, the populist and zealously observant faction of Palestinian Judaism.[10] He had sat at the feet of Gamaliel (*fl.* mid-first century) in Jerusalem,[11] where he had been sent by his parents to study. His mother tongue was Greek (*koine*), but he

---

[8] Stephen Neill, *A History of Christianity in India* (Cambridge: Cambridge University Press, 1984), p. 28.
[9] Neill, *A History of Christianity*, p. 29. There was a lot of multicultural exchange in these areas, to judge by the simple reference in *Acts* 2:9–11 to the many foreigners present in Jerusalem at the time of Pentecost.
[10] *Acts* 13:9 and 23:6.
[11] *Acts* 22:3. See *Mishnah*, Fourth Division, 3:9.

knew Aramaic as well. He may not have studied Greek philosophy, especially Stoicism, since this was not in the curriculum of a Jewish *yeshivah*, but he may have picked its tenets just by living in Tarsus, well-known for the Stoic philosophers Athenodosius and Nestor.

Two experiences seem to have been formative in young Saul's life: being accessory to murder and being blinded by a divine revelation. When zealots in Jerusalem stoned Stephen to death, Saul kept their coats and afterward approved of their deed.[12] Later, when he was between eighteen and twenty-six years old and was proceeding to Damascus, empowered to bring the members of the new sect back to Jerusalem for trial, he was struck down, heard the voice of Jesus, and was blinded by the brilliance of the revelation.[13] Between three and nine years later, after a long sojourn in the desert, he embarked on his first missionary journey, and from then on he would be constantly on the move until he was accused of sedition and ordered by the Roman authorities to be scourged. Paul identified himself as a Roman citizen and thus avoided the beating, but he was brought before Felix, then governor of Judea, who incarcerated him for two years. In the meantime, Festus succeeded Felix as governor, and when he planned to have Paul tried in Jerusalem, Paul appealed to Caesar (as was his right as a Roman citizen). After conferring with his advisers, Festus replied, "You have appealed to Caesar: to Caesar you shall go."[14]

In Rome, Paul seems to have spent about two years confined to his own house. It is not clear whether he was freed after the burning of Rome (highly unlikely, given Nero's blaming of the Christians for the sad event) or whether he was kept a prisoner until his death. At

---

[12] *Acts* 7:58 to 8:1.

[13] *Acts* 9:1–19. It is not clear why Paul would have been "officially" entrusted with the mission of going to Damascus to bring Jesus's followers to Jerusalem for trial. But there is some validity to a tradition that he was a temple guard. If this was so, he may even have witnessed the crucifixion of Jesus, and this may explain his tortured reaction to Stephen's claim and then his bewilderment when confronted by the vision of a Jesus whom he had seen ignominiously put to death on a cross.

[14] *Acts* 25:12.

any rate, he seems to have been executed in Rome under Nero, perhaps in 68 CE, and was buried beside the road to Ostia.

———— ✴ ————

In one of his sermons, John Donne said the following about Paul's visionary experience: "*Saul* was struck blind, but it was a blindness contracted from light; it was a light that struck him blind… That powerful light felled *Saul*; but after he was fallen, his own sight was restored to him again."[15] Two thousand years before Donne, Plato had explained that one can be blinded, or fail to see, because there is no light at all, or because there is a superabundance of light, as happens when we walk from a dark room into the brilliant light of the midday sun.[16]

What was the light that suffused Paul's eyes and made him blind, causing him to stumble and fall? It was the realization that his own conception of God and his elect, the fellowship of the Temple, on the basis of which he meant to persecute and bring to trial and death any dissenters, was mistaken and wrong. These people, who followed Jesus and identified with him, were the real thing, the ordinary Galileans who, according to Daniel's vision, were to inherit the Kingdom of God. This was an overwhelming insight, one that challenged everything that young Saul had studied, learned, and practiced. It would require of him to change his entire perspective on life and religion. It would also demand from him years of intense and solitary self-examination in the desert before he could really become Paul.

———— ✴ ————

Paul was not a convert to Christianity, since Christianity did not exist then. Moreover, in *Galatians* 1:11–17, Paul specifically claims

---

[15] John Donne, Sermon preached at St. Paul's the Sunday after the Conversion of St. Paul. January 30, 1624–25, in John Donne, *Complete Poetry and Selected Prose,* ed. Charles M. Coffin (New York: The Modern Library, 1952), pp. 503–504.

[16] Plato, *Republic* VII. 518A.

that his message is *not* the same as that of the Jerusalem group, for it comes from his own private revelation. In fact, Christianity arose as the Paulinization of Jesus's message took place in and through the Pauline epistles. Only about half of the letters attributed to Paul were written by him; the rest were clever anti-Pauline forgeries using his name to have their message accepted.[17] But in the matter of the formation of Christianity, this distinction is irrelevant, for the counterfeit were accepted as real, and the effect was the same as if all the letters had been genuine.

From the Jerusalem community, Christianity took the idea that men are better than women and the only ones fit to perform the mysteries, and though there were a few women leaders in the early communities, they disappeared "bye and bye" (or, as seems more likely, were deliberately put down) as patriarchy continued its relentless march. Paul preached the equality of all, but this was one of the issues in which the pseudo-authors disagreed with him, so their letters, attributed to Paul, confirmed the misogynist trend with the injunction that women should obey their husbands and be silent and veiled in church.[18] In addition, there are at least three major ideas that the Pauline letters injected into the Western tradition, and these must be spelled out in some detail.

First is the concept of sin. Having aided and abetted the murder of Stephen, and having approved of it, Paul must have been guilt-ridden and remorseful. How could he, who had sat at the feet of Gamaliel, have done such a thing? The obvious explanation was to be found in the congenital weakness of human nature. Adam and Eve, the originators of the human race, had disobeyed God, and in so doing they had lost the privileges that adorned their nature— immortality and the innocence needed for communion with nature. What they lost for themselves, they lost for us, too, since they were the origin of us all, and their nature is our nature. Sin at the origin (or

---

[17] The letters to the *Romans, Galatians, Corinthians, Philippians, Philemon,* and *I Thessalonians* are generally considered authentic, though even they may have additions not from the pen of Paul. They are the oldest Judeo-Christian documents we possess.

[18] *I Timothy* 2:12; *I Corinthians* 11:10.

"original sin," as it is called) made us liable of sinning and explained the moral weakness that made us succumb to temptation. But by becoming man in Jesus, God had repaired human nature, and it was now up to us to take advantage of God's presence among us. We achieve this, wrote Paul, by believing in Jesus and his resurrection. In this faith alone is atonement; in it alone is salvation.[19] Despairing of self-forgiveness, Paul cast his belief and hope upon Jesus and the resurrection, and he forcefully counseled the same to all his readers.[20] The message caught on. In fact, in so far as the sin of Adam and Eve had eventually necessitated God's intervention in the guise of Jesus, the Church learned to glorify sin and to sing on the Easter Vigil, *O felix culpa quae talem ac tantum meruit habere redemptorem.*[21] From this time on, Christianity would be obsessed with sin and salvation.

Paul felt compelled to preach this message to all and sundry, that salvation "does not depend on man's will or effort, but on God's mercy."[22] In fact, he felt he would be damned if he did not preach, and he came back to this theme again and again in the letters. His *mission*, he claimed, was to preach,[23] not to baptize or discuss philosophy. He had a mandate to preach, the idea of which he derived, at least partially, from the proselytism of Jews in the diaspora.

---

[19] The Protestant dictum that we are saved "by faith alone" is often contrasted with the Roman Catholic belief that works also contribute to salvation. But in rejecting "works," Paul meant actions under the old Jewish Law, not good actions in general. So the overemphasis on "by faith alone" is a misunderstanding of Paul.

[20] Tarsus was famous for the cult of Mithras and for celebrations of the death of Herakles and his descent to the underworld, from which he ascended as a savior. It must be remembered that Herakles was the son of god (Zeus) who battled Death in order to bring Alkestis back to life. Paul must have known all this and even witnessed some of the rituals as a child growing up in Tarsus. Such rich backgrounds did in no small measure contribute to his theological elaborations. See A. N. Wilson, *Paul: The Mind of the Apostle* (New York: W. W. Norton, 1997), pp. 25–28.

[21] "O happy sin which deserved to have such a great and wonderful redeemer!"

[22] *Romans* 9:16.

[23] *1 Corinthians* 1:17.

This sense of mission will soon pervade the entire Christian movement. Missionaries will go to the four corners of the world carrying the message of God's mercy and of the necessity of conversion. The missionary endeavors did not cease with the deaths of the immediate followers: mission continued through the following centuries. Thus Ulfilas (*ca.* 311–383) will preach to the Barbarians, Patrick (*ca.* 385–461) to the Irish, Xavier (1506–1552) to the Japanese, and every conquistador will be accompanied in his travels of discovery by a missionary. There are today more than 300,000 Evangelicals engaged in missionary work. To these must be added the envoys of Mormons, Roman Catholics, Anglicans, Methodists, Lutherans, and Presbyterians.[24] Mission in such grandiose terms is an idea that comes into the West through the Paulinization of Jesus's message.

Finally, Paul introduced into the ideologies of the West the notion of a faith that is not subject to the canons of reason. Not that it is irrational, but that it obeys a different logic because it is paradoxical. In a celebrated passage, he wrote:

> Christ did not send me to baptize, but to proclaim the Gospel; and to do it without relying on the offices of worldly wisdom, so that the fact of Christ on his cross might have its full weight. This doctrine of the cross is sheer folly to those on their way to ruin, but to us who are on the way to salvation it is the power of God. Scripture says, "I will destroy the wisdom of the wise, and bring to nothing the cleverness of the clever" [*Is* 29:14]. Where is your wise man now, your man of learning, or your subtle debater—limited, all of them, to this passing age? God has made the

---

[24] Many missions were established centuries ago at a time when Christianity saw itself as the only and best religion in the world. That the effort continues today among Evangelicals and Mormons is surprising in many ways, because it hints at the fact that these Christian groups disdain other religions and do not respect their traditions. On the other hand, given their fanaticism, it is understandable, though regrettable.

wisdom of this world look foolish. As God in his
wisdom ordained, the world failed to find him
by its wisdom, and he chose to save those who
have faith by the folly of the Gospel. Jews call for
miracles, Greeks look for wisdom; but we proclaim Christ—yes, Christ nailed to the cross; and
though this is a stumbling-block to the Jews and
folly to the Greeks, yet to those who have heard
his call, Jews and Greeks alike, he is the power of
God and the wisdom of God.[25]

There was, of course, an idea of faith in the Judaism of the
time, exemplified perhaps in the pseudo-Pauline *Letter to the Hebrews*
11:1–3: "Faith gives substance to our hopes, and makes us certain of
realities we do not see." But the paradoxicality that Paul insisted was
constitutive of the faith of this emerging sect was new, and it would
have tremendous repercussions in the subsequent developments
of the relationship between religion and science (and philosophy),
because the interpretation given to it was—and continues to be—
that Christian faith is irrational, and that in so far as the Christian
religion is based on such irrational faith, it is incompatible with the
rational methods and conclusions of science (and philosophy). This
interpretation of Christian faith as irrational was helped later by a
much quoted passage from Tertullian (*ca.* 160–235). Addressing
Marcion, he wrote:

> Why do you destroy the indispensable dis-
> honor of our faith? Whatsoever is unworthy of
> God is of gain to me: I shall be saved if I be not
> ashamed of my Lord! The Son of God was cru-
> cified: I am not ashamed because people must
> needs be ashamed of it. And the Son of God
> died: it is by all means to be believed because it

---

[25] *1 Corinthians* 1:17–24.

is absurd. And he was buried and rose again: the
fact is certain because it is impossible.[26]

Tertullian's *Credendum est quia absurdum* was taken as the proof
that Christian faith—indeed, all faith—concerned the irrational and
relished in it. Most scholars did not stop to examine what Tertullian
might have meant by the *quia* ("because") in the celebrated phrase.
In the context of his work, and taking into consideration the fact
that Tertullian was discussing the Pauline passage quoted above, the
meaning can only be this: since a god's birth, crucifixion, death, and
resurrection are unprovable and absurd according to the canons of
reason, the only way to affirm them is through faith. Faith, thus, is
essentially a way of dealing intellectually with paradoxical religious
statements.[27] This way of understanding faith is another Pauline
contribution to the intellectual culture of the West.

---

Being closely associated with Judaism (of which it was thought
to be a mere sect), Christianity moved around for a little while in
Jewish circles and suffered the same fate as the Jews when they were
dispersed after the overthrow of Jerusalem by Titus in 70 CE and
later in 116–117 and 130–133. The Jewish Diaspora, begun at the
time of the Babylonian Exile, was thus completed. The followers of
Jesus moved out with them. But they sought strenuously to sever

---

[26] "*Non pudet quia pudendum est... Credendum est quia absurdum... Certum est
quia impossibile est*" (*De Carne Christi* 3, 5).

[27] This is like moving to a larger and more encompassing system as the way to
deal with propositions that cannot be proved (that is, which are undecidable)
but which appear nonetheless to be true. See Kurt Gödel, "Über formal
unentscheidbare Sätze der *Principia Mathematica* und verwandter Systeme,
I," *Monatshefte für Mathematik und Physik* 38 (1931): 173–198. Also Barkely
Rosser, "An informal exposition of proofs of Gödel's theorems and Church's
theorem," *The Journal of Symbolic Logic* 4:2 (June, 1939): 53–60; and Harry
J. Gensler, *Gödel's Theorem Simplified* (Lanham: University Press of America,
1984), 64. Also George Boolos, "Gödel's Second Incompleteness Theorem
Explained in Words of One Syllable," *Mind* 103:409 (January 1994), 1–3.

their connections with the Jewish revolutionaries that precipitated the strong, military Roman reactions. In some ways this was not difficult, since many, perhaps most of them, were Gentile converts. But they felt that only in a disassociation from the Jews would they stand a chance of surviving the tumultuous events taking place around them. At the intellectual and religious level, Marcion (*ca.* 85–144) preached a radical version of the new faith that denied the Jewishness of Jesus, severed all connections with Judaism, rejected the Hebrew Bible, and put together a Gospel based almost exclusively on Luke's, which proclaimed a totally non-Jewish Jesus. Here, and not on the crucifixion, one must place the budding of an anti-Semitism that accompanied Christianity for the past two thousand years.

The destruction of the Second Temple and of much of Jerusalem in 70 CE doomed the Jewish faction and its ideological influence among the followers of Jesus. Deprived of a center in Jerusalem, they dispersed, and while from a certain perspective this fact accounted for the spread of the new movement to outlying regions of the Roman Empire, from another perspective it weakened their sway and allowed the Hellenistic converts to gain importance and ultimately to dictate the content of the new faith. The belief in the divinity of Jesus, for example, is intimately tied to this development. Thus, the simple facts of the Jewish revolts and the downfall of Jerusalem are significantly responsible for the type of religion Christianity eventually became.

———◆———

The deification of Jesus was a central part of the project of severing the nascent faith from its Jewish roots. This, as I have explained, was deemed necessary because of the revolutionary turmoil fanning through Judea and the Jewish Diaspora, and the concerted attacks by Gentile intellectuals. Docetism, the claim that Jesus had only an apparent physical body, was part and parcel of the process of deracinating Jesus from his Jewishness. The opposition to Docetism and to the views of Marcion and Hermogenes was mounted by Tertullian, Cyprian, and Origen—all Gentile Christians. Their arguments affirmed, not so much the Jewishness of Jesus as his humanity. As Tertullian wrote, "The common people know of Christ as truly a man, as the Jews thought of him."[28] Jesus, they argued, was a true human being, truly born, who would eventually truly die. Tertullian, again, writing against Marcion (who had died some fifty years before): "He [Jesus] has a body derived from a body. You may, I assure you, more easily find a man born without a heart or without brains...than without a body."[29] Again: "If Christ was the truth, he was flesh; if he was flesh, he was born."[30] The theological idea of human nature—that is, that which we all share as human beings—became the key to a solution of the problem raised by Docetism and by Marcion. Jesus had a *human* nature like ours, but he also had a *divine* nature. He was, as Tertullian put it, "a man mixed with God" ("*homo Deo mixtus*"[31]). The formula, "two natures in one person," which the Council of Nicaea would enshrine in the Nicene Creed, was a neat solution, except that it treated as irrelevant the Jewishness of Jesus: "We see a twofold state, not confounded but conjoined in one person, Jesus, God and man...and the property of each substance is wholly preserved."[32] Jesus was human, the formula declared, but it conveniently forgot to add "and Jewish." This is important because human nature does not exist in the abstract: no human nature in general was "mixed with God," but the actual and particular human nature of Jesus the Jew.

The theology of the two-natures-in-one-person achieved several things in one stroke: it cemented the physical reality of Jesus (against Docetism); it explained how Jesus was both God and man; and it dropped the Jewish issue out of the picture. This last conse-

---

[28] Tertullian, *Apologeticum* 3.

[29] Tertullian, *Adversus Marcionem* IV, 16.

[30] *Adversus Marcionem* III, 9.

[31] *Apologeticum* XXI, 14; also *De Carne Christi* XV, 6; *De Praescriptione Haereticorum* XX, 1; *Adversus Marcionem* IV, 13, 6.

[32] *Adversus Praxeam* XXVII, 6 *ff.*, esp. lines 60–65. Also *De Carne Christi* V, 7. Pope Leo the Great (*ca.* 400–461) will use Tertullian's words in his *Letter to Flavian*, chapter 3. His formula became canonical by its adoption by the Council of Chalcedon in 451.

quence may not have been intended by Tertullian, but it fit neatly into the anti-Jewish trend that, for political and theological reasons, had developed through the second century. It should be noted that the theological conceptualizations that developed during the first three or four hundred years had, as an (probably) unintended consequence, the further distancing of Christianity from Judaism. Judaism was, and has remained, much more imaginative and personalistic than Christianity. The rejection of mythology and imagery, therefore, is part and parcel of the anti-Semitic trend begun already in the late first century. While the history of ideas records this movement toward conceptualization and abstraction, it often forgets the Jewish and Gnostic context from which it arose and against which it battled.

It is not difficult to understand why this theology could not have been developed by the Jews who had known Jesus in the flesh, followed him, and given their lives for his cause. James, Judas "the Twin," Simon, Mary of Magdala, could not have constructed a theology that postulated the divinity of Jesus. But a theology they must have constructed, for some doctrine was carried to India and preached there by Judas "the Twin." In fact, the *Gospel of Thomas*, a sayings gospel contemporary with the *Gospel of Mark*, may approximate such a repository of doctrine, especially because the Coptic version may have escaped the bias present in versions of the original gospels written during the anti-Jewish period of the second century, from which time the earliest extant copies of Christian documents derive. But whatever it was, it was swallowed up in the haste to Hellenize Jesus and his message and to extricate his memory from the Jewishness, which was his by birth.

The thing is that, like it or not, the Christianity that grew up knowing itself to be Christianity is not the way that Jesus preached and that his early disciples followed. We have known this for some time, but millions of Christians still cling to the Gentile-developed version, which fundamentally altered the character of its founder.

Tertullian, Cyprian, Origen, Irenaeus, Athanasius—all spent their lives preserving the faith they believed to be authentic and orthodox, and it never seems to have occurred to them that this was the Gentile faith that the numerically superior Gentile Christians had developed, not that of the original poor Jews of the Galilee.

———— ◈ ————

As the years passed, persecutions ensued, most of them unsystematic, local, and sporadic. Around 50 or 53, there were riots in Ephesus against Paul and his followers, some of whom were Gentile converts. The issue was the fear that the new religion would bring the end to the worship of Artemis (= Diana) of the Ephesians (*Acts* 19:23 *ff.*). Then Nero, blaming Christians for the fire of Rome and in order to deflect blame from himself, had many Christians crucified along the Appian Way. Trajan allowed Christians to be brought to trial, among them Ignatius of Antioch (*ca.* 117), and so did Antoninus Pius, under whose reign Polycarp was martyred in 156. Marcus Aurelius countenanced some martyrdoms at Lyons, and the Scillitan Martyrs were executed at Scillium, Africa, under his reign in 177 or under that of Commodus in 180. Septimius Severus forbade conversion under pain of death, and so Perpetua, Felicitas, and their companions were martyred at Carthage in 203.[33] Decius decreed a persecution in 250, which was continued under Valerian and Diocletian. But in 313 Constantine and Licinius agreed on a policy of toleration and signed the Edict of Milan. A short while after this, Christianity would become the quasi-official religion of the Roman Empire, and although it had always viewed with suspicion and often overt antagonism the learning of Greek philosophers,[34] it became the carrier of the classical tradition into the West.

---

[33] On the interesting records of this martyrdom, see CJMJ, *Passio Sanctarum Perpetuae et Felicitatis* (Bonn: Hanstein, 1938). For a different perspective, see John Boswell, *Same-Sex Unions in Premodern Europe* (New York: Villard Books, 1994), p. 139 *ff.*

[34] Witness Tertullian's celebrated "What has Athens to do with Jerusalem?" (*De Praescript.* 7; *Apolog.* 46). See Henry Chadwick, *Early Christian Thought and the Classical Tradition* (New York: Oxford University Press, 1966). See Bart D. Ehrman, *The Triumph of Christianity* (New York: Simon & Schuster, 2018), chapter 9.

The spread of Christianity was not halted by the persecutions, which were, in fact, minor in comparison with those the Christians themselves instituted later against their own (for instance, against the Donatists, the Pelagians, the Arians, and the Albigenses). Yet, rather than halt the conversion movement, the persecutions hastened it. As Tertullian noted in a celebrated phrase, "the blood of martyrs is the seed of Christians."[35]

---

[35] Tertullian, *Apologeticum* 50, 13.

# CHAPTER 14

# Faith and Paradox

Most Christians think of faith in terms of doctrine, whether dog-
matic or traditional. Faith, they think, is *what* you are supposed or
expected to believe. For some this is contained in the Catechism or
in the various denominational Disciplines, for others in the Nicene
Creed (as revised by the second Council of Nicaea in 787 to include
the clause affirming that the Holy Spirit proceeds from the Father
"and from the son." This is the version most popularly recited at
church services). Fundamentalists, of course, believe at least the
five "fundamental" tenets agreed to in 1895, and Roman Catholics
believe in a host of additional materials like the assumption of Mary,
the infallibility of the pope, the "real presence," and the existence of
hell.

A number of beliefs are paradoxical, something I shall deal with
in greater detail later. Suffice it to say here that they demand assent
even though they do not make sense logically. The assent is given
because God is assumed to have revealed these tenets, so that God
becomes the guarantor of their truth. He is also supposed to be the
primary reason for believing, so that faith becomes an assent given
*propter auctoritatem Dei revelantis* ("because of the authority of the
revealing God"). Reason and discussion merely persuade one that
belief is reasonable, that it is the thing to do; they do not prove *what*
one is to believe. As Augustine put it, "people do not believe unless

they first believe they ought to believe,"[1] and this is all that reason achieves.

Faith, thus, is supposed to precede the assent to the propositions, in the sense that what one believes is not a conclusion arrived at after a conceptual process. One does not first prove and then believe; in fact, if one did that, as Augustine claimed, one would not be talking of faith at all. Moreover, faith is a gift of God, a grace. In Augustine's words: "To be able to believe and to be able to love are part of human nature; but to have faith, and to actually love, is a gift of the faithful."[2]

The relation between faith and understanding is explained by Augustine in reference to a passage in *Isaiah* 7:9, which reads, in the Septuagint version Augustine was using, "Unless you believe, you will not understand." This formula is repeated by Anselm in a famous passage: "I do not seek to understand that I may believe, but I believe that I may understand. For this also I believe, that unless I believed, I would not understand."[3] But this *credo ut intelligam* ("I believe that I may understand") gives the impression that once one believes, one will come to understand what one believes. This is not the case. The formula is beautiful and concise, but it is misleading, because what is thus believed is not thereby understood any better than it was understood before it was believed. This is one reason many people say they believe this or that, and yet they entertain doubts about the reasonableness of what they believe, or seek further explanations from others, because they cannot explain to themselves rationally what they believe. The Anselmian formulation requires that one step by faith into the realm of beliefs, and thereafter simply believe without questioning everything that is presented for acceptance as revealed by God.

Without meaning to be disrespectful, this traditional understanding of faith guarantees that whatever the religious leaders and theologians present to the faithful believers as beliefs, will be believed,

---

[1]  Augustine, *De Praed. sanct.* 2, 5; ML 44, 962.
[2]  Augustine, *De Praed. sanct.* 5, 10; ML 44, 968.
[3]  Anselm of Canterbury, *Proslogium*, 1.

because belief must precede every understanding. The Anselmian formula guarantees the acceptance of a body of beliefs or dogmas, and it requires one to behave according to those accepted beliefs. It also justifies the exclusion as heretical of everything not included in the beliefs. For heresy can exist only when there is an official body of belief from which certain opinions depart. Before beliefs are included in such compilations, they are merely opinions, and they must be judged according to the force of the arguments in their support. This distinction is important because the views about Jesus and about the texts that describe his life and sayings were controverted up until the time the hierarchy made some views orthodox and some not, and chose some texts to be canonical and some not. Up to then, they could not be excluded by simple recourse to a canon or to ortho-doxy, because neither the canon nor the orthodoxy existed. But the creation of a canon took several centuries of give and take. For exam-ple, today we call a "Docetist" someone who denies that Jesus had a real body, and we call this view heretical; but at the time shortly after the death of Jesus, this was one view of him that was held by many of his followers, though it was also opposed by many. It did not become a heresy until the fact of Jesus's physical body was affirmed as a dogma.[4]

Another result of the application of the formula *credo ut intel-ligam* is that matters are left unexamined, since once one believes, one is supposed to have achieved what is expected: one has faith. Asked *what* it is that one believes, the most one can do is to recite the tenets of one's faith (that is, what is in the Catechism, which is one reason Roman Catholics insisted the children learn the Catechism by heart), since believing in them is all that matters. In fact, reciting these tenets in the Nicene Creed, for example, seems to many to be all that is expected of them. More, the Creed seems to many to be the

---

[4] Karl Barth stated that "there are only relative heretics," since beliefs are pronounced orthodox or heretical in relation to views held at the time. See his *Die protestantische Theologie im 19. Jarhundert* (Zollikon-Zürich: Evangelischer Verlag, 1952), p. 2 *ff.*

essential compendium of beliefs, so that to recite the Creed publicly or privately is taken to be the basic expression of Christian belief.

———◈———

As one of the great religious traditions, Christianity has sought to lead Christians to what lies beyond the scriptures, the rites, the commandments, and the dogmas. Things like scriptures and dogmas have value, not in themselves, but only in so far as they lead Christians into the mystery of God.[5] In Western Christianity, paradox has been the preferred way to entice the spirit beyond the letter and into the mystery, just as in the Zen tradition it was the *kôan*, "that great baffler of reasoning" (as Suzuki called it[6]), which was used to break the stranglehold of logic on the thinking mind in order to open it to the beyond. A mind that always looks for reasons, that always wants answers, is an obstacle to enlightenment. Enlightenment is an experience, not a conclusion or the answer to a question or problem. Enlightenment is an awareness, not of things not seen before, but a seeing in a different way. *Kôans* are paradoxical statements conceived by the masters precisely for this purpose. They are logically intractable, intellectually incomprehensible, but they are not "false." Any effort to find their meaning through discursive reasoning is bound to end nowhere. It is only when this is realized experientially that logic is transcended and enlightenment ensues.

The fundamental paradox by means of which Christianity has sought a way to the mystery has been that of the birth and death of Jesus-as-God. Saying that a god can be born and that a god can die is paradoxical, not irrational or anti-rational, but paradoxical. A paradox is a mode of thinking that diverges from the usual, thus creating a conflict of sorts. Logical thinking goes straight to the point; paradoxical thinking makes a detour or changes dimensions. Paradoxes are not false, they just require a different mode of thinking. A com-

---

[5]  Patrick Laude, "An Eternal Perfume," *Parabola* 30: 4 (Winter 2005), pp. 4–5.
[6]  Daisetz T. Suzuki, *Manual of Zen Buddhism* (New York: Grove Press, Inc., 1960), p. 307.

mon mistake made by both Christians and their opponents is that of trying to "understand" conceptually, or to explain logically, the paradox of God-become-man. This cannot be done, though theologians have spent gallons of ink trying to do so. The purpose of the paradox is to catapult the mind (and the heart) beyond the walls and parapets of logic.

The Christian paradox *par excellence* is Christ nailed to the cross (*1 Corinthians* 1:18–31). The Jews could not accept Jesus as God because the Torah insisted that there is only one God; and the Greeks could not accept Jesus-as-God dead on a cross because gods just do not die (though at some point a rumor was circulated that "the great god Pan" had died). Yet Christians maintained that these logically untenable propositions could be *believed*, that is, that faith was the one way of going beyond the paradoxes and affirming them as true.

Paul affirmed the paradox, but it was Tertullian who drove it in:

> There are, to be sure, other things quite as foolish as the birth of Christ, which have reference to the humiliations and sufferings of God. Or else let them call a crucified God "wisdom"... For what is more unworthy of God, what more likely to raise a blush of shame, that God should be born, or that he should die? that he should bear the flesh, or the cross? be circumcised, or be crucified? be cradled, or be coffined? be laid in a manger, or in a tomb?... But, after all, you will not be "wise" unless you become a "fool" to the world by believing the "foolish" things of God... Spare the whole world's one only hope! Why do you destroy the indispensable dishonor of our faith? Whatsoever is unworthy of God is of gain to me. I am saved if I be not ashamed of my Lord... The son of God was crucified: I am not ashamed because people must needs be ashamed of it. And the son of God died: it is by all means to be believed because it is absurd. And he was

buried and rose again: the fact is certain because it is impossible. But how will all this be true in him if he was not himself a true man, if he really did not have in himself that which might be crucified? that which might die, might be buried, and might rise again? I mean this flesh suffused with blood, built up with bones, interwoven with nerves, entwined with veins, a flesh which knew how to be born and how to die, human without a doubt, as born of a human being. It will therefore be mortal in Christ because Christ is man and the son of man.[7]

There is a graffito found scratched on a wall of what may have been the kitchen of a Roman mansion. It depicts a human figure with an ass's head hanging on a cross. On one side stands another figure making with uplifted hands a gesture of devout reverence. Underneath is written in Greek, "Alexamenos worships [his] god." The graffito may have been a way to mock a kitchen slave who was Christian, and it conveys the attitude pagans had toward the worship of Christ as God-crucified. The legend seems to imply that it is asinine to worship such a powerless god that would allow himself to be crucified. But to the side of the original legend, another hand has written, "Alexamenos is faithful." This would be the Christian response, and it conveys what Paul was trying to show was the distinctive mark of Christianity, the paradoxical belief in a suffering God.[8] Tertullian, characteristically, has written: "I claim for myself Christ, I maintain for myself Jesus...whatever that poor despised body was, however it looked to the eye or felt to the touch. Be he inglorious, be he ignoble, be he dishonored, he shall be my Christ."[9] And he added, "Fortunately it is part of the Creed of the Christians to believe

---

[7] Tertullian, *De Carne Christi* V.
[8] G. L. Prestige, *Fathers and Heretics* (London, 1940), p. 85.
[9] Tertullian, *Adversus Marcionem* III, 16, 7–17, 2.

even that God died, and yet that he is alive for evermore."[10] The paradox at the heart of Christianity can hardly be stated with greater succinctness and passion!

————— ✳ —————

But if we see Jesus as "the son of the man," as a throughly human being, what happens to the paradox of the dead God-man? And if this paradox is eliminated, what happens to Christianity as a religious faith?

The initial experience of the followers of Jesus when he was crucified must have entailed disappointment, as we read in the episode narrated in *Luke* 24:18 *ff.* A couple of disciples are on their way to Emmaus when unbeknownst to them Jesus joins their trek. To him they express their letdown, saying, "We had been hoping that he was the man to liberate Israel." But they also acknowledge that Jesus "had been powerful in speech and action before God and the whole people." The expectation and the disillusionment go hand in hand.

Two things are manifest here: first, there is the realization that a good man has been made to suffer even unto death on the cross. This is the perennial paradox, why the good suffer, "why bad things happen to good people." The story of Job is relevant here, but there was a tradition of a Job-like figure in ancient Sumeria,[11] which would indicate that the concern was not exclusive to the Hebrews.

The second point is the interpretation of this paradox—that a good man should suffer and die—in Jewish terms; or the formulation of some kind of explanation with specific application to Jesus by his immediate followers, who were Jews. According to this view, Jesus-the-good-man is identified also with the *'ebed Yhwh* ("suffering servant") of *Deutero-Isaiah* 42:1 *ff.* This appears explicitly in a passage like *Acts* 8:26 *ff.*, where the eunuch is reading *Isaiah* 53:7–8 and cannot understand the meaning of the passage. Philip explains

10 Tertullian, *Adversus Marcionem* II, 16, 3.
11 D. Winton Thomas, ed., *Documents from Old Testament Times* (New York: Harper Torchbooks, 1958), p. 98 *ff.*

it and applies it specifically to Jesus. Such also is the implication of *Mark* 8:31, "He began to teach them that the son of the man had to undergo great sufferings." It should be noted also that the expression *ho pais theou*, which is the Septuagint translation of *'ebed Yhwh* (but which was taken to mean "son," not "servant" of God by the Gentile Christians), appears repeatedly in *Acts*.[12]

All this would lead one to conclude that early, even pre-Gospel Christianity, "preserved the memory that Jesus himself was conscious of having to realize the work of the *'ebed Yhwh*."[13] Paradoxical though this may have seemed to them, it afforded an explanation of why Jesus, good man that he was, had to suffer and die on the cross: he had to be the "servant of God." This tradition, which some scholars attribute to Peter and his circle, disappeared very early as a separate interpretation of the life of Jesus, and it was supplanted by the more explicitly Greek theologizing associated with Paul.

The contrast may have been even more stark if Jesus and his Jewish followers were aware of the tradition of "a son of the man" in *Daniel* 7:13 and in *Ezekiel* 1:26–2:1.[14] This "son of the man" (the same exact words Jesus uses for himself) is an exalted figure bathed in a mystical light. It would be almost impossible to deny that Jesus and his followers knew the references to these texts of the Hebrew Bible, which they might have used to signify Jesus's greatness, the greatness that was tied also to his humiliation and suffering as the *'ebed Yhwh*. Though the terms are biblical and the contexts are mystical, this is as legitimate a way to express the paradox surrounding Jesus as the later, Greek-derived theologizing that made him divine.

Surely, this paradoxical amalgamation in the person of Jesus of the glorious "son of the Man" of Daniel and Ezekiel with the suffering *'ebed Yhwh* of Isaiah possesses a more restricted meaning than the later formulas that detail Jesus's divine "preexistence," but it has the advantage that it reflects an earlier Jewish mode of thinking and

---

12  See *Acts* 3:13, 3:26, 4:27, 4:30.
13  Oscar Cullmann, *The Christology of the New Testament* (London, 1959), p. 79.
14  See Walter Wink, *The Human Being: Jesus and the Enigma of the Son of the Man* (Minneapolis, MN: Fortress Press, 2002), chapter 2.

that Jesus himself may have used it. It also has the advantage that it offers a true Christology without divinizing Jesus, as one would have expected from Jewish interpreters. At a later date, and possibly under the influence of Gnosticism, a further component was added that conceived of a descent from the glory of the Danielic "son of the Man" to the humiliation of the 'ebed Yhwh and then, again, to a reaffirmation of the former glory. This descent-ascent pattern is that of the "hero with a thousand faces," and it is stated here in Judaic terms (and therefore in a metaphorical sense), and in reference to Jesus.

Thus the early Jewish followers of Jesus produced a Christology with endemic Jewish (and later Gnostic) themes. The main characteristic of this approach was the aspect of descent. Jesus descends metaphorically to the human world (the *logos* becomes flesh). In traditional hero stories, the descent is often followed by suffering and even death, and then by an ascent that restores the "hero" to his pristine glory. In the case of Jesus, later theology will speak of incarnation, death, and resurrection, but we are not there yet. In fact, the original Jewish-Gnostic versions stand for themselves as viable theologies, and therefore can be taken as carriers of the Christian paradox.

The earliest explicit exponent of this Christology is the *Ascension of Isaiah*, a first-century work. It describes how the *logos* descended through the seven heavens (the seven spheres of the Ptolemaic astronomical system), making himself one with the angels who presided over each sphere and being unrecognized by them all: "He was hidden to the heavens and to all the princes and gods of this world."[15] Ignatius of Antioch, in his letter to the *Ephesians* 19:1, similarly maintains that "the prince of this world was in ignorance of the virginity of Mary and of her childbearing, and also of the death of the Lord, three mysteries loudly proclaimed to the world, though accomplished in the stillness of God." The reason for this hidden descent is, as Paul states in *1 Corinthians* 2:8, that if "the princes of this world" had known of it, they would have impeded it, and salvation would not have been effected. In other words, they allowed their own

---

[15] *Ascensio Isaiae* XI, 17. Also III, 13–20; IX, 12–18; X, 8–15 and 18–31; XI, 23–33.

destruction to take place unawares. Irenaeus comments: "Because the Word came down invisible to creatures, he was not known to them in his descent."[16] This theme is repeated many times, perhaps most tellingly in the *Odes of Solomon*, where God's word is described as having become a letter that descended from on high. Innumerable hands were raised to snatch it and read it, but the letter escaped through their fingers.[17] *Physiologos*, a work of the fourth century, summarizes the tradition as follows: "Our Lord Jesus...when sent by the Father, covered up his spiritual qualities, that is, his divinity. For he emptied himself and descended into the womb of Mary that he might save deluded humanity. And the logos became flesh and dwelt among us. And so, those who saw him descended from above, kept asking, 'Who is this king of glory?' And the Holy Spirit answered, 'The Lord of power, he is the king of glory!'"[18]

By this time the theologizing has become explicit in its affirmation of the divinity of Jesus. Metaphor has given way to "truth." Still, the descent is perceived as a humiliation, a *kenosis*.[19] It is the enduring of the fate of the ʿ*ebed Yhwh*; it is a sharing in the human experience and in the paradox of the suffering just. The basic original paradox of Daniel's and Ezekiel's "son of the man" becoming Isaiah's ʿ*ebed Yhwh* is maintained, and Christianity's distinctness is preserved.

———✼———

So, to recast the question of chapter 6, who *was* Jesus? Jesus's followers on their way to Emmaus, representing ordinary Jews, said it

[16] Irenaeus, *Demonstr.* 84. Also *Adversus Haeres.* I, 23, 3.
[17] *Ode* 23, 5–9. See chapter 6.
[18] *Physiologos* I; MG 43, 517–520.
[19] The theme of humiliating or kenotic descent and glorifying ascent recurs often in the Christian scriptures. Here are some passages from the canonical records only: *Matthew* 18:4, 20:28, 23:12; *Mark* 8:31; *Luke* 14:11, 18:14 and 31–33, 24:26 and 44–46; *John* 1:1–14, 12:26, 13:12–17, 16:18; *Acts* 26:23; *Romans* 8:32–39, 15:3 and 7 ff., 8:17b; *1 Corinthians* 2:8 and 16; *2 Corinthians* 4:11, 8:8–9, 13:4; *Galatians* 2:20; *Ephesians* 1:18–23, 2:4–7, 4:8–10, 5:2; *Philippians* 2:1–12, 3:10–11, and 20–21; *2 Timothy* 1:10, 2:1–14; *Hebrews* 1:3–4, 2:9, 5:8, 12:1–2; *1 Peter* 2:21, 3:18–22, 4:13, 5:6; *Revelation* 5:12.

well: he was "a prophet powerful in speech and action" (*Luke* 24:19) who was "handed over by the chief priests and rulers to be sentenced to death and crucified" (*Luke* 24:20).

Peter put it this way: he was "a man singled out by God" (*Acts* 2:22) "whom heathen men crucified and killed" (*Acts* 2:23).

In the metaphorical way that became the foundation for later theologizing and the construction of a philosophical Christology, Jesus was like "the son of the man" sitting on the throne (*Ezekiel* 1:26) who accepted suffering unto death like a true servant of God ('*ebed Yhwh*; *Isaiah* 42:1) for the sake of his vision of what it means to be human, that is, to have been created in the image of God.

———— ✳ ————

I should add that the divinization of Jesus attested to in the Nicene Creed and recited by millions of Christians every Sunday had its final seal of orthodoxy imprinted on it partly as the result of the struggle with Arianism, which denied it. Arius († *ca.* 335), a Lybian deacon, maintained that Jesus was just a human creature whose title as "son of God" was accorded to him as a mere courtesy. While some Christians did not see much of a problem with this formulation, others discerned in it a threat to the belief in the redemptive work of Jesus. For, as Athanasius (*ca.* 295–373) argued, if Jesus was not God from the beginning, he could not have communicated the divine grace to us. As the old Latin adage has it, *nemo dat quod not habet* ("you can't give what you don't have"): if he was not God, he could not save us. "He was not," Athanasius argued, "first man and then became God; but he was first God and then became man in order that he might better deify us (*theopoiese*)."[20]

The divinization of Jesus, begun during the decades after his death, culminated in the dogmas proclaimed by the ecumenical councils.

———— ✳ ————

[20] Athanasius, *Orat.* 1, 39.

I should also like to add that faith may be something entirely different from what I have hinted to above. It may have nothing to do with tenets and dogmas, creeds and professions of faith. Faith may be an opening of oneself to the mystery of the divine, an opening as simple as the blossoming of a rose. This is clear from the fact that faith is supposed to precede believing, as was mentioned above. Moreover, since faith is a grace of God, this grace connects the believer to God even before there is anything explicit to believe.

Furthermore, from this point of view, it could be legitimate to engage in study and research and to seek to understand before believing (the reverse of the Anselmian formula), because believing is not concerned with what one understands but with what lies beyond, in a realm where understanding is totally irrelevant. In this instance, one seeks to understand as much as possible of the dogmas and statements pertaining to one's tradition in a straightforward pursuit of the truth, with respect for but without subservience to established dogma, because one's faith is not really concerned with those tenets and creeds but with the *one* who stands beyond all the creeds of the world. One seeks to understand everything that is said about *him*, because one cares for *him*, but in the end, one simply moves ahead to love, because what one is truly interested in is *him*. This is the profound understanding that flourishes at the end of Dante's *Paradiso*, where, after all the theological and ethical considerations of the previous two books, the mind fails, even in poetry, but the soul still moves on toward the *one* simply "impelled by love," the love that makes the world go round.[21]

Confirmation of this view of faith is ready at hand. In *1 Corinthians* 13:13, Paul asserts that the trio faith, hope, and charity, remains (forever), and that the greater (= greatest) of them is love. If faith were a matter of believing what is paradoxical and unexplainable here and now, then clearly faith would not remain once everything is explained (*1 Corinthians* 13:12); so faith must be something more, so that it can remain even in heaven. Faith, then, is what unites us to God. It is the opening of a channel before any communication

---

[21] Dante, *Commedia*, "Paradiso," XXXIII, 142.

come through it; it is the switching on of a line to the divine. I knew an old bishop who rose every morning at four o'clock to pray—or, as he put it, to turn his radio on to the God station.[22]

Therefore, following Kierkegaard, I have come to understand that faith unlocks the doors to an undiscovered country wherein dwells the Divine Incognito (as Barth named God),[23] the Beloved. Faith is the link to the Unknowable Presence about which we stammeringly affirm our articles of belief. In truth, dogma tells us little about the divine, but whatever it tells links us to *it* beyond the very details of belief. These details, for whose truth we have killed millions of people, are truly secondary, for what is most important is the connection with the divine opened to us in the act of faith. As a blind person comes to see by touching, we come to know by believing,[24] but what we know is not primarily the tenets of faith, but the unfathomable beyond all utterances, the indescribable behind all descriptions, toward whom we speed ardently in love along the tracks laid down by faith. Faith, truly, is like a wormhole between our human/ earthly dimension and that of the divine. In faith, blind acrobats hurtling through circus heights, we somersault into the outstretched hands of the beloved whose presence we sense and whose allure we feel, but whom we cannot see. This was the fate of Psyche, the beautiful maiden whose lover, the divine Eros, came to her in the midst

---

[22] Augustine reads *1 Corinthians* 13:13 differently in *De perfect. just. hom.* 8, 19; ML 44, 300. This is because he misreads the passage, which in the Latin translation has a different meaning from the original Greek. So, on strictly philosophical grounds, he claims that heaven is the full revelation of what we believe and hope here on earth: "It belongs to the act of faith to believe what is not yet seen, and the reward of faith is, precisely, to see what you believe" (*Sermo* 43, 1; ML 38, 254).

[23] Karl Barth, *The Epistle to the Romans* (London: Oxford University Press, 1933), I, 16, p. 39.

[24] *Contra* St. Anselm, *Proslogium*, Ch. I: "I believe in order to understand; for this also I believe, that unless I believe, I shall not understand." The same idea in St. Augustine's *In Ioannis Evangel.*, tract. 29, 6; ML 35, 1630. See also Karl Barth, *Fides quaerens intellectum: Anselms Bewis der Existenz Gottes* (Munich: Kaiser Verlag, 1931). For a further elaboration of this view of faith, see Ignacio L. Götz, *Faith, Humor, and Paradox* (Westport, CT: Praeger, 2002).

of blackest night so that she heard his manly voice murmuring sweet nothings, felt his warm caresses, but was not permitted to gaze on his wondrous beauty—and therefore was ignorant of his true nature.[25] But behind that ignorance blossomed a love stronger than all the trials and tribulations of life.

—⟶⟨⟩◀—

To conclude: the relation between faith and reason, or revelation and reason, has been the subject of protracted debate over centuries of Christianity.[26] The burden has been to justify the *fact* of revelation and thereby the *content* or *what* of it before the court of reason. I believe this is a misplaced effort. As Kant proved, and as subsequent scientific inquiry has confirmed, no knowledge of God in Godself is possible because we are always and invariably confronted by prior knowledge of appearances or phenomena, which are impossible to penetrate. Many theologians still function as if Kant, Gödel, and Heisenberg had not existed, and they continue to practice their hermeneutic arts in total disregard of the contrary evidence. But the simple solution to the search for divine, or divinely revealed truth, is to accept it all as paradox, and to use paradox as a springboard for mystical contemplation.

---

[25] This marvelous story by Apuleius contains many levels of meaning, one of which, surely, reflects the ancient belief that no mortal could see God and live. This was the answer YHWH gave to Moses (*Exodus* 33:20) and to Elijah (*1 Kings* 19:10–13), and Krishna gave Arjuna (*Bhagavadgītā* XI). Psyche did eventually see Eros, and she was severely punished as a result, though she did not die, perhaps because she only saw the mortal shape of her immortal lover.

[26] Among many citations, see Emilio Brito, *De Dieu: Connaissance et inconnaissance* (Leuven: Peeters, 2018). Also William J. Abraham, "Divine Revelation," in Christopher C. Green and David I. Starling, eds., *Revelation and Reason in Christian Theology* (Bellingham, WA: Lexham Press, 2018).

# Esoteric Escapes

The death of Caesar on the Ides of March, 44 BCE, led to the formation of the second triumvirate consisting of Antony, Lepidus, and
Caius Octavian (who was only a teenager at the time). The conspir-
ators were defeated at Philippi in 42, with Cassius and Brutus com-
mitting suicide. The Empire was then divided: Lepidus took Africa,
Octavian the West, and Antony took Egypt and Cleopatra for wife.
But this state of affairs did not last. Lepidus was removed from the
triumvirate in 37, and Octavian defeated Antony and Cleopatra at
the battle of Actium in 31. Both killed themselves, Cleopatra in a
rather original way, coffined with poisonous asps. This victory left
Octavian in sole control of the Empire, which he ruled from 29 BCE
until his death in 14 CE. During these years he became "the Great
One," *Augustus*, the name by which he is commonly known. In his
short will and testament, he gloried that he had been reelected every
year for forty-three years, thus preserving at least the semblance of
republican government. But in fact, the elections were contrived, and
Rome had moved solidly into dictatorships that would last until the
final disintegration of the Empire.

Interestingly, Rome had gone through the cycles described by
Plato: from monarchy to oligarchy to democracy to dictatorship
and back to monarchy again. The emperors were kings, but they
could not be called so because of the oath taken by the founders of
the Republic upon the death of Lucretia, that anyone who called

himself king would be put to death.[1] So they chose the title of emperor (*imperator*[2]), commander in chief, for they were in effect the supreme commanders of the Roman armies, and their fate would often hinge upon their good relationship with the military.

—————✻—————

By this time—around the beginning of the Common Era—the Empire extended from England to Persia. Its population is estimated at some 100 million people, and the city of Rome itself boasted between 1 and 1½ million inhabitants.

The emperors had discovered that they could pretty much do what they liked as long as the people enjoyed plenty of food and entertainment, "bread and circus" (*panem et circenses*), a fare they provided in plenty. The theater of Pompey seated 17,000,[3] and that of Marcellus 20,000. The audience was kept cool by the evaporation of trickles of water running down the aisles, and occasionally they were sprayed with perfume. Both of these theaters were dwarfed by the Colosseum, which seated 50,000, and by the Circus Maximus, which accommodated 180,000 spectators. It must be remembered that the Colosseum housed an intricate underground complex of cells for prisoners and cages for wild animals to be used in the "spectacles," and that it could be filled with water so that naval battles might be fought in it.

The city of Rome boasted some 1,352 public swimming pools, 800 private baths, and 9 public ones. The "baths" were enormous edifices containing everything from exercise locations to steam rooms. Nero's accommodated 1,600 people in each shift, and Caracalla's and

---

[1] The fear that Caesar would have himself crowned king was one of the motives for the conspiracy that killed him. See Suetonius, *The Twelve Caesars*, "Caesar," 78–80.

[2] Addressing the emperors as "Caesar" became a custom after the death of Gaius Julius Caesar. "Caesar" was the surname of the Julian family.

[3] With characteristic cynicism, Tertullian remarked that Pompey was smaller only than his own theater (*Pompeius Magnus, solo theatro suo minor*) (*Spectac.* 10, 5).

Diocletian's 3,000 in each shift. There were shifts from sunrise to 1:00 p.m. for women, and from 2:00 to 8:00 p.m. for men. The amount of burning wood needed to produce steam for such facilities simply boggles the mind, but this was the price paid to keep the people satisfied.

The great prosperity of the people was made possible by heavy taxes levied against Rome's vanquished enemies, but also from its aristocracies. The bureaucracy needed to administer this machine was staggering.

It goes without saying that prosperity and bureaucracy were accompanied by great corruption. The public treasury was alternately full and empty depending on the recklessness or conservatism of the reigning emperor. Reign followed reign, terror followed terror, and moral turpitude was everywhere visible, even in the royal family. In fact, Caligula and Nero were models of impropriety and lewdness.[4]

The general decay of morals had disastrous social effects. Rome had a state religion, and the emperor was its chief priest who offi-ciated at the major religious festivals. These grew more and more extravagant as the empire extended itself into the first centuries of the Common Era, relegating the ordinary citizen to the periphery. Moreover, the knowledge that the officiant emperor was morally cor-rupt must have made participation repugnant. As this public area became more meaningless (and therefore empty), a vacuum was cre-ated for the growth of private worship.[5] Augustus made an effort to

---

[4] The best source for studying the moral decadence of the first century of the Empire is Suetonius's *The Twelve Caesars*, which contains individual lives of Caligula and Nero.

[5] In the US, there is no official or public religion. In fact, there is even an amendment to the Constitution that forbids the "establishment" of religion, that is, the creation of a state religion. This separation between church and state is taken as a strength of American democracy, but its obverse is the relegation of religion to the private sphere, where it then proliferates endlessly, creating divisions in the body politic not always easy to bridge and heal, as the recent presidential elections have shown. It remains to be seen whether the First Amendment's disestablishment clause will prove to be beneficial or eventually pernicious. In Rome, the divisions caused by the proliferation of religions was a major cause of the fall of the Empire.

stem the moral decay by banning Egyptian and Eastern cults (except Judaism), but the reprieve was short-lived. Zeus, emperor, and state became so far removed that the simple citizens felt alienated and filled with a certain acosmism, a sense of unbelonging. The vacuum of meaning, the rising individualism that resulted, the repudiation of the official religion, the reassertion of the East, the rising bureaucracy—all of these factors created a climate ripe for the appearance and multiplication of private cults and religious movements. These went beyond philosophy into mythology, and they were largely experiential or mystical.[6] A search thus developed among rich and poor alike for the secret bridge to meaning, the path to God. Caught in the wheels of fate and bureaucracy, the only way was to trust in an otherworldly deity. Moreover, the emerging religious sects were often connected with older religious forms practiced in remote parts of the Empire, and because of this, they offered to the ethnically displaced and those living in various diasporas a sense of belonging and home.

---

The age still produced outstanding thinkers like Seneca (5 BCE–65 CE), Epictetus (*ca.* 50–138 CE), Philo (*ca.* 25 BCE–40 CE), Marcus Aurelius (121–180), Tertullian (*ca.* 160–*ca.* 230) and Plotinus (205–270). The prevailing conditions still allowed the flourishing of philosophy, though philosophers were banished from Italy by Domitian in 90 or 93, and while Stoicism saw its heyday during these years, philosophy generally began to acquire a more mystical and otherworldly orientation.

Philo was a Jew living in Alexandria, which was slowly overtaking Athens as the intellectual capital of the ancient world. His main concern was in bringing Jewish revelation in accord with Greek thought, especially that of Plato. To this end he distinguished between the literal and the allegorical meanings of the Torah, believing that the latter form of exegesis would be more compatible with the abstrac-

---

[6] To them might be applied the words of Rabbi Moses of Burgos (*ca.* 1290), "The philosophers whose wisdom you praise end where we begin."

tions of Greek thought. Thus, for example, he saw *Genesis* as an allegory of the creation of intelligence and soul by God, together with the intelligible and the sensible, and he saw the Fall as the seduction of intelligence by the senses. Perhaps influenced by nascent Gnostic trends (and in turn contributing to them), he placed God in a realm far removed from the world, which therefore needed intermediaries to access the divinity. Thus the divine Logos was introduced as the rationality of the deity, responsible for divisions, limits, plans, and instrumentalities, but also as the mediator back to the godhead. Humans were created by God as creatures of intelligence and sense into whom God breathed his spirit (*pneuma*), which therefore is higher than the merely psychological psyche of philosophy.

This trend toward allegory and mysticism continued in Plotinus, perhaps the most difficult of the Greek philosophers. Born in Egypt, he went to Alexandria in his late twenties and studied with Ammonius Saccas for eleven years. At thirty-nine he traveled through the East, Persia, and Mesopotamia, and upon his return settled in Rome (245), where he taught until his death, probably of some illness akin to leprosy.

The details of Plotinus's life come to us from his secretary, Porphyry (233–*ca.* 304), who also edited his works, and who mounted one of most thorough attacks on Christianity. Through him we know that Plotinus "seemed to be ashamed of being in a body, and hence refused to tell anyone about his parents, his ancestry, or his country."[7] We also know that he was a terrible speller, and that his aim in life was the attainment of intimate union with God— which, Porphyry says, he attained four times during the seven years he was in Plotinus's service. His last words are reputed to have been, "Now I shall endeavor to make that which is divine in me rise up to that which is divine in the universe."

Plotinus developed a kind of rational mysticism that from then on will characterize Neoplatonism (the revival of Platonism but with a mystical tinge). Reason alone is divine, and the world evolves as reason contemplates itself. The structure is Platonic but, in some

---

[7]  Porphyry, *Life of Plotinus*, chapter 1.

ways, more concerned with the human place in it. He strenuously opposes Gnosticism, especially its dualism of matter and spirit as evil and good.[8] The mystical orientation he gave to Platonism made it much more appealing to Christianity, as can be seen in the influence it exerted on later Christian writers all the way to the Renaissance. On the other hand, its strict philosophical treatment made it at times difficult to isolate from the rest of Greek philosophy; Muslim writers of the eighth and ninth centuries will mistakenly refer to his work as "the theology of Aristotle"!

$$\text{---} \rightarrow\!\!\ast\!\!\ast \text{---}$$

The influence from the East came in the shape of cults, often referred to as Mystery Religions because of their similarities with the ancient Mysteries of the Great Goddess. And indeed, they tended to be Mother-Goddess oriented or at least to be cognizant of the feminine dimensions of the divine; to arise within a community of believers; to be open to all and sundry regardless of race or nationality (though the more localized ones attracted sectaries from the area); they were secretive and esoteric, requiring initiation rites and even an oath of secrecy, which accounts for the fact that our information on some of them is still sketchy. The initiation rites tended to symbolize patterns of death and rebirth, both in the mythological narratives of the central figures of the cults as well as in the specific ritual practices. They were purificatory in the sense that they involved a cleansing from previous lifestyles; they included the delivery of secret doctrines, texts, and experiences;[9] they often culminated in some vision or ecstatic moment that was taken to mean that the initiate was "born again" and that salvation had been attained.[10]

There were many of these mystery religions, and although most of them found their way to Rome where they counted often with

---

8  *Ennead* II, 9.
9  See Marvin W. Meyer, ed., *The Ancient Mysteries: A Sourcebook* (New York: Harper & Row, 1987), p. 10; Plato, *Symposium* 211C.
10  Meyer, pp. 8–9.

a substantial number of adherents, they were also celebrated in the provinces, especially in the places where they had originated. The most famous ones were the Eleusian Mysteries, dating back to the celebrations in honor of Demeter and Persephone at Eleusis, west of Athens. The Orphic ones combined celebrations of the Orpheus myth with those of Dionysus-Zagreus. Isis and Osiris had their followers, and not exclusively among Egyptians. Attis, originally a god of vegetation, had been so devoted to the goddess Kybele that he had castrated himself under a pine tree in fear of being unfaithful to her. Violets had sprung from the droplets of his blood. He was remembered every year in his death, mourned by his followers, and celebrated by his priests who castrated themselves during the public parades of the Hilaria in March, flinging their severed organs as a blessing to the houses along the streets through which the procession passed.

As the Empire decentered itself politically and moved its center to the East, the cult of Mithras acquired importance. Mithras was an Indo-Iranian god, the creator of light,[11] and therefore of life, for without light, there cannot be life. The bull was the symbol of his worship, and the slaying of the sacrificial bull (*taurobolium*) whose blood was drunk and whose meat was eaten was a powerful ritual even in towns such as Tarsus, where Paul was born. The worship of Mithras was a favorite among the Roman legions, for this was a supermasculine religion open only to men and boys. It will be remembered that Maxentius's troops went to battle against Constantine swinging over their heads the standards of Mithras.

But perhaps the most important and lasting of the esoteric religions were the various Gnostic sects that sprang up among Jews, Pagans[12] and Christians, remnants of which have endured till today

---

[11] See *Avesta*, Yasht X.
[12] See Prudence Jones and Nigel Pennick, *A History of Pagan Europe* (London: Routledge, 1995), pp. 1–4. On Gnosticism, among many excellent studies, see Hans Jonas, *The Gnostic Religion* (Boston: Beacon Press, 1967); Antonio Orbe, *Estudios valentinianos* (Rome: Gregorian University, 1958–1966); Giovanni Filoramo, *A History of Gnosticism* (Oxford: Blackwell, 1990); Robert M. Grant, *Gnosticism and Early Christianity*, 2nd ed. (New York: Columbia University

in the Kabbalah, in Theosophy and Anthroposophy, in the Cathari pockets in southwestern France and Canada, and among present-day Mandaeans in Iraq.

Gnosticism is the common label applied to a variety of movements that incorporated elements from the Mystery religions, from Christianity and Judaism, from Zoroastrianism, and probably from Jainism. The label is often applied indiscriminately, but it is still somewhat useful, so I have kept it. What follows is a very simplified version of this religion.

Zoroaster (Zarathustra) (either 628–551 BCE or 660–583 BCE) was a priest and prophet who, driven from his own people, settled in the realm of King Vistaspa, ruler of Eastern Iran. His god was Ahura Mazdah (Ormuzd), creator of spirit, who, at the dawn of the world, had chosen good, while his counterpart, Ahriman, creator of matter, had chosen evil. Spirit was good, therefore, and matter evil, and people were hard put to choose between the two. This moral dualism became typical of sects influenced by Gnosticism.

Gnosticism generally centered around *gnosis*, the special, mystical knowledge promised the initiates: knowledge of the secrets of existence enshrined in their myths; knowledge of the complex theologies developed over time by each new leader (Marcion, Valentinus, Mani, to name a few[13]); knowledge of the way back to pure spirit

---

Press, 1966); Gershom Scholem, *Jewish Gnosticism, Merkabah Mysticism, and Talmudic Tradition* (New York: Jewish Theological Seminary of America, 1960); Karen L. King, *What Is Gnosticism?* (Cambridge, MA: Harvard University Press, 2003); and Willis Barnstone, "The Inner Light of Gnosis," in Willis Barnstone and Marvin Meyer, eds., *The Gnostic Bible* (Boston: Shambhala, 2003), pp. 765–799.

[13] Among the many minor figures of Gnosticism, Simon Magus occupies an interesting place. According to *Acts* 8:9–24, he saw the healing power of the Apostles as a possible source of money; he was a magician, always on the lookout for newer and more effective tricks, and so he asked the Apostles to sell him the secret of their power—a sin since called "simony."

Simon traveled with a woman named Helen (or Selene, the moon goddess), whom, in proper Gnostic fashion, he called Ennoia, and who, he claimed, was a reincarnation of Helen of Troy as well as of the heavenly Ennoia. He himself claimed to be an incarnation of God. This Ennoia had become a prostitute in

after the prevarication of spirit into matter (or after the "fall" of spirit into matter); and finally (in some sects) knowledge of the rituals and sacraments. According to Irenaeus's account of the Valentinians, "Perfect salvation is the cognition itself of the ineffable greatness."[14]

For whatever reason, the Gnostics had an almost existential sense of the alienation of people in the world.[15] They had, wrote Bultmann, "a sense of the radical otherness of man, of his loneliness in the world."[16] They believed that God was totally transcendent; in fact, he was defined as the "not-world"; therefore this world was not divine, but radically different and separate from God; and it was not destined to be saved—in fact, it was the enemy of salvation.

If God is "No-thing," then the strict adherent must in turn be "no-thing"; that is, not identified with any country, group, language, religion. Human individuality was acknowledged and fostered. Moreover, it was believed that the norms and rules of "the world" did not apply to those who were enlightened, who "knew," who were spiritual (*pneumatikoi*) and had preferred spirit to the flesh (*sarx*). In fact, the "spirituals" could not be soiled by deeds involving the material, because by their radical choice of spirit they had isolated their selves from evil matter, so that material deeds—such as sex—did not affect them anymore.[17]

---

Tyre, and he claimed to have come down for her salvation, and in hers, that of the whole world. See Hans Jonas, *The Gnostic Religion*, 2nd ed. (Boston: Beacon Press, 1963), p. 107.

Simon was nicknamed *Faustus* ("the Lucky One") by the Romans for his daring magical escapes, which he performed until a cable he was using for a flying trick snapped and he fell to his death.
In him, part of the Faust legend seems to originate.
[14] Irenaeus, *Adversus Haereses* I, 21, 4.
[15] Jonas, *The Gnostic Religion*, p. 320 *ff.*
[16] Rudolf Bultmann, *Primitive Christianity in Its Contemporary Setting* (New York: Meridian, 1957).
[17] Echoes of this belief are to be found in Paul's epistles; for example, *1 Corinthians* 2:14 and 15:44. Obviously, such beliefs were strenuously attacked by nascent orthodox Christianity. Irenaeus's book *Adversus Haereses* is principally devoted to an attack on Gnostic beliefs and practices.

This doctrine is very similar to the spirituality commended by Krishna in the *Bhagavadgītā* as "karma yoga," the yoga of action without attachment to the

Each Gnostic sect produced an elaborate mythology designed to explain how spirit had come to be trapped in matter, how light had come to be linked with darkness, and how deliverance was to take place. Final redemption of spirit was to take place in an eschaton at the end of the world.

Jewish Gnosis gave rise to what is called *Merkabah* (that is, throne-chariot, from Ezekiel's vision in chapter 1) mysticism. Its great exponents were Rabbi Akiba (40–138), the main spokesman in the *Lesser Hekhaloth*; Rabbi Ishmael (flourished *ca.* first century), speaker of the *Greater Hekhaloth*; and Johannan ben Zakhai (flourished *ca.* 100) and his disciples. Jewish Gnosticism gave rise to the *Kabbalah* and culminated in the *Sefer ha-Zohar*, the "Book of Splendor," written by Moses ben Shemtob de León between 1280 and 1286.

Christian gnosis endured despite the strenuous attacks from the hierarchy. It distinguished itself by its mystical and allegorical understanding of the Scriptures. As Clement of Alexandria wrote, "Gnosis is the knowledge of the Name and the understanding of the Gospel."[18] It emphasized the need for "conversion" (*metanoia*) in order to understand the unity of all humankind in the spirit of God, who is both male and female, and as such it preserves best the social message of Jesus—one more reason it was damned as heterodox.

It was not easy for Christianity to get rid of Gnosticism; therefore, many of the early Christian Fathers adopted an orthodox form of *gnosis*, claiming that theirs was the only true one. Thus Justin Martyr (100–165), Origen (185–254), Clement of Alexandria (†215), and Irenaeus (125–202) saw themselves a proponents of this "true gnosis." Irenaeus claimed that it was the apostles who had received the only true mysteries: "If the Apostles had known any hidden mysteries which they taught to the perfect apart and in secret, they would have transmitted them to the very leaders to whom they entrusted

---

fruits of action. This doctrine itself is grounded on the belief that the Brahman-Atman, the Supreme Self of which we are all scintilla, is not really enmeshed in the world, and therefore does not act in it.

[18] *Stromata* IV. iv. 15.

the Church." As for the rest, he claimed, "Let us not be embarrassed because God has reserved for himself things that are beyond us."[19]

———⟶⟨⟩⟵———

Gnosticism is important for many reasons. First, it preserves the tradition of the femininity of the deity, a tradition going back to the Goddess worship of the Neolithic and later times. Even though occasionally the feminine is described in an unfavorable light, the very mention of it maintains the tradition alive so that it can be handed down to subsequent generations. The ambiguity of the picture is captured, perhaps, in this hymn:

> I am…the honored one and the scorned one
> I am the whore and the holy one
> I am the wife and the virgin
> I am the mother and the daughter
> I am the members of my mother…
> I am the bride and the bridegroom,
> and it is my husband who begot me
> I am the mother of my father and the sister
> of my husband,
> and he is my offspring.[20]

Many of the Gnostic leaders were women. In fact, part of the struggle within the early Christian Church may have had to do with the sharing of power, something the male leadership was unable to do.[21] Moreover, Gnostic writings are a most important source for our understanding of the doctrinal changes taking place within the Judeo-Christian community during the decades following Jesus's

---

[19] Irenaeus, *Adversus Haereses* II. 2 and 39.

[20] *The Thunder, Perfect Mind*, in James M. Robinson, ed., *The Nag Hammadi Library* (New York: Harper & Row, 1981), pp. 271–272.

[21] See John A. Phillips, *Eve: The History of an Idea* (New York: Harper & Row, 1984), p. 162.

death. Even though rejected by the orthodox hierarchy, they are a window into a most important past in the history of Christianity.

Second, Gnosticism explicitly envisaged the deity as male-female and gave expression to this belief in numerous ways: the Unspeakable (*En-Sof*) and its Presence (*Shekinah*), Mind (*nous* [m.]) and Thought (*epinoia* [f.]), to name but a few.[22] Even the notion of the "Eternal Feminine" finds its expression in the *Zohar* I. 228b and in Dante, in Kabbalist writings, and eventually in Goethe and Hesse.

Third, the notion that matter is evil and that therefore any material activity is also evil, led to the view that sexuality is evil, since it is physical or material. Moreover, spiritual leaders counseled all men and women to become "male," that is, to avoid conception by having "spiritual marriages," giving up sexual desire as material and, therefore, evil, and striving for the realization of androgyny.[23]

Fourth, Gnosticism emphasized the importance of the individual self at a time when the masses threatened to engulf every individual. It took many centuries for this emphasis to bear fruit, but it eventually did in the eleventh century when the troubadours and mystics of the Languedoc sang the exploits of individuals in their spiritual quests in epics like the search for the Holy Grail.

Finally, Gnosticism, in the same manner as the other religions and sects that sprang up during the early centuries of the Empire, represents a sort of escape from the anguishing reality and disintegration prevalent at the time. Faced with a similar breakup of the traditional sources of identity, city states and their armies, the Greeks of the Hellenistic period had turned to education as a way of sustaining their identity. If the group was no longer available, at least the Greek language and Greek philosophy and education could identify one as Greek. During the beginning of the breakup of the Roman Empire, its citizens took a more esoteric way out to identity, the unity of the religious sect and its beliefs.

---

[22] See Jonas, *The Gnostic Religion*, p. 105.
[23] Phillips, p. 166–167. The words "male" and "female" are not to be taken literally as meaning gender, but as referring to what is human and divine.

But in the long run, such a search for identity and belonging proved to be countercultural. It turned religion into a source of disunity, each sect looking after its own and endeavoring to persevere by itself. After Christianity became predominant, religious disagreements led to fratricidal wars (as they still do), and thus one more factor was introduced into the political fabric that would eventually contribute to the breakdown of the Empire. Whether or not the current multiplicity of religious sects in the West will lead to a similar disintegration is a matter for conjecture and speculation.

———— ✶ ————

In our own day, the Evangelical community has devised a distinctive escape[24] in the fanatical adherence to beliefs that deny the facts of science. This escape is as religious as the ancient ones described above, for it invokes the Bible as justification, and it survives only among members of the same religious group.

There is nothing more shamefully escapist than the vaunted ignorance of the facts of evolution. Denying evolution is like denying one had parents. A visit to any great museum of natural history would disabuse anyone of the view that evolution is a belief. Evolution is a *fact* visible in the many specimens that crowd the halls of these museums.

The ancient Greeks themselves, who possessed fossils found while digging in their mines, already knew that species evolve through time. They began a patient accumulation of data, most of it, together with thousands of parchments and manuscripts, unfortunately destroyed by Christian fundamentalists rioting in Alexandria. The Barbarians finished whatever the rioters had left. The Greeks, however, had not developed a theory to explain why and how evolution took place, even though Empedocles (484–424 BCE) had come up with a primitive version of natural selection. Also, they had no

---

[24] On the Evangelical refusal of science by clinging to the Bible as an escape, see Walter Kaufmann, *Without Guilt and Justice* (New York: Dell Publishing Co., 1973), and Erich Fromm, *Escape from Freedom* (New York: Rinehart, 1941).

fossil evidence that evolution had produced the human species. But in the fourteenth century, scholars like Ibn Khaldûn (1332–1406) had speculated that "the higher stage of man is reached from the world of the monkeys."[25] Four centuries later, Buffon (1707–1788) and Lamarck (1744–1829) proposed the theory that evolution had taken place through the transmission of acquired characteristics bequeathed to successive generations. A while later, and writing independently of each other and in different parts of the world, Charles Darwin (1809–1882) and Alfred Russel Wallace (1823–1913) came up with the notion of random selection of those members best fitted to survive in their environments. Ernst Haeckel (1834–1919) in Germany and Thomas Huxley (1825–1895) in England cemented the findings of their contemporaries. This is what the *theory* of evolution is about: a plausible explanation, based on painstaking research, of the *facts* of evolution known since antiquity.

While Darwin and Wallace were presenting the results of their research in England, the Roman Catholic monk Gregor Mendel (1822–1884) was conducting his experiments in the garden of his monastery of Brünn, in Moravia. This novel understanding of genetics further clarified and buttressed the theory of evolution. The discovery of DNA by Watson (1928–) and Crick (1916–2004) in the twentieth century completed the genetic picture.

At this point, the *facts* of evolution are not questionable; the *theory*, like all scientific theories, is, though it would be rash to do so given the experimental research behind it. But *Genesis 1–2* is *not* a scientific theory that might be substituted for it—certainly not any more than the *Enuma Elish* (the ancient Mesopotamian creation story), or the *Theogony* (the ancient Greek creation account), or the *Qur'ân* (the Islamic version of creation). They are not scientific theo-

---

[25] Ibn Khaldûn, *The Muqaddimah*, trans. Franz Rosenthal (Princeton, NJ: Princeton University Press, 1967), book 1, chapter 1, "Sixth Prefatory Discussion," p. 75.

ries because their statements regarding the origin of the world are not subject to empirical and independent verification.[26]

———✺———

Recently I heard an Evangelical minister say on TV that he could not understand how a Christian could believe in the theory of evolution. I was surprised. I learned how to put together Christianity and evolution when I was in sixth grade in the Third World country of Venezuela. I had an excellent science teacher, a Jesuit who was able to explain clearly why the data of science and the beliefs of religion need not repel each other.

The essence of the *Genesis* story is that God is "in the beginning." The details are secondary. After all, as God told Job (*Job* 38:4), none of us were there when the heavens and the earth came to be. How could we prove, then, that God did not create the world to evolve? How can we assert that he did not infuse a human soul into a ready primate much as *Genesis* 2:7 says he did into a lump of clay? And if one were to answer that Scripture says otherwise than Darwin, on what grounds could one prefer the *Bible* to the *Theogony* or to the *Qur'ân*?

The Evangelical escape into the safety of Scripture is but an avoidance of the responsibility that comes with knowledge, and of the *angst* that accompanies it. Better not to know, they seem to say, than to be filled with anguish. But in ancient times the Valentinians had already understood that if anguish is not fought, it can become dense

---

[26] Evangelicals keen on introducing religion into science have sought to substitute the *Genesis* account of creation for the theory of evolution. But *Genesis* is not science. If they were really interested in a more inclusive perspective, they could have gone to A. R. Wallace, who preferred a "guided" evolution over Darwin's random selection. They could also invoke the "anthropic principle," which claims that if the universe were different, we would not be here to perceive it. But even Wallace's views are influenced by religion. So are those of Teilhard de Chardin (1881–1955), the Jesuit paleontologist who proposed a view of evolution guided by a God who has become incarnate in it. These views are interesting and worth discussing, but *not* in a science course.

like a fog, and it can then engender error.[27] This is what has happened among devout Evangelicals and Fundamentalists, who have been led into all manner of obscurantist and unscientific positions because they have refused to countenance the anguish that comes with knowing; even though Jesus himself, while acknowledging that true seeking would engender anguish, added that after the anguish would come amazement (*Gospel of Thomas* 3).

God is a God of knowledge (*1 Samuel* 2:3). Concern about anguish should not stop us from learning, especially since Jesus promised that knowing the truth will set us free (*John* 8:32). To paraphrase Wiesel, people are defined by what troubles them, not by what reassures them.[28]

───✦───

There is a danger in holding on to beliefs against all manner of reason and empirical evidence simply because they are found in the Bible. This danger is made most clear in a story from the Babylonian Talmud, *Hagigah* 14b. The book of *Genesis* 1:6–8 describes the creation of the heavens as a kind of dome to separate the waters above it from the waters below—something like the creation of a living space in the bottom of the ocean by the erection of a glass bubble. The implication was, of course, that there was water above the firmament (that is why rain came down from it!), and since Paradise was above the firmament, it was reasonably assumed that Paradise was watery. Against this background, we have the simple story of the Talmud:

> Four men ascended into Paradise, Ben Azzai, Ben Zoma, Acher [Elisha ben Abuyah], and Rabbi Akiba. Rabbi Akiba said to them: "When you arrive at the stones of pure marble do not exclaim, 'Water! Water!' for it is written, 'He

---

[27] *Gospel of Truth* 17, 10–16, in Robinson, ed., *The Nag Hammadi Library*, p. 38.
[28] Elie Wiesel, *All Rivers Run to the Sea: Memoirs* (New York: Knopf, 1995), p. 124.

that tells lies will not tarry in my sight'" [*Psalm 101:7*].

> Ben Azzai gazed and died. Ben Zoma gazed and became demented. Acher cut the plants [that is, lost his faith]. Rabbi Akiba departed in peace.

Rabbi Akiba ben Yoseph (early second century CE) knew that one must not take the *Genesis* passage literally: heaven is not water. He warned his friends that such a literal belief was a lie, but they did not listen to him. So, when they came face-to-face with the divine reality, which was entirely different from what *Genesis* had implied, one died, one went crazy, one lost his faith. Only Rabbi Akiba, who combined knowledge and belief, retained his faith and his peace.

———— ✳ ————

Faith is not *ever* a substitute for knowledge. We do not have faith simply because we cannot have knowledge. As St. Anselm elucidated, faith does not explain knowledge for the simple reason that it abides in a different realm, though faith does help us comprehend the entire range of understanding that extends from opinion to belief: without faith, the human spectrum of knowing is incomplete.[29] But faith is nowhere a substitute for knowledge. It is a rank or step or state above or beyond knowledge. Faith breaks out above us when the clouds of knowing and unknowing are surpassed and diaphanous skies lie infinitely open before of us.

When people have questions, it is *not* appropriate ever to say, "Never mind. Believe!"

---

[29] Anselm of Canterbury, *Proslogium*, 1.

# AFTERWORD

*Nothing is true that forces one to exclude.*
—Albert Camus

The religious literature of the East and the West is replete with stories and comments on "seeing." John Ruskin wrote once that "the greatest thing a human soul ever does in this world is *see* something... to see clearly is poetry, prophesy, and religion,—all in one."[1] This is the primary concern of Zen, of Buddhism and Hinduism (especially the Vedanta), of Platonism and its successors, of Judaism and Islam, and of Christianity in its many forms. The Hindu *Vedas* contained those things "seen" (from Sanskrit *ved*, "to see or know," akin to Greek *oida*, past-perfect of *eidô*, "to see," and to Latin *video*). Plato developed his "Allegory of the Cave" as an example of how we can become enlightened,[2] and he suggested that the role of the true teacher is not to put knowledge into those who do not have it, but in knowing how to turn the soul in the right direction so that it itself should come to see.[3] St. Augustine, who was a Neoplatonist at the time of his conversion, adds:

> If wisdom and truth are not desired with one's whole strength, they cannot, in any way, be found. But if they are sought after as they should,

---

[1] John Ruskin, *Modern Painters III* (Chicago & New York: Bedford, Clarke and Co., 1873), p. 286.
[2] Plato, *Republic* VII. 514A.
[3] Plato, *Republic* VII. 518.

they cannot hide or withhold themselves from their lovers… By love desire is kindled, by love the search takes place, love knocks at the door, by love the revelation takes place, and in love, finally, one dwells on that which has been revealed.[4]

And this is the condition that St. Augustine believes will characterize eternal life in Paradise: "There we will rest and see, see and love, love and praise. This will be in the end without end. For what other end do we propose to ourselves than to dwell in that Kingdom of which there is no end?"[5]

But in today's world, many teachers block the vision of truth with fear and threats of damnation. Some Evangelicals forbid their followers to read books like the Harry Potter and the Lord of the Rings series, prompted by God-knows-what qualms, in effect blinding them to the multifaceted truth of Jesus, afraid that his truth would set them free (*John* 8:32) with the result that they would no longer be subservient to the ignorant whims of their leaders.

---

Why is this so? Why are Fundamentalists and Evangelicals so adamantly opposed to learning? Fundamentalists are spiritually illiterate. This condition is caused by failure to grow up morally and religiously. Research shows that it is possible—indeed, *very* common—for people to get stuck at certain developmental stages in life from which they fail to move on. According to St. Paul, we all are expected to outgrow childish speech, outlook, and thinking as the years pass (*1 Corinthians* 13:11), and to adopt the stance of a mature faith. Fundamentalists and Evangelicals come up short in that they, as they grow up in age, continue to believe in ways that are appropriate to children. Their faith continues to be defined by their church groups, however big or small these be, long after

---

[4]  St. Augustine, *De mor. Eccl. cath.* I, 17, 31; ML 32, 1324.
[5]  St. Augustine, *De civ. Dei* XXII 30, 5; ML 41, 904.

they should be thinking independently, and they do not take personal responsibility for their beliefs. These beliefs remain generally unexamined, a condition achieved by the rejection of scholarship and, simultaneously, by their blind allegiance to the Bible as interpreted by their ministers, many of whom are poorly trained and have an obvious interest in maintaining their congregations' lack of informed knowledge. Emotion, in the form of fervor and devotional effusion, often whipped up by popular music, helps them to avoid intellectual self-criticism: nothing is more convincing than a heart that has been strangely warmed! Critical reflection figures nowhere in this landscape, and this in itself ought to be an indication that something is not right.

Whenever authority is preferred, whether that of the Bible or other religious scriptures, or of a person, preacher, priest, or pope, and reason and argument are downplayed or peremptorily rejected when they conflict with authority, the seeds are being sown of a weed that stifles every shrub and flower-bearing plant. This weed is authoritarianism. Years ago Piaget concluded that reciprocity is the only soil where moral and religious autonomy can grow,[6] because reciprocity allows for reason and argument, while authority eschews both; but Fundamentalist upbringing, whether in the home, the sectarian school, or the church, is typically authoritarian, concerned as it is with conformity, not autonomy. In this it is most unchristian, since Jesus explicitly stated that the truth, the object of all learning, would set us free, not bind us (*John* 8:32). No Christian should be afraid of the truth.

Now, just as the condition of spiritual illiteracy is caused by authoritarianism, it can be cured by open-minded literacy. However, it is extremely difficult to break out of this pattern of authoritarian upbringing, unless a dramatic event were to take place that would wake people up from their complacent comfort and propel them unto the freedom of the spirit Jesus preached and promised to his

---

[6]  Jean Piaget, *The Moral Judgment of the Child* (New York: The Free Press, 1965), p. 196; Jürgen Habermas, *Communication and the Evolution of Society* (Boston: Beacon Press, 1979), p. 88.

true followers. Such an event was the Scopes Trial, but its salutary effects have been superseded and no longer hold ignorance in check. Even the recent scandals among some of the Evangelical clergy and the several rebukes by the academic communities and by the courts have been explained away, and we look in vain for a cataclysm that will shake the Fundamentalist church to its foundation and expose the weakness of its edifice.

———⋗⋆⋖———

The Fundamentalist condition is not unique. Toward the end of the nineteenth century, the Theosophical Society was excited by the expectation that the Lord Maitreya, the World Teacher, would appear again soon in mortal garb as he had done before in the shape of Sri Krishna, of Buddha, and of Jesus. The leaders of the Society, Annie Besant and C. W. Leadbeater, were on the lookout for young boys who might show any signs of being the chosen vessel for the appearance of the great master. Some children were provisionally singled out and then abandoned, especially when, in 1909, Leadbeater spotted Jiddu Krishnamurti in Adyar, near Madras, India, one of the Society's major centers. Krishnamurti was then fourteen years of age, the son of a local Brahmin who had belonged to the Society since 1881.

Young Krishnamurti was taken to England and educated in the best schools and universities. He and his entourage were given full access to the Society's centers in England, America, The Netherlands, and India, and all the resources of the organization were placed at his disposal. As he grew up in years, he did also in wisdom and spirituality, and people around him became more and more expectant of the time when he would make his big announcement to the world and reveal himself as the expected World Teacher.

This is why there was great expectation when Krishnamurti prepared to speak at the Society's summer Camp at Ommen, the Netherlands, on August 2, 1929. But to the consternation of all,

Krishnamurti did not declare himself to be the expected teacher. Instead, he said:

> Truth is a pathless land... You cannot and must not organize it. If you do, it becomes dead, crystallized... This is what everyone throughout the world is attempting to do. Truth is narrowed down and made a plaything for those who are weak... If an organization is created for this purpose, it becomes a crutch, a weakness, a bondage, and must cripple the individual and prevent him from growing, from establishing his uniqueness, which lies in the discovery for himself of that absolute, unconditioned Truth... The moment you follow someone you cease to follow Truth.[7]

In accord with this belief, he declared that he was nobody's teacher and that he did not want to have disciples anymore because he did not want to stand in the way of anyone's spiritual development. Even though he continued to lecture widely to large audiences, he maintained this decision until the end of his days.

———✢✢✢———

Another thing. Some people may be apprehensive that the picture of Jesus presented in the preceding pages will entail a loss, real or imagined, of what Christianity has treasured for centuries. But the truth is that the old traditions need not be jettisoned simply because they are understood in a different light. The beautiful rituals that Christians have developed through the centuries must continue to inspire devotion and call forth dedication. The artistic achievements of Christianity need not be forgotten or downgraded. The musical gems, the literature, the architecture and paintings that various times

---

[7]  Mary Lutyens, *Krishnamurti*, 2 vols. (New York: Avon Books, 1975, 1983), vol. 1, pp. 293–294.

and cultures have produced need not be rejected. No achievements must be forgotten or bypassed. They are, after all, the fruits of the inspiration that fueled Christianity for two thousand years. So let me say, again, that none of this must be confined to the dustbin of history as no longer relevant simply because our faith has matured, as St. Paul said his had too (*1 Corinthians* 13:11). All this is part of us, of who we are in both East and West, and hopefully it will continue to inspire our children and our children's children for many generations still to come. The only thing we must give up is the fear of knowledge.

———✳———

In one of my college courses, I used to hold up to the class a set of puzzle rings. I would first show them the rings entwined, then I would disentangle them, and finally I would merge them together again. I would repeat this process in silence two or three times, making sure the three steps were clear. Then I would ask the class, "What is the difference between the first stage and the third stage?" Most of the time there was at least one student who would explain that in the first and the third stages, the rings were identically twined, but that by the third stage, we knew they could be disengaged and had actually gone through the process of untangling them and putting them back together again. Thus, there *was*, indeed, a difference, a cognitive and procedural difference, between the first and the third stage.

To apply this example to the case at hand: it is one thing to believe that Jesus is God because preachers say he said he was God, and quite another to believe that he is God *after* one has researched what the early church community believed when they called Jesus God. As with the example given above, there *is* a difference between belief in the first stage and in the third. The first belief is ignorant and naive; it is not faith at all because it has not pushed reason to the limits. The third belief is tenable without compromising scholarship or belief. What is the difference between the first and the third stages of belief? A process of untangling beliefs and traditions and of placing them in their historical contexts has taken place between the first and the third stage of belief, as a result of which the third stage of belief is quite different from the first. Consequently, if, after reading this book, you want to continue to believe that Jesus is the son of God, and that this is the best explanation of who Jesus was historically and in fact, your faith will be mature, and it will have been strengthened and enlightened.

————— ✻ —————

This is precisely what Marcus Borg does. As a scholar, he acknowledges the few facts of Jesus's life, what Jesus thought of himself and what his followers thought of him; and he distinguishes all this from what the Christian community subsequently thought of him, the story (the *mythos*) they told about him; and he accepts this story as a summary of his own belief in Jesus. He writes:

> [Jesus] was a flesh-and-blood, corpuscular and protoplasmic Galilean Jew; he weighed around 110 pounds and was a bit over five feet tall; he had to eat and sleep; he was born and died. *This* Jesus…is a figure of the past, dead and gone, nowhere anymore.[8]

Jesus did not think or speak of himself as "son of God" or "messiah," and he did not proclaim himself to be so. The Gospels report only what some of his followers thought and said of him after he died.[9] However, Borg thinks that "these affirmations are true. They are the post-Easter testimony of early Christian communities, and as a Christian I agree with them—this is who Jesus is for me."[10]

This confession comes after years of painstaking scholarly study, and differs *toto coelo* from the emotional preachings of Fundamentalists and the beliefs of ignorant Christians.

————— ✻ —————

[8]  Marcus J. Borg, *Jesus* (San Francisco, CA: HarperSanFrancisco, 2006), p. 44.
[9]  Ibid., pp. 47–48.
[10]  Ibid., p. 315, note 11.

You see, faith begins where reason ends. Reason is like a diving board, and faith is the leap divers take from its farthest edge. To believe before stepping up to the limits of reason is like attempting to dive from the middle of the diving board: the board will hit you hard as it rebounds.

How can one believe after confronting the results of scholarship and research? The answer is clearly yes: *because belief steps into the clearing that reason has contrived.*

Many years ago John Wisdom proposed a parable designed to gain perspective on disagreements regarding matters of fact interpreted in conflicting ways. The parable concerns two friends who return to their long neglected garden and, as they examine it, discover that some plants have prospered while others have been displaced by weeds. One of them assumes that a gardener has been taking care of the garden, but when they inquire of the neighbors, no one has seen him. They then construct various assumptions that he has worked at night quietly and noiselessly, and so forth. Moreover, they study everything they can find about gardens and what happens to them when they are left untended. In the end, they both know the same facts about their garden, and yet one still believes a gardener comes unseen and unheard while the other says there is no gardener. At this point, the gardener hypothesis has ceased to be experimental.[11]

One thing is definite about this story: both friends have exhausted everything that scholarship and research can tell them about gardens. They have pushed reason to the limits. Their positions, therefore, are not unreasonable, since they have looked at *all* reasons. They have thus entered the realm of belief, and only now are they truly justified in taking a leap.

I should add that it would be quite as reasonable to believe that Jesus was *not* the son of God, just as one of the friends continued to maintain that no one had come to take care of the garden. Why would one decide to believe that Jesus was just a human being, "the son of the man" (as he called himself)? Perhaps because

---

[11] John Wisdom, "Gods," in *Religion from Tolstoy to Camus*, ed. by Walter Kaufmann (New York: Harper Torchbooks, 1964), pp. 391–406.

of a strong commitment to historical truth, which suggests, as I have tried to show, that the divinity of Jesus was a later construct of the church. There may also be issues of consistency and fairness as well, for believing Jesus to be the son of God would involve commitment to the belief that Gilgamesh (the king of Uruk) was the son of the goddess Ninsun, that Aeneas (the Trojan prince) was the son of the goddess Aphrodite, that Achilles (the Greek hero) was the son of the gods Zeus and Thetis, that Dionysus (son of Zeus) was "the son of God," as he himself proclaimed publicly and demonstrated by miracles to the citizens of Thebes, and that Helen of Troy was the daughter of Zeus and Leda. It would not be fair to claim that one's beliefs are true while those of others are fake.

—————➤✤◄———

But I still must say a final word about the picture of Jesus that I hope has emerged in the preceding pages. Tertullian, the passionate second-century apologist of Christianity, argued against Marcion and his followers that Jesus was truly human, and as such, he was truly born, truly lived on earth, and truly died on the cross. He forgot about Jesus's Jewishness, but he did not consider the humanity of Jesus to be an impediment to his faith. In fact, he felt that those who denied the humanity of Jesus were minions of the Antichrist.[12] "I claim for myself Christ," he wrote, "I maintain for myself Jesus... whatever that poor despised body was, however he looked to the eye and felt to the touch. Be he inglorious, be he ignoble, be he dishonored, he shall be my Christ!"[13] And elsewhere he said, "I am safe if I be not ashamed of my Lord!"[14]

While not as extreme as the Marcionites and the ancient Docetists, many contemporary American Christians are willing to emphasize the divinity of Jesus even to the detriment or neglect of

---

[12] Tertullian, *De Carne Christi*, XXIV, 3, quoting *2 John 7* and by implication *1 John* 4:2–3.

[13] Tertullian, *Adversus Marcionem* III, 16 *ff*.

[14] Tertullian, *De Carne Christi*, V.

his humanity and, of course, his Jewishness. They would assert that Jesus was truly the son of God *incarnate*, but the stress would be placed on his divinity much more than on his life and his actions as a truly human being. It is almost as if they were ashamed of being the followers of a mere man, especially a Jew, the one who repeatedly called himself "the son-of-the-man," who lived and died in Palestine two thousand years ago. And yet, as Bonhoeffer wrote, "the Christian is not a *homo religiosus* ["a religious person"], but simply a human being as Jesus…was a human being."[15] Actually, no Christian is just "a human being" in the abstract but a concrete human—Peter, John, Mary, or whatever; and Jesus was not just "a human being," in the abstract, but quite concretely Jesus, a Jew.

This is the Jesus I have tried to present in this book, truly a good man who "went about doing good" (*Acts* 10:38) while trying his best to reproduce or incarnate in himself, and particularize, the image of humanity hidden in the sacred mystery of God. Even though nearly two thousand years separate us, I feel I can and must assert, with Tertullian, that I, too, will be safe if I be not ashamed of *him*, the Jew from Nazareth.

---

[15] Dietrich Bonhoeffer, *Das Zeugnis eines Boten*, ed. Visser 't Hooft (Geneva, 1945), pp. 46–47, quoted by G. Leibholz, "Memoir," in Dietrich Bonhoeffer, *The Cost of Discipleship* (New York: Macmillan, 1963), p. 24. I have altered the translation slightly to conform to current nonsexist language.

# Fundamentalism

*Absolute faith corrupts as absolutely*
*as absolute power.*
—Eric Hoffer

In 1895 a conference of Christian conservatives[1] met at Niagara Falls to discuss the perceived threat to their faith coming from Modernism, Darwinism, and what was being called "Form (or Text) Criticism," the scholarly study of the biblical texts. The threat, really, was to their ignorance, though they perceived it to be to their Christian faith. Millions of other Christians with sound and well-developed theological systems did not feel threatened but, rather, strengthened by such developments. At any rate, out of this meeting, a set of five fundamental beliefs was adopted that, according to the participants and thousands like them, defined the Christian faith. The five tenets were (1) the complete inspiration and literal inerrancy of the entire Bible, (2) the divinity of Jesus, (3) the virginal birth of Jesus, (4) substitutional atonement, and (5) the physical and bodily resurrection of Jesus. This was the official beginning of what we call Fundamentalism, though its spirit had been roving through the American countryside for more than a century.

---

[1] I dislike using this term because calling anyone, or any idea, "conservative" (or "liberal," for that matter) does not say anything about the truth of the views in question. The moniker implies that views have been researched impartially and the truth has been ascertained, but we do not really know if this is the case. See "A Note on Conservatives and Liberals."

Now, Fundamentalism is today the major obstacle to a clear understanding of Jesus and his message. As Seyyed Hossein Nasr explains, "Fundamentalism today refers to a literalism that came out of Protestant Christianity in the late nineteenth and early twentieth centuries *as a result* of the onslaught of another kind of fundamentalism, which is modernism."[2] But it should be pointed out again that only certain Protestant sects experienced modernism as an onslaught, those which did not have a solid theology and therefore felt vulnerable to the new views of science and scripture that were being propounded by modernism. Other "higher" Christian denominations encountered modernism and overcame its threat—if threat it was— and surpassed it in time. Many people, however, succumbed to their fears and latched on with incredible tenacity to those tenets of their faiths that seemed essential to them.

We call these people Fundamentalists, whether in Islam, Judaism, Hinduism, or Christianity. They do not exist only in other countries, as we often delude ourselves into thinking. They dwell among us—in fact, they are almost half of the American population. According to Karen Armstrong, Fundamentalists "have no time for democracy, pluralism, religious toleration, peace keeping, free speech, or the separation of church and state. Christian fundamentalists reject the discoveries of biology and physics about the origins of life and insist that the Book of Genesis is scientifically sound in every detail."[3] Already in 1934, Dewey had written:

The fundamentalist in religion is one whose beliefs in intellectual content have hardly been touched by scientific development. His notions about heaven and earth and man, as far as their

---

[2]  Seyyed Hossein Nasr, "The Sacred World of the Other," *Parabola* 30:4 (Winter 2005), p. 31. See also Edward Farley, "Fundamentalism: A Theory," *Cross Currents* 55, No. 3 (Fall 2005), pp. 378–403. The description of Fundamentalism here highlights its refusal of scholarship. For a more thorough account of it, see Martin Marty, ed., *Fundamentalism and Evangelicalism* (New York: K. G. Saur, 1993).

[3]  Karen Armstrong, *The Battle for God* (New York: Alfred A. Knopf, 2000), p. ix.

bearing on religion is concerned, are hardly more
affected by the work of Copernicus, Newton,
and Darwin than they are by that of Einstein.[4]

Fundamentalists stand to biblical scholars in the same relationship as Flat Earth Society members stand to geologists and geog-
raphers. They have, as Hofstadter puts it, a "generically prejudiced
mind."[5] One step more, and we enter the realm of fanaticism.

According to William James, fanaticism is "loyalty carried to a
convulsive extreme."[6] Eric Hoffer identifies fanaticism with blind
faith, the kind of faith that has no eyes to see the complex truth, for
that would be its demise; so all fanatics are willing to die basically
for the same thing, blotting out the truth. True believers are unwill-
ing to confront their own obscurity, religious or otherwise, for it is
themselves they seek under cover of religious bigotry. Fanatics cannot countenance the possibility of being wrong; therefore, they block
vehemently any and all ideas that might discomfit them. They label
these as liberal or conservative, democratic or republican, in a desperate effort to dull their impact as if by some incantatory magic. This
is their ploy. It is typical of fanatics that they try to win arguments by
shouting and sloganizing rather than by reasoning.

Fanaticism is not merely a matter of theoretical belief: fanatics pursue their ideas in utter disregard for the interests of others.
According to Hare, if "to have an ideal is *eo ipso* to have an interest in
its fulfilment [then] to make one's ideals override other people's interests is to make them override their ideals as well,"[7] and to do this
is to enter the realm of fanaticism. Now, Fundamentalists of every
kind enter this realm the moment they actively seek to impose their
ideals on students in the public schools and on society at large. In
fact, fanaticism has been called a terrorism of the mind, and though

---

[4]   John Dewey, *A Common Faith* (New Haven: Yale University Press, 1934), p. 63.
[5]   Hofstadter. *Anti-Intellectualism*, p. 133.
[6]   William James, *Varieties of Religious Experience* (New York: Mentor, 1964), p.
      265.
[7]   Richard Hare, *Freedom and Reason* (New York: Oxford University Press, 1965),
      p. 176.

it does not necessarily lead to overt violence, it does so whenever certain sociopolitical conditions exist and the appropriate leadership arises. This is the threat that fanaticism brings to our world, a threat that is important given the intimate connection between fanaticism and terrorism. Terrorism is fanaticism carried into violent action. It is an outburst born of feelings of impotence.

Many years ago, in India, I discovered a monkey in the pantry of the boarding school in which I was teaching. The pantry was a secure room. It had only one door, a very high ceiling, and a small, square window very high up the back wall, which made it impossible for anyone to gain access through it, so how the monkey came to be there, I never really found out.

The monkey I encountered was a big monkey, a rhesus (as they are called), and I obviously disturbed the feast he was having consuming the edibles stored there. The place was a mess. I left the room and returned quickly with a hockey stick, determined to beat the thief, but when it realized the threat, it jumped agilely and escaped through the high window, an unbelievable feat, but an understandable one considering the threat. Fundamentalists, I believe, react to the perceived threats from ideas as if their lives were in danger, and they make ready to defend them even by a recourse to violence.

Now, "violence," comments Anne Twitty, "argues (always) a lack of faith…that is less easily discerned, that arises among those who cling to 'faith.' Faith is defined precisely by texts and creeds and practices. A lack of faith in the ungraspable essence from which these texts and creeds and practices arose. A lack of faith in the realm of experience that is open to allusion, not to definition. A lack of faith in the as yet inchoate, uncreated what-is-to-come."[8]

———————

As I mentioned above, one of the basic dogmas of Fundamentalism is "substitutional atonement," namely, that Jesus redeemed us from our sins through his own death and resurrection.

---

[8]   Anne Twitty, "Lines in the Sand," *Parabola* 30: 4 (Winter 2005), p. 25.

This view of the work of Jesus, however, is the result of a later theology based primarily on Greek philosophical and theological concepts. It is not necessary to espouse this view in order to accept that Jesus "died for us." What he did was to show us how to die so that we ourselves would be able to die to our sins ourselves. Of course, this view puts salvation squarely on our shoulders, while the Fundamentalist one relegates the burden of salvation to Jesus. All one has to do is believe in Jesus, and that is it, one is saved; no work of self-mortification, of self-sacrifice, of endurance in the face of evil, and so on. "Substitutional atonement" makes Christianity "easy," the religion of the dispirited poor who have dropped off. Marcus Borg explains: "I don't think that Jesus literally died for our sins. I don't think he thought of his life and purpose that way; I don't think he thought of that as his divinely given vocation... But I do have faith in the cross as a trustworthy disclosure of the evil of domination systems, as the exposure of the defeat of the powers, as the revelation of the 'way' or 'path' of transformation, as the revelation of the depth of God's love for us, and as the proclamation of radical grace. I have faith in the cross as all of those things."[9]

"Substitutional atonement" is "easy faith," as Staal calls it, because it relies for salvation on someone else's work, not on our own hard effort.[10]

---

Another basic tenet of Fundamentalism is the literal inerrancy of scripture, whether Bible or *Qu'rân*, which consequently must be interpreted literally. But though Fundamentalists believe that by being literal they show reverence to "the word of God," they actually betray this very word, because "to reduce reality to the outward, or to the literal, or to the most external, is to destroy its depth, and its

---

[9] Marcus Borg, *The Heart of Christianity* (San Francisco: HarperCollins, 2004), p. 96.
[10] Frits Staal, *Exploring Mysticism* (Berkeley, CA: University of California Press, 1975), chapter 13.

height."[11] As Marcus Borg says, "There is always something missing in it,"[12] in the literalness. And he adds: "Fundamentalism is partial and superficial while claiming an artificial perfection."[13]

In being narrowly "literal," Fundamentalism betrays the letter, because the literal includes the cultural as it brings meanings and contexts to the letters that are used in the text. A narrow claim of literalness, therefore, is a betrayal of literalness. An example may be given. The *'ebd YHWH* ("servant of God") of Isaiah was translated by the Septuagint as *pais theou* ("child of God") and by the Vulgate as *filius Dei* ("son of God"), which was then read as "son of God" by the Gentile Christians, who therefore reinterpreted an early Judaeo-Christian theology and laid the foundation for the divinization of Jesus. "Son of God" meant for the Gentile Christians something quite different from what it means to us. Without knowing this, one cannot know why Jesus was called "the son of God."

As Patrick Laude says, "Fundamentalism could be characterized as a blind adherence to forms that imposes upon them the passional limitations of the individual ego—and the collective ego with which it identifies…[it] freezes the understanding of the 'letter' and worships this icy idol to the point of death."[14]

---

I should add that while I have pretty much lumped together all sorts of Fundamentalisms, Jewish, Christian, Hindu, and Muslim, there are marked differences among them. For one thing, Islamic Fundamentalism has taken hold among many college-educated youth who long for social justice and see in a return to primitive Islam a formula or scheme for redress. The Fundamentalism they seek is social, a return to what they, perhaps inaccurately, conceive as a pristine age in which the Prophet was the arbiter of morality and religious faith.

---

[11] Borg, *The Heart of Christianity*, p. 96.
[12] Ibid.
[13] Ibid., p. 9.
[14] Patrick Laude, "An Eternal Perfume," *Parabola* 30: 4 (Winter 2005), p. 8.

Such recourse to the past is understandable even though mistaken in its interpretation of history and, in truth, impossible to achieve again today. Moreover, the reading of Qu'ranic texts in support of such backward visions is often unenlightened and literal, and in fact contrary to more orthodox interpretations of the holy writ. But at least the spirit animating Muslim Fundamentalism is healthy and inspired by justice, even though its terrorism is sinful.

Christian Fundamentalism, on the other hand, is born out of a deliberate refusal to be enlightened. Christian Fundamentalism is obscurantist from the get go. It rejects the application of any scholarship to the biblical texts and to events as narrated in the Bible, whether Jewish or Christian. Christian Fundamentalism is born of a deliberate ignorance. In this it is very different from Muslim Fundamentalism, which at least is inspired by a concern for welfare. Christian Fundamentalism is powered by a fear of knowledge, a belief that sees knowledge as a threat to the faith. The Reverend Billy Graham has said, with a tinge of regret, that as a young man he abandoned his theological studies because he was afraid they might threaten his faith: this is the stance of Christian Fundamentalism, a refusal of knowledge because of a fear of what such knowledge may entail.

———◈———

In beating this hasty retreat from knowledge, Fundamentalists have taken the stance of the proverbial ostrich burying its head in the sand. They went along with the general feeling that the Darwinian theory of evolution "lowered" human dignity and made us similar not to angels but to apes. Instead of taking up the challenge to their views, they hid behind a veil of ignorance. Scholars all over were striving to understand evolution in humanistic, even religious and spiritual terms, but they remained stuck in their ignorance. Alfred Russell Wallace and Ernst Häckel, to mention just two, each in his own way, strove to interpret evolution in ways that included the spiritual, and somewhat later Teilhard de Chardin constructed a synthesis of evolution and Christian spirituality that turned out to be religiously satisfying and intellectually consistent; but in all this, the Fundamentalists were nowhere to be found.

Further, biblical scholars in various Christian denominations were able to absorb the results of textual criticism of the Bible into their own religious traditions, and in this way, they contributed immeasurably to our current understanding and appreciation of the Bible. Fundamentalists and Evangelicals, on the other hand, instead of taking the opportunity of making the Bible again a living thing, turned it into a fossil, irredeemable, incapable of updating no matter how many new translations are published, believing that in this facticity they would find security from the onrushing stream of evolution in which science says we are immersed.

This same latching on to the dead letter of Scripture prevented them from exposing and correcting the sexism that permeates many of the texts of *Genesis*. At a time when American society was finally recognizing and appreciating the role of women, Fundamentalists and Evangelicals remained stuck in their atavistic ideas about women, and therefore they have been bypassed by the empowering march of the feminine into all areas of life. The chauvinistic view of women still based on understandings of *Genesis* long ago revised and updated has been a major reason America has lagged behind so many other countries all over the world in which women are queens, presidents, prime ministers, scholars, and scientific and political experts, striding *pari passu* with men in their pursuit of happiness and on the way to heaven. The same unlettered literalism has prevented Evangelicals from undertaking the protection of the earth that we were charged with by God to preserve and by St. Paul to divinize, and not simply to misuse in selfish pursuit of shortsighted ends. Like a collective "Sleeping Beauty," Fundamentalists and Evangelicals have wasted a whole century in the sleep of ignorance and refusal.

———⋗⋖———

At the height of the Protestant Reformation, Martin Luther introduced the notion that the interpretation of Scripture is not dependent on the pope and the bishops but on the individual, but it never occurred to him that every unlettered individual would have the final word. He himself was a scholar, trained as a professor, and he was actually teaching at the University of Wittenberg when the famous discussion about indulgences took place. Moreover, with great vigor he set himself to the task of creating public schools (*Volkschule*) in order to equip children with the intellectual tools to do at least minimal study of Scripture. Our age, however, has misapplied democracy, which essentially is a system for making practical decisions regarding government, to the pursuit of truth and meaning. But truth is not determined by majority vote, nor is the meaning of Scripture fathomed by those ignorant of textual criticism and exegesis. Still, thousands upon thousands of Sunday school teachers do not hesitate to enter church classrooms, week after week, to teach what they truly know very little about. We accept in Bible study what we would never condone in any other field of intellectual endeavor, the assumption that anyone can teach what they hardly know. Imagine seeking advice on the building and running of atomic submarines from people with no knowledge whatever of atomic physics, or on setting up and positioning satellites in the sky from people totally ignorant of jet propulsion and guidance systems.

———⇒✦⇐———

Years ago I lived in an area of Long Island, New York, where the Jehovah's Witnesses came regularly on Sunday mornings preaching their message of salvation. As they stood outside my door, I would listen to them while sporting a benevolent if slightly sardonic smile on my face, and then I would ask them how they knew that the Bible said what they were telling me the Bible said. Their response was to show me in their Bibles the texts they were reading that day. To this I would reply that those texts were in English, and did they know that the Bible had been written in Hebrew (or Greek, as the case might be), and did they know Hebrew? To this they invariably replied that they did not. Then I would ask them how they knew that the translation was accurate and that the English text said exactly what was written in the Hebrew text. To this they had no answer but a kind of dumb murmuring, and with vague excuses, they would take their leave and move on through the neighborhood. I am not sure many got my message, but it may be that my style of conveying this truth about the Bible was not the appropriate one. Still, my point has been made with utmost clarity by Bart Ehrman in his recent book, *Misquoting Jesus*:

> If the meaning of the words of scripture can be grasped only by studying them in Greek (and Hebrew), doesn't this mean that most Christians, who don't read ancient languages, will never have complete access to what God wants them to know? And doesn't this make the doctrine of inspiration a doctrine only for the scholarly elite, who have the intellectual skills and the leisure to learn the languages and study the texts by reading them in the original? What good does it do to say that the words are inspired by God if most people have absolutely no access to these words, but only to more or less clumsy renderings of these words into a language, such as English, that has nothing to do with the original words?... How does it help us to say that the Bible is the inerrant word of God if in fact we don't have the words that God inerrantly inspired, but only the words copied by the scribes—sometimes correctly but sometimes (many times!) incorrectly?[15]

It seems to me unpardonable that thousands upon thousands of ministers and preachers who have gone for training to evangelical so-called Bible colleges can come out hardly touched by the scholarship that is taken for granted in major seminaries and universities throughout the world where the full study of the Bible—textual, lin-

---

[15] Bart D. Ehrman, *Misquoting Jesus* (San Francisco, CA: HarperSanFrancisco, 2005), p. 7.

guistic, stylistic, anthropological, archaeological, historical, cultural, and theological—is conducted. Ehrman mentions the fact that at the Moody Bible Institute in Chicago, which he attended as a young man, both students and professors had to sign a statement obliging them to one, and only one, view of Scripture; namely, that the Bible is totally and completely inspired and inerrant to the very last word, even though we do not have a single original manuscript of it![16] This is what they, then, preach. In this respect they are blind leaders of the blind, and as Jesus once said, when the blind lead the blind, both will end up in some ditch (*Matthew* 15:14).

I should add that today, Fundamentalist (and Evangelical) leaders worry openly about losing adherents among the young members of their denominations. They blame the unchristian culture all around for what they see as prevarication, and they conduct meetings and devise strategies to stem the flow; but more likely than not, the loss of membership is due to their own anti-intellectualism in matters of religion and the Bible. When young people and adults come face-to-face with the world of scholarship and with the fact that it is not devilish or anticlerical, they realize that they have been duped and forced to deny a God-given right to exercise their intelligence; and they bolt. The leaders have no one to blame but themselves.

---

One more thing. Fundamentalists claim, as justification for the lack of interest in scholarship, that salvation comes from faith alone. But, one may ask, faith in whom? And what *is* faith?[17] Let me explain the relevance of these questions. There was a time, during the first half of the twentieth century, when people believed that Nietzsche

---

[16]  Ibid., p. 4.
[17]  James Charlesworth, *Jesus within Judaism*, p. 22. Julian the Apostate (*ca.* 331–363), Roman emperor and scholar, is reputed to have complained in desperation against the Christians, "There is nothing in your philosophy beyond the one word, 'Believe'!" Quoted in E. R. Dodds, *Pagan and Christian in an Age of Anxiety* (Cambridge: Cambridge University Press, 1965), p. 109. Belief was reputed by the philosophers to be an inferior form of knowing.

was an anti-Semite. I ran into such an opinion in some of my gradu-
ate lectures. Middle-aged and older Jews, especially, were convinced
that Nietzsche had been one of the progenitors of Nazi anti-Semitism. And Nietzsche's works were there to prove this! It was only
after his sister Elizabeth Förster's death in 1936, when her tight-fist
control over her brother's manuscripts ceased, that people realized
that she had expurgated his works of all passages praising the Jews
and had left only those that might be interpreted as anti-Semitic.[18]

Now, the texts of the New Testament have been in the control
of people who had an ax to grind, who favored one interpretation
over others, and who therefore controlled the translations that most
people read. For an example, one could take all the phrases in the
Gospels and *Acts* that refer to "the Holy Spirit" and check the Greek:
one will find that in nearly all instances, the Greek text clearly has "a
holy spirit." Why is the wrong translation used still? Because it fits
a particular theological view of Jesus's relation to the Trinity. This, it
seems to me, is inexcusable. Is it not time for all of us, and not just
the scholars, to have full access to the truth? to see for ourselves what
the words say in all their naked simplicity?

# A Historical Note

Beginning in the 30s and 40s of the last century, there was in biblical theology a movement to "demythologize" the New Testament,
to peel off from the Gospel narratives the mythological accretions
that were thought to belong to the ancient times in which the New
Testament documents were written. A major argument in support of
this bracketing was that modern people, grown mature and scientific
in their understanding of the world and of themselves, were turned
off by mythologies of miracles, resurrection, and the like, and this led
them to reject the whole message of Christianity. Rudolf Bultmann,

---

[18] Elizabeth and her husband were so virulently anti-Semitic that they bought
land in Paraguay to found a colony of pure Aryans. The colony still exists.
Incidentally, Hitler himself delivered a eulogy at Elizabeth's funeral in 1936.

as explained in the introduction, was a principal advocate of this "demythologizing" project, but there were others.

Bultmann's proposal engendered a lively and scholarly debate regarding his definition of myth and the extent of the bracketing he advocated. Generally, however, the rationale offered, that modern people were turned off by the mythologies in which the Christ-event was couched, was not questioned. This is interesting because in America, consistently since the early part of the twentieth century, 30 percent to 40 percent of the population still clamor for the old New Testament mythologies, which even today they embrace with a sincere if naive faith. At the same time, these same people disown evolutionary theory, biblical scholarship, theological speculation, feminism, and scientific understandings of the world. Proof of this is easily found in Fundamentalist and Evangelical movements, from the times of the Scopes Trial in 1925 to the current efforts to ban the teaching of evolution in the public schools and to introduce "creationism" and other lightly veiled religious viewpoints into the curriculum.

Why this state of affairs, this refusal so prevalent in America, and only in America? Historians have argued that this anti-intellectual trend has its roots in the past of Puritan America. It was implied in the voluntarist tradition that saw the Christian primarily as a creature of will, not intellect, so that sin and virtue depended on the will wrongly or rightly configured rather than on the knowledge of what is necessary for salvation. For Augustine, from whom the tradition drew inspiration (and who knew nothing about the law of gravity), the human will is the gravity by which we are drawn wherever we are drawn.[19] "An ill will," he wrote, "is the cause of all evil."[20] The will, therefore, concluded the Puritans had to be trained in the right manner of living from earliest infancy; discipline and authority were

[19] Augustine, *Confessions* XIII, 9, 10.
[20] Augustine, *De libero arbitrio* III, 17, 48–49.

essential in this process, and the Evangelicals devoted most of their spiritual energies to this shaping of the will.[21]

Moreover, this trend was exacerbated by certain conditions attending the spread of Christianity in the United States after the Revolution. From the late eighteenth century on, a move began toward the West, a great pioneering enterprise that put a premium on "rugged individualism." Where there were few or no resources, people had to count on themselves alone to succeed against great odds. In this venture, the established Christian denominations, Catholics, Anglicans, Lutherans, were slow to venture out; the bulk of Christianizing activity was left to itinerant, often unlicensed and unlettered preachers who actually brought with them a virulent repudiation of the educated clergy whom they labeled authoritarian, rigid, stuck up, and bigoted. In other words, this so-called second Great Awakening was carried out by preachers who, in the words of a contemporary writer, "imagine they are able, and without Study too, to speak to the spiritual Profit of such as are willing to hear them."[22] This ministry legitimized "ignorance & her squalid brood," to quote Colin Goodykoontz,[23] and led to the sentiment reflected in Billy Sunday's angry remark, "When the word of God says one thing and scholarship says another, scholarship can go to hell!"[24]

It is obvious that whatever else it was, this anti-intellectual attitude was part of a rejection of the social classes from which the established clergy usually arose. There is also a kind of *ressentiment* at work in this repudiation of what one cannot have. Today, add to this the fact that the moral obscurantism of Fundamentalists and Evangelicals has received serious setbacks in the fields of censorship, evolution, Prohibition, feminism, racism, and abortion, by the efforts of more

---

[21] See Norman S. Fiering, "Will and Intellect in the New England Mind," *William and Mary Quarterly* 29 (1972); Philip Greven, *The Protestant Temperament* (Chicago: The University of Chicago Press, 1977).

[22] Charles Chauncy, *Seasonable Thoughts on the State of Religion in New England* (Boston, 1743), p. 226, quoted in Richard Hofstadter, *Anti-Intellectualism in American Life* (New York: Vintage, 1963), p. 70.

[23] Hofstadter, *Anti-Intellectualism in American Life*, p. 78.

[24] Ibid., p. 122.

enlightened people, and one can understand, if not condone, the militant hunger for comforting mythologies present among such a large segment of the American population.

———— ⋙⋘ ————

It should be added that the refusal to engage in a scholarly study of the Gospels is not new. St. Augustine mentions people in his own time who disdained the study of Scripture because they imagined they already understood all there was to know about the Gospels, and therefore did not need any further consultation.[25] To this, St. Augustine answered that there is always something more to learn from others, and that to deny this is to succumb to the dangerous temptation of pride,[26] thinking that our own views of the texts are the only possible ones.

Moreover, he argued that we should never be satisfied with any interpretation of the text, but should constantly seek new meanings; because, after all, the text is not the object of our final search, but he whom the texts lead to, God, for whom we are made, so that we are forever restless until we rest in him.[27] For, St. Augustine argues, Jesus himself said he was "the way" (*John* 14:6), but nobody loves the way for its own sake, but rather for the sake of the journey's end, the love of God. Hence, he writes, "We may learn how essential it is that nothing should detain us on the way, when not even our Lord himself, who condescended to be our way, was willing to detain us, but wished us rather to press on."[28]

---

[25] St. Augustine, *On Christian Prayer*, preface, 2.
[26] *On Christian Doctrine*, preface, 6.
[27] St. Augustine, *Confessions*, I, 1.
[28] *On Christian Doctrine*, I, 34 [38]. See Randi Rashkover, "Cultivating Theology," *Cross Currents* 55, 2 (Summer 2005), p. 244.

# A Note on "Softies"

The title comes from one word Paul uses in *1 Corinthians* 6:9 to describe, probably, his version of homosexuals, *malakoi*, which is often translated as "softies." One question is, Why are homosexuals so hated and despised by some segments of American society? The answer: Because many people are locked into the one-dimensional view that only heterosexual relations are natural and normal, a view that prevailed more than two thousand years ago, but which, through the advances in the sciences of human biology and genetics, was shown to be erroneous almost a century ago and has therefore been abandoned by most well-informed people. This is not a unique case. Not too long ago, people believed that left-handedness was unnatural, and they forced left-handed children to become right-handed. We no longer hold this view because we understand that handedness, left- and right-, and even ambidexterity, are part of the natural spectrum of human ability. But unfortunately many Americans still hold to the anachronistic opinion that only heterosexuality is natural, and they think this way because they misread the Bible,[1] which they think teaches these erroneous beliefs. I shall try to show that the Bible does no such thing. Many American Christians today despise homosexuals and object to marriage between them. A lot of this opposition is

---

[1] Bishop Alexander maintains that one could argue that Paul is right in condemning sex between heterosexual men, because he did not understand that there are also homosexual men. This is an interesting way of having your cake while eating it! See J. Neil Alexander, *This Far by Grace* (Cambridge, MA: Cowley Publications, 2003), p. 44.

based on ignorance of the biology and genetics of sexual differences. Many ignorant people have strongly held opinions that are not any less false because they are strongly held. It is understandable that people will condemn what they do not understand, simply out of fear of the unknown or dislike of differences, but in America, especially, this opposition claims the Bible as justification, and in this, those who reject homosexuals are plainly wrong. Their claim that the Bible condemns homosexuality is clearly in error, and for several reasons.

To begin with, the Bible knows nothing about homosexuality *as we understand it today*. The very term "homosexual" did not exist until the late nineteenth century. By homosexuality we, in the West generally, mean today a sexual orientation toward and attraction for people of the same sex, based on a prenatal disposition. Whether or not this prenatal disposition is also genetic is still unclear, but that the inclination originates *in utero* is scientifically unquestionable today. Homosexuality, in other words, is not just a matter of same-sex *acts* between heterosexuals: it is much more. It is the actualization of an inborn tendency, the actualization of desires some people, men as well as women, are born with. For a homosexual to have sex with a person of the same sex is as natural as it is for a heterosexual to have sex with a person of the opposite sex. Homosexual sex is not sex between consenting heterosexuals (as St. Paul saw it), it is sex between consenting homosexuals.

The Bible knew nothing of this. The only sex the biblical writers knew was between heterosexuals, whether of the same or of another sex. Ancient peoples, including the Greeks (among whom *paiderasteia* was commonly practiced), had no conception of a sexual orientation different from heterosexuality. The reason for this is simple: they had no knowledge of genetics or of hormones. They *did* understand that some people were born different—for example, left-handed (*Judges* 3:15) or without sexual organs (*Matthew* 19:12)—but they did not know what we term prenatal dispositions, such as giftedness, addictive personalities, fetal alcohol syndrome (FAS), dyslexia, heterosexuality—and homosexuality.

The Bible writers also knew about homosexual acts—actually, what they considered to be heterosexual acts between people of the

same sex—but they thought them to be mere expressions of unbri-
dled lust, as in the case of the men at Gibeah who lusted after a visiting male Levite, but were satisfied with the gang rape of the visitor's
concubine (*Judges* 19:22–26). A parallel case, but with a different
outcome, occurred when Lot received some male visitors that the
men of Sodom lusted after (*Genesis* 19:4–11).[2]

Some texts, such as *Deuteronomy* 23:17–18; *1 Kings* 14:24,
15:12, 22:46; and *2 Kings* 23:7 object to *cultic* same-sex prostitution,
not to homosexuality *per se*. The texts of *Leviticus* 18:22 and 20:13
do make homosexual acts between consenting adults punishable by
death because the Israelites must observe a ritual purity that is more
stringent than that of the surrounding peoples, but this prohibition
applies *only* to men, not at all to women. So, theoretically at least,
lesbianism would not have been objectionable. Moreover, other practices are equally condemned, such as incest (various types, clearly
specified), adultery, child sacrifice, cursing one's parents, intercourse
with a menstruating woman, shaving one's head and/or the edges of
one's beard, and getting a tattoo (*Leviticus* 21:5). But significantly,
as Jacob Milgrom notes, these restrictions applied only to the people
of Israel as a condition for inhabiting the Holy Land, and therefore,
Milgrom thinks, "It is incorrect to apply this prohibition [against
homosexual acts] on a universal scale."[3] Finally, homosexual acts
between consenting adults are forbidden only if they are illicit, that
is, "with males who are of the equivalent degree [of consanguinity]
of the females prohibited in these lists."[4] That is, homosexual relations are forbidden only within the immediate circle of the family.
Same-sex acts with unrelated males are not forbidden, nor are they
penalized.

---

[2] This episode has given rise to the view that the people of Sodom were
"homosexuals," and that their sin was "homosexuality." But the Sodomites were
condemned because they were uncaring and stingy with the poor, as Ezekiel
says specifically (*Ezekiel* 16:49). See Mark D. Jordan, *The Invention of Sodomy
in Christian Theology* (Chicago: The University of Chicago Press, 1997).

[3] Jacob Milgrom, *Leviticus: A New Translation with Introduction and Commentary*,
3 vols. (New York: The Anchor Bible, 2000), vol. 2, p. 1786.

[4] Ibid.

As should be clear from this very sketchy overview of pertinent texts, same-sex acts are not unambiguously forbidden in the Hebrew Bible, and people who claim they are, are either ignorant or malicious—or both.

---

Idan Dershowitz maintains that earlier versions of *Leviticus* than the one we now possess may have been entirely silent in the matter of sexual acts between men, because like all ancient texts, *Leviticus* took at least a hundred years to arrive at its present text. Moreover, Dershowitz thinks that the additions to the text can be traced with careful detective work.[5]

The main point is that the current text presents a biased editor's emendations, and therefore it should not be taken as the Bible's final and peremptory word on the matter.

---

At the beginning of Christianity St. Paul writes to the Corinthians that "neither fornicators, nor idol worshipers, nor adulterers, nor softies, nor men who bed men, nor thieves, nor the avaricious, nor drunkards, nor the accursed, nor robbers will inherit the kingdom of God" (*1 Corinthians* 6:9–10; also *1 Titus* 1:10 and *Romans* 1:27). Here, again, it is men (*ársên*, "male") performing such acts who are to be banned from the kingdom, together with a host of other "sinners" we most often choose to ignore when invoking the Bible as the source of prohibitions against homosexuality. But why would homosexual acts be worse than adultery or fornication or drunkenness? One could even argue that adultery is a sin of choice, while homosexual attraction is inborn, and therefore natural, though St. Paul could not have known that.

---

5   Idan Dershowitz, "The Secret History of Leviticus," *The New York Times*, July 21, 2018.

One should add that current translations often display a bias that is not found in the texts, and that therefore contribute greatly to the perpetuation of the bias against homosexuals. *Malakoi*, for example, a term used by St. Paul, simply means "softy," or perhaps "effeminate," in the sense in which Cardinal Newman used it in his *The Idea of a University*.[6] *Arsenokoitai* (which the Latin version translates as *masculorum concubitores*) means "people who sleep with men," which could refer to same-sex intercourse, prostitution, or simply to overindulgent sex (excessive sexual intercourse). Here, again, the meaning is not unambiguously clear.[7]

There are other considerations that could be given to explain why some same-sex relations were objected to by the ancients. These have to do with perceptions of the social relations between older and younger men, and between women and men. Men were at the top of the social scale, and women were below. Free men were higher than slaves. A free man could force sex upon a woman simply because he was superior to her. If two men had sex with each other, it was assumed that one of them was behaving like a woman or a slave, and *that* was objectionable, not on moral grounds but on hierarchical ones. As Ehrman puts it, "When ancient texts…condemn same-sex relations, it is important to understand what it is they're condemning. They are condemning a man for acting like a member of the weaker sex."[8] Today, most of us reject such social hierarchies, but we should know that they existed, and should also understand how they colored the judgments of the people of those times; but since those grounds are no longer considered valid, the judgments should also be revised.

---

[6] John Henry Newman, *The Idea of a University* (Garden City, NY: Image Books, 1959), VIII, 10, p. 219.

[7] Se Charles D. Myers Jr., "What the Bible Really Says about Homo-sexuality," *Anima* 19:1 (Fall 1992), pp. 47–53.

[8] Bart D. Ehrman, *Peter, Paul, and Mary Magdalene* (New York: Oxford University Press, 2006), p. 213.

Finally, there was another dimension to the opposition to homo-sexual acts between men. For a man to submit himself to another man in a homosexual encounter was to become a woman. As Meeks puts it, "Many people thought of the female as an incomplete male, while a man was always in some danger of having his masculinity diminished or weakened."[9] In other words, men could become "soft-ies," as St. Paul calls them. Brown writes:

> It was never enough to be male: a man had to strive to remain "virile." He had to learn to exclude from his character and from the poise and temper of his body all telltale traces of "soft-ness" that might betray, in him, the half-formed state of a woman.[10]

St. Paul would have wanted to prevent his Christian men from losing their virility, and homosexual acts would have betrayed in them a womanish softness that was to be avoided at all costs. The condemnation of "softness," therefore, would not have been due to (homo) sexual acts *per se* but because they had the potential to turn men into women, or to make men effeminate.

⸻ ❖ ⸻

Actually, homoeroticism is not as removed from Christianity as many seem to think. The entire theological structure of Christianity conceives Jesus as a man and the Church as his bride—a heterosexual model; but the actual members of this church are not all women: in fact, about half of them are men who, according to the model, owe their love to Jesus, another man. However spiritualized this encounter with Jesus may be, the fact is that for men, the model is homoerotic, and therefore the devotion men are encouraged to give to Jesus is,

---

[9] Meeks, *Origins of Christian Morality*, p. 141. See also Margaret A. Farley, *Just Love* (New York: Continuum, 2008), pp. 275–276.
[10] Brown, *The Body and Society*, p. 11.

paradoxically, homosexual. I say paradoxically because Christianity publicly condemns same-sex desire yet elicits it in its men's prayers and devotion to the man Jesus. Mark Jordan calls this "the paradox of the Catholic Jesus, the paradox created by an officially homophobic religion in which an all-male clergy sacrifices male flesh before images of God as an almost naked man."[11]

St. Bernard of Clairvaux spoke of being united to Christ in a holy kiss,[12] and St. John of the Cross used highly charged homoerotic language when, in his *The Living Flame of Love*, he wrote:

> When the soul is transpierced with that dart, the flame gushes forth, vehemently and with a sudden ascent, like the fire in a furnace or an oven when someone uses a poker or bellows to stir and excite it. And being wounded by this fiery dart, the soul feels the wound with unsurpassable delight... The fire issuing from the substance and power of that living point...is felt to be subtly diffused through all the spiritual and substantial veins of the soul in the measure of the soul's power and strength.[13]

The orgasmic symbolism of this passage should be quite clear. Contemporary "Christian rock" songs, belted powerfully by male leads, are full of homoerotic suggestion. Hymns like the Evangelical classic "I Come to the Garden Alone" describe suggestively a secret meeting with Jesus:

> I come to the garden alone
> While the dew is still on the roses
> And the voice I hear falling on my ear

---

[11] Mark Jordan, *The Silence of Sodom: Homosexuality and Modern Catholicism* (Chicago: The University of Chicago Press, 2000), quoted by Jeffrey J. Kripal, "Heroic Heretical Heterosexuality," *Cross Currents* 54, 3 (Fall 2004), p. 85.
[12] Bernard of Clairvaux, *Super Cantica Canticorum* iii, 5.
[13] Kripal, "Heroic Heretical Homosexuality," p. 86.

The Son of God discloses.
And He walks with me, and He talks with me,
And He tells me I am his own;
And the joy we share as we tarry there,
None other has ever known.

A more traditional hymn intones:

Jesus, thy boundless love to me
No thought can reach, no tongue declare;
O knit my thankful heart to thee
And reign without a rival there.

Prothero comments: "In these hymns, believers lay down their heads on their Savior's breast and rest in the shadow of his sheltering wings. Jesus responds by putting his loving arms around them, and in some cases the embrace lasts until dawn."[14] Prothero does not think that hymns such as these are homoerotic; he thinks that "piety overwhelms passion here."[15] But he explicitly assumes a woman singing, not a man. When the singer is a man, I believe that passion overwhelms the simple, innocent, and self-deluding piety.

But there is more. As I mentioned in chapter 1, the *Gospel of Mark* was probably the first one to be written down, but the version of it we have today may not be the one that Matthew and Luke employed as a blueprint in the composition of their own Gospels. Mark seems to have added to the one original version of his Gospel, and one of these versions is the *Secret Gospel of Mark*, which contains passages not found in either the version used by Matthew and Luke or the one we read today. This *Secret Gospel*, according to ancient testimony, was current among select and more spiritually advanced Christians in Alexandria, where Mark had gone to live after the death of Peter *ca.* 65 CE. The restricted circulation was due to some obvious

---

[14] Stephen Prothero, *American Jesus* (New York: Farrar, Straus & Giroux, 2003), p. 78.
[15] Ibid.

313

reasons: some of the additional secret passages might have appeared scandalous to the uninitiated. For example, *Secret Gospel of Mark* adds a story after *Mark* 10:34 about a young man who has died. Jesus walks up to the tomb, rolls away the stone at the entrance, goes in, grabs the corpse by the hand, and raises him up. Resuscitated, "the young man looked at Jesus, loved him, and began to beg him to be with him... Six days later, Jesus gave him an order, and when evening had come, the young man went to him, dressed only in a linen cloth. He spent that night with him, because Jesus taught him the mystery of the Kingdom of God."[16] Was this a reference to a ceremony like that of later baptism in which, as Hippolytus explains (*Apostolic Tradition* 21, 11), both the minister and the catechumen stood naked in the baptismal water? or did this have to do with an initiation mystery, the sacrament of "the bridal chamber" described in *Gospel of Philip* 67, 27–30? or was this part of a homoerotic tradition that only now is being self-consciously explored by male scholars? Anyway, it is understandable why this passage would not have been included in the Gospel text used more popularly.

---

One more thing. A heated controversy has developed lately over the subject of same-sex unions. Historically, Christian priests have solemnized same-sex unions among their congregants for some seventeen hundred years. Current leaders of the various Christian churches either do not know this historical fact or they choose to ignore it and cover it up while assailing those who try to avail themselves of the privilege by invoking the secular law, which in some states allows them to be so united. The whole current spectacle of opposition offers a disgusting example of bigotry and hypocrisy.

The truth is that same-sex unions were blessed by the Church, and with enough frequency to have required the provision of an official ritual ceremony. The texts of these rites are preserved in

---

[16] Robert J. Miller, ed., *The Complete Gospels* (Sonoma, CA: Polebridge Press, 1994), p. 411.

many extant liturgical books. They resemble the traditional rites of heterosexual marriage, but they have their own distinctive form.[17] Montaigne witnessed one such ceremony in Rome at the Church of Saint John at the Latin Gate in 1578,[18] and there are studies and references to such celebrations in other parts of Europe well into the early part of the twentieth century. One can argue that the church solemnized these same-sex unions because it chose to ignore what might happen behind the closed doors of the contrahents' homes and to respect their privacy, but the fact is that the rituals existed, that they endured for centuries, and that therefore they may be said to form part of the hallowed traditions of Christianity.

---

One final point. Marriage between a man and a woman has not remained unaltered through the centuries, as some opponents of same-sex marriage seem to proclaim. The fact is that changes have been taking place at a steady pace, so that the very institution of heterosexual marriage has changed considerably. For example, among the Romans, a wife was considered to be the property of her husband. This concept passed into the European and later American traditions as "coverture," the idea that a wife's rights were covered by or included in those of her husband. However, this is no longer the case. Husbands and wives exercise their rights equally, and only some Fundamentalists insist on the subordinate status of their wives.

To cite other examples: in the US, race restrictions existed at some point, so that whites could not marry blacks, and society generally supported this practice; but this is no longer the case. Similarly, no-fault divorce applies equally to both husbands and wives, so that gender is no longer relevant. Again, divisions of labor between hus-

---

[17] For the texts, see John Boswell, *Same-Sex Unions in Premodern Europe* (New York: Villard Books, 1994), pp. 283–363, and a list of manuscripts on pp. 372–374.
[18] See Michel de Montaigne, *Journal de Voyage en Italie par la Suisse et l'Allemagne en 1580–1581*, ed. Charles Dédéyan (Paris, 1946), p. 231, cited in Boswell, *Same-Sex Unions*, pp. 264–265.

bands and wives are no longer applied along gender lines: wives engage in whatever occupation they want, and can, and often are the primary breadwinners. As Judge Walker concluded in his decision on the constitutionality of California Proposition 8, today "marriage under law is a union of equals" (p. 113). Thus, in effect, marriage has been "transformed from a male-dominated institution into an institution recognizing men and women as equals" (p. 112). Given this fact, same-sex marriage—that is, marriage that does not abide by the differences of gender—is perfectly legitimate under the law, and should be so recognized even by the churches.

---

The conclusion to all this? When Martin Luther proposed the principle of the individual interpretation of Scripture, he did not envision the degree of ignorance that today prevails among both the leadership and the populace. In fact, Luther was an accomplished professor of biblical studies; he translated the Bible into German, and he encouraged the formation of a system of local schools to make sure ordinary people learned what they needed in order to read the Bible and interpret it for themselves. Today, most leaders among Fundamentalists and Evangelicals, and even among other higher denominations, cannot read the Gospels in the simple Greek in which they were written. They despise such studies, preferring a passionate and devout ignorance instead, and out of this negative background, they dare provide guidance to millions of people who themselves have no knowledge at all of the results of exegesis.

But, as one can see from *Matthew* 25:44–45, Jesus is not very forgiving of those who claim ignorance as the justification for their actions (or lack thereof) or beliefs.

# A NOTE ON CONSERVATIVES
# AND LIBERALS

*Words like… "conservative," "liberal"…*
*seem more like political battles for power*
*than spiritual searches for truth.*
—Henri J. M. Nouwen,
*In the Name of Jesus*

Not too long ago, at a wedding reception dinner, I overheard someone mention the words "conservative" and "liberal." I inquired,
"What does this mean? What do these words mean?" and immediately became tangled in a discussion of TV personalities and politi-
cians who were reputed to be liberal or conservative. I also was told
that most people in America were conservative, and that many repu-
table opinion polls bore this out; only disreputable ones, sponsored
by the liberal establishment, expressed a different opinion. As I was
swept away by this avalanche of facts I was supposed to know (unless
I was a liberal, of course), I could only dimly remember what I had
wanted to say in the first place, for right now I was tumbling down
in the swirl of seemingly convincing utterances, unable to gain a sure
footing or say the right thing. Only much later did I come to realize
where I had first missed my step, and why.

"The devil made me do it," I thought to myself, as I concluded
that I must have been tempted by a clever and devious pupil of the

great and redoubtable old teacher of tempters, Screwtape himself.[1] And the temptation, I saw, was twofold. First was the use of the terms "conservative" and "liberal" as incantations in order to distract from the real point at issue, namely, the truth. For these terms mean nothing, really, when one zeroes in on matters of truth and the evidence for it. Calling some view or some person "conservative" or "liberal" (as the case may be) settles nothing about the truth of the views the person in question holds, which truth ought to be the focus of any and every serious discussion. For this is the important thing, is it not? to get closer to the truth or to move at least into the inner courtyard, so as to gain a glimpse of it sooner rather than later, as one might steal a peek at the lady of the castle as she walks quietly at night along the moonlit corridors before withdrawing to her private chambers. To be conservative or liberal is profoundly irrelevant in respect to the truth, just as whether the lady is blonde or brunette is immaterial to her beauty, and whether a fox is brown or red is of no consequence whatever to the hunters galloping after it, much less to the dogs who, I am told, are color-blind anyway. No, the point is to bag the critter, and the sooner the better. One must banish useless distractions. There are many ways of hunting, but the basic one is to hunt.

This is not to deny that there are different perceptions of the truth, just as there are foxes with pelts of various colors. Women, too, sport different complexions. According to Ambrose Bierce, a conservative is someone enamored of existing evils, and a liberal is someone who wishes to replace those evils with new ones.[2] The point is that simply to emphasize, as we often do, the existence of conservatives and liberals in our midst, is to miss the very subject about which there are differences of opinion; it is, in the case of fox hunting, to put the pelt before the fox.

Also, it is to confuse method with substance. Conservatism and liberalism are methods of pursuing the truth. One functions with

---

[1]  See C. S. Lewis, *The Screwtape Letters and Screwtape Proposes a Toast* (New York: The Macmillan Co., 1962). See also Ignacio L. Götz, *Faith, Humor, and Paradox* (Westport, CT: Praeger, 2002), chapter 7.

[2]  Quoted by Russell Kirk, "Introduction" to *The Portable Conservative Reader*, ed. Russell Kirk (New York: The Viking Press, 1982), p. xi.

greater regard for tradition and established beliefs, the other with a more open stance and a willingness to be surprised. But both of them are methods, and they should not be confused with the results of the search. The same thing happens with the term "democracy," which is a way of making political decisions, but which we popularly confuse with the results obtained by the method. We do this often when we criticize other nations for not being "democratic" because they arrive at results different from the ones we have obtained, or would have liked for them to obtain. But methods do not guarantee truth—certainly not *our* perception of it!

I should add that it really does not make much difference whether we call people conservative or liberal: at bottom, in most matters, both views are almost exactly alike; the difference between them is minimal. It is a matter of perspective, not of truth; like seeing a glass as half full or as half empty. Not that there are no real differences: both liberals and conservatives think they are promoting the Kingdom of Heaven, but they think it is to be promoted in a different manner, and the different manner makes it quite a different Kingdom;[3] though how different can drinking a half-empty glass of water be from drinking a half-full one? The *tertium quid*, glasses always filled to the brim, is part of the utopian nature of human aspirations.

But all this is beyond the ken of most people who bandy about the terms "conservative" and "liberal"; they usually do not know what the terms mean, because this knowledge requires a good amount of philosophical and political sophistication, which most journalists and ordinary people do not possess. In fact, more often than not, people use these words to encapsulate ideas or practices they like or dislike; but since likes and dislikes are purely personal and idiosyncratic, the use of the labels is arbitrary and therefore meaningless. As Russell Kirk puts it, "they hold their convictions somewhat vaguely,

---

[3] Richard S. Peters, *Authority, Responsibility, and Education* (London: George Allen & Unwin, Ltd., 1963), p. 95.

as prejudices rather than reasoned conclusions," because "their minds are not susceptible to temperate argument."[4]

The second part of the temptation was to believe that opinion polls have any relevance to the pursuit of truth. They do not. They are simply statistical samplings of the opinions of certain groups or classes of people about a particular question, not about the evidence that may or may not ground these opinions. Whether or not 50 percent of a certain polled population opine one way or another is of no concern to those who wish to pursue the truth, for truth is not a matter of majority vote. It is said that when Einstein first proposed the theory of relativity, only about nine scientists in the whole world understood what he was talking about. The fact that this was a minuscule percentage of the total world population did not make their views wrong, just as the fact that, during the Middle Ages, most people believed that the sun moved round the earth did not make them right. Truth, simply put, has nothing to do with polls. Truth has to do with evidence and with the reasons given in its support. Reasons matter, opinion polls do not.

———— ❧ ————

So this is what had happened: I had been tempted to engage in the usual charade about conservatives and liberals and opinion polls, and I had fallen into temptation. By the time I realized my error, it was too late to steer away from the trap. Mercifully the entrapment did not last long, and I was able to recover my composure and review the events leading to my fall.

But how has it come to pass that in America, arguments about politics, religion, education, and the like are settled by labeling the positions of the discussants (or the discussants themselves) "conservative" or "liberal"? How have we come to fall in love with the ubiq-

---

[4] Russell Kirk, "Introduction," p. xxiii. The term "Conservative" has been politicized to the point that, as Anita Renfroe says, "it is almost synonymous with 'Please check your brain at the door.'" See Mimi Suarez, "Did you hear the one about the Christian comedian?" *The New York Times Sunday Magazine*, February 24, 2008.

uitous polls, even though they tell us nothing about the truth of the questions we are asked about?

In his famous retirement speech at the annual dinner of the Tempters' Training College, Screwtape, that most experienced of devils, floated the idea that the misapplication of democracy to all areas of life (and not just to the political system) would, as a result, lead people to believe that their opinions were of equal value and worthy of equal notice regardless of the reasons that might be mustered in their support. Opinions were like votes; if all votes were equally valid, so were opinions. "One person, one vote," would become "one person, one opinion." Once this belief system was in place, he suggested, one could dispense with the truth, with reasons and with evidence, for none of this was important if all views were of equal value and importance. Numerical sampling was all that was required, and if further distinctions were needed, all views could be neatly packaged into conservative and liberal ones, whether this made any sense or not. Screwtape explained:

> You are to use the word [democracy] purely as an incantation; if you like, purely for its selling power. It is a name they venerate. And of course it is connected with the political ideal that men should be equally treated. You then make a stealthy transition in their minds from this political ideal to the factual belief that all men *are* equal. Especially the man you are working on. As a result you can use the word *democracy* to sanction in his thought the most degrading (and also the least enjoyable) of all human feelings. You can get him to practice, not only without shame but with a positive glow of self-approval, conduct which, if undefended by the magic word, would be universally derided.

The feeling I mean is of course that which
prompts a man to say *I'm as good as you*.[5]

In our context, this means *My ideas are as good as yours*. This is, of course, untrue; not all ideas have the same value, nor are they all equally true. In fact, many of them are false. But since everyone, or nearly everyone, believes all ideas are equal, no one notices, and we can continue with the business of our daily lives without much concern for the fact that we have based the entire enterprise on a lie. Because no one who says *My ideas are as good as yours* really believes it. People would not say it if they really believed it. Einstein never said it to his students, nor does the pope say it to his conclave, nor the genius to the dunce, nor the boss to his/her employees.

Another way of explaining this is by the example of the common form we use for ending discussions in which agreement is not easily forthcoming. "That is your opinion, this is mine," we say, as if all opinions were of equal value, so that people could hold one or another, and the world would not be any the worse for it. But this is patently false, and we ourselves do not really believe it, or else we would not have gone to war against Hitler and *his* opinions, or against Saddam Hussein and *his*.

But why would we be willing to act this way? Screwtape again: "The claim to equality, outside the strictly political field, is made only by those who feel themselves to be in some way inferior. What it expresses is precisely the itching, smarting, writhing awareness of an inferiority which the patient refuses to accept."[6] That is, the claim of equality is usually made by people who feel unequal and who resent this feeling. In America we can usually countenance all kinds of differences of talent, of beauty, of prowess in sports, of financial success, without letting the facts of inferiority interfere with our lives; we can accept millionaires and wealthy movie stars even though most of us scramble to make a living, but we cannot tolerate the very thought of people having better ideas than ours. In other countries, scholars are

---

[5] C. S. Lewis, *The Screwtape Letters*, p. 162.
[6] Ibid., pp. 162–163.

respected and esteemed; but in America, they are generally resented because of the supposition that they may have ideas that are better than ours. And what is peculiar of our age and place, according to Screwtape, is that we sanction our feelings of jealousy for other people's ideas by calling *them* undemocratic. It is commendable to aspire to be successful in business, in athletics, in the field of communications, but not in that of ideas. Intellectual excellence is, as we say, "elitist," the pursuit of the few, and therefore it is undemocratic. I once ran a discussion group for undergraduate students, and many of the best in the college refused to join because of the fear of being called "elitists." And theirs was a real fear, a sincere and deep repugnance of appearing to be more scholarly than their peers, of seeming to be different in their regard for ideas, so thorough was the conditioning and brainwashing that had been effected in them through the misuse of the concept of democracy and its application to the realm of ideas.

⟶✴︎⟵

Now, the terms "conservative" and "liberal" are used also in the context of Christian views and theological positions, and here again I am afraid they are meaningless, because the point—the *real* point—in matters of religion is also the truth. In terms of biblical scholarship, the truth is the textual one of the original manuscripts in so far as this can be ascertained, for there are literally thousands of manuscripts with hundreds of thousands of variants. The textual truth is not that of the translators, who, in spite of themselves, must always interpret as they translate, *but* there *is* a text, and words *do* have meanings defined in dictionaries so that translators cannot act like Humpty-Dumpty who claimed that words had the meaning *he* chose them to have, neither more nor less.[7] When the truth of the text is in question (or the truth that *is* the text!), it makes little, if any, sense to call some scholars conservative and others liberal, for the

---

[7] Lewis Carroll, *Through the Looking Glass*, in *The Annotated Alice*, ed. Martin Gardner (New York: Clarkson N. Potter, Inc., Publisher, 1960), p. 269.

point is what the words mean without any preconception or bias. To give just one example: most current translations say that Mary was pregnant "from *the* Holy Spirit" (*Matthew* 1:18, *Luke* 1:35), interpreting this spirit to be the Third Person of the Trinity; but the Greek text says clearly "*a* holy spirit." Anything beyond this is biased theological interpretation.

In theological and denominational matters, things are a bit more complicated because by definition we are dealing with interpretation from start to finish, and interpretations are likely to differ, at times considerably. But here again the terms "conservative" and "liberal" are of little use because they presuppose a norm or standard accepted by all Christians from which the interpretations in question would depart to the right or to the left, as the case may be. This is precisely the point, that Christian denominations are a whole unto themselves, each to be judged by its own standards, which are adhered to by all members of the denomination. Moreover, in cases of dissidence, the point of reference is still the truth, and how distant a view is from the central truth can be established without labeling it conservative or liberal.

On the other hand, when we come to religious practice, the terms may be meaningful, because (as I mentioned above when discussing conservatism and liberalism as "methods') some denominations are more "conservative" in their approach to the religious life—that is, more wedded to tradition—than others in particular matters, like Roman Catholics with regard to the issue of the ordination of women to the priesthood, while others are more "liberal"—that is, more willing to adjust practice to new understandings of how the practice originated—like the Episcopal Church in the very same issue of the ordination of women. Still, the labels do not automatically convey the thinking and scholarly research behind every position, and these are the crucial matters. Most denominations do not adjust their practices on a whim or simply because their hierarchies are reputed to be liberal, so sloganizing is really inappropriate and misleading, as it is in the other cases I have mentioned here.

———✷———

And maybe it is here that Screwtape's advice to his young train-
ees has been most damaging. He knew what was being wrought by
the superficial preaching and the interfaith jealousies that have agi-
tated Christianity from its beginning. He knew the seeds of discon-
tent that were being sown by labeling people we disagree with "conservative" or "liberal." He knew that even the practice of religion as a
way to avoid the truth can very well pave the way to hell. This is why
he recommended an emphasis on the superficial—on "this atrophy
of substance to slogan," as Catherine Madsen has termed it[8]—and on
a consequent and divisive sloganizing in order to avoid the search for
truth. "All said and done, my friends," he explained as he concluded
his speech, "it will be an ill day for us if what most humans mean by
'religion' ever vanishes from the Earth. It can still send us the truly
delicious sins. The fine flower of unholiness can grow only in the
close neighborhood of the Holy. Nowhere do we tempt so successfully as on the very steps of the altar."[9]

———✤———

But here someone may object, "What is wrong with using labels
like 'conservative' and 'liberal'? After all, we all perceive the world
according to our own prejudices. Perception is reality." To a great
extent, such a view is correct: things are as we perceive them to be.
This is what prejudice achieves, a *re*vision of reality, whatever it be.

This position has a long pedigree. Bishop George Berkeley
(1685–1753) argued that the reality of a thing consists in the fact
of its being perceived—*esse est percipi.*[10] Perception, in other words,
*is* reality, though perhaps not *all* of reality. Samuel Johnson (1709–
1784) was once asked what he thought of this problematic view of
Berkeley's, and he is reported to have answered, "It is solved thus,"

---

[8]  Catherine Madsen, "Editorial," *Cross Currents*, 56, No. 3 (Fall 2006), p. 300.
[9]  C. S. Lewis, *The Screwtape Letters*, pp. 171–172.
[10]  George Berkeley, *A Treatise Concerning the Principles of Human Knowledge*,
3, in *Great Books of the Western World*, ed. Robert M. Hutchins (Chicago:
Encyclopaedia Britannica, 1952), Vol. 35, p. 413.

while kicking a stone. In other words, the stone is not just the perception of it we have when kicking it; *it* is there.

The plausibility of the view that perception is reality was undermined already in the sixteenth century with the publication of Copernicus's *De revolutionibus orbium coelestium* (1543). We all perceive the sun as rising in the east and setting in the west, and if perception were constitutive of reality, this would mean that the sun moves round the earth. But Copernicus argued that this perception was in error: it is the earth that moves round the sun. Our perception notwithstanding, this is the truth. The being of the solar system is not made up by our perception of it.[11]

Therefore we must not hide behind the facile quote, "Perception is reality." Similarly, having recourse to the identification of views as "conservative" or "liberal" is a quick way to avoid an encounter with the reality of whatever it is we are confronting: abortion, war, a woman's right to choose, same-sex unions—or a stone. Ideally, we should drop the labels and the slogans and cut through the perceptions to the reality, however difficult and unpleasant this may be. As Tertullian wrote, "Truth blushes at nothing except at being hidden." Personal perceptions are often shameful concealments of the truth.

---

[11] The role of perception in the being of reality is a fundamental cornerstone of contemporary physics. Schrödinger (1887–1961) has amply demonstrated this. What I am arguing against is the popular *mis*application of the theory as a justification for prejudice and for the refusal to look for the facts.

# BIBLIOGRAPHY

Aflākī, Shams ad-Dīn Ahmad. *Manāqib al-'Ārifīn.* Tehran: Duniyā-yi Kitāb, 1983.

Albright, W. F. and C. S. Mann. *Matthew.* Garden City, NY: Doubleday & Co., 1971.

Alexander, J. Neil, *This Far by Grace.* Cambridge, MA: Cowley Publications, 2003.

Alighieri, Dante. *The Divine Comedy* [*La Commedia*]. Chicago: Encyclopaedia Britannica, 1952.

———. *La Vita Nuova.* New York: Penguin Books, 1980.

Anselm of Canterbury. *Proslogium; Monologium, An Appendix; Cur Deus Homo,* translated by Sidney Norton Deane. Chicago: Open Court, 1939.

Aquinas, St. Thomas. *Opera Omnia,* edited by E. Fretté and P. Maré. Paris: 1872–1880.

Aristotle. *The Complete Works,* edited by Jonathan Barnes. 2 vols. Princeton: Princeton University Press, 1995.

Armstrong, Karen. *The Great Transformation.* New York: Alfred A. Knopf, 2006.

———. *The Battle for God.* New York: Alfred A. Knopf, 2000.

Athanasius. "Opera Omnia." In *Patrologiae cursus completus,* Series Graeca, edited by J. P. Migne. Paris: Garnier, 1844–1855.

Attridge, Harold W., trans. "Dialogue of the Savior." In *The Nag Hammadi Library,* edited by James M. Robinson. San Francisco: Harper & Row, 1978.

Augustine, Saint. *The City of God.* Chicago: Encyclopaedia Britannica, 1952.

———. "Opera Omnia." In *Patrologiae cursus completus,* Series Latina, edited by J. P. Migne. Paris: Garnier, 1844–1855.

Bachelard, Gaston. *The Poetics of Reverie.* Boston: Beacon Press, 1971.

Baer, Richars A. *Philo's Use of the Categories Male and Female.* Leiden: E. J. Brill, 1970.

Baigent, Michael. *The Jesus Papers.* San Francisco: HarperSanFrancisco, 2006.

Balthasar, Hans Urs von, SJ. *Prayer.* New York: Paulist Press, 1976.

Barnstone, Willis and Marvin Meyer, eds. "Secret Book of James." In *The Gnostic Bible.* Boston: Shambhala, 2003.

Barnstone, Willis and Meyer, Marvin, eds. *The Gnostic Bible.* Boston: Shambhala, 2003.

Barth, Karl. *Die protestantische Theologie im 19. Jarhundert.* Zollikon-Zürich: Evangelischer Verlag, 1952.

———. *Fides quaerens intellectum: Anselms Bewis der Existenz Gottes.* Munich: Kaiser Verlag, 1931.

———. *The Epistle to the Romans.* London: Oxford University Press, 1933.

Bede, Venerable. "Opera." In *Patrologiae cursus completus,* Series Latina, edited by J. P. Migne. Paris: Garnier, 1844–1855.

Berger, Peter L. *A Rumor of Angels.* Garden City, NY: Doubleday, 1969.

Berkeley, George. "A Treatise Concerning Human Understanding." In *Great Books of the Western World,* edited by Robert M. Hutchins. Chicago: Encyclopaedia Britannica, 1952.

Bhaktivedanta, A. C., Swami Prabhupāda. *KṚṢṆA: The Supreme Personality of Godhead.* London: The Bhaktivedanta Book Trust, 1986.

Bonhoeffer, Dietrich. *The Cost of Discipleship.* New York: Macmillan, 1963.

———. *Das Zeugnis eines Boten,* edited by Visser't Hooft. Geneva, 1945.

Boolos, George. "Gödel's Second Incompleteness Theorem Explained in Words of One Syllable." *Mind* 103:409 (January 1994), 1–3.

Borg, Marcus J. *Jesus.* San Francisco: HarperSanFrancisco, 2006.

————and John Dominic Crossan. *The Last Week*. San Francisco: HarperSanFrancisco, 2006.

————. *The Heart of Christianity*. San Francisco: HarperCollins, 2004.

Boswell, John. *Same-Sex Unions in Premodern Europe*. New York: Villard Books, 1994.

Brito, Emilio. *De Dieu: Connaissance et Inconnaissance*. 2 vols. Leuven: Peeters, 2018.

Brock, Ann Graham. *Mary Magdalene*. Cambridge, MA: Harvard Divinity School, 2003.

Brown, Peter. *The Body and Society*. New York: Columbia University Press, 1988.

Brown, Raymond E., SS. *The Death of the Messiah*. 2 vols. New York: Doubleday, 1994.

————. "The *Pater Noster* as an Eschatological Prayer." *Theological Studies*, 22 (1961): 175–208.

————. *The Birth of the Messiah*. New York: Doubleday, 1993.

————. *The Community of the Beloved Disciple*. New York: Paulist Press, 1979.

————. *The Gospel According to John*. 2 vols. Garden City, NY: Doubleday & Co., 1970.

Buber, Martin. *Between Man and Man*. New York: Macmillan, 1965.

Bühler, G., trans. "Manusmṛti: The Laws of Manu." *Sacred Books of the East*. Vol. 25. Oxford: Oxford University Press, 1886.

Bullough, Vern L. and James Brundage. *Sexual Practices and the Medieval Church*. Buffalo: Prometheus Books, 1982.

Bultmann, Rudolf. *Primitive Christianity in Its Contemporary Setting*. New York: Meridian, 1957.

————. *Jesus Christ and Mythology*. New York: Scribner's, 1958.

Burke, James. *The Day the Universe Changed*. Boston: Little, Brown & Co., 1985.

Camus, Albert. *The Rebel*. New York: Vintage, 1956.

Casanovas, Ignacio, SJ. *Comentario y explanación de los Ejercisios Espirituales de San Ignacio de Loyola*. 4 vols. Barcelona: Balmes, 1945.

Chadwick, Henry. *Early Christian Thought and the Classical Tradition.* New York: Oxford University Press, 1966.

Charlesworth, James H. *Jesus within Judaism.* New York: Doubleday, 1988.

Chauncy, Charles. *Seasonable Thoughts on the State of Religion in New England.* Boston, 1743.

Chilton, Bruce. *Rabbi Jesus: An Intimate Biography.* New York: Doubleday, 2000.

Clement of Alexandria. "Stromata." In *Patrologiae cursus completus,* Series Graeca, edited by J. P. Migne. Paris: Garnier, 1857–1866.

Coathalem, Hervé, SJ. *Ignatian Insights.* Taichung, Taiwan: Kuangchi Press, 1961.

Collins, John J. *The Scepter and the Star.* New York: Doubleday, 1995.

Connolly, Myles. *Mr. Blue.* Chicago: Loyola Press, 2005.

Crenshaw, James L. *Education in Ancient Israel.* New York: Doubleday, 1998.

Crossan, John Dominic. *God and Empire.* San Francisco, CA: HarperSan-Francisco, 2007.

———. *The Birth of Christianity.* San Francisco: HarperSanFrancisco, 1998.

Crouzel, Henri. *Théologie de l'Image de Dieu chez Origène.* Paris: Aubier, 1956.

Cullmann, Oscar. *The Christology of the New Testament.* London, 1959.

Cyril of Alexandria. "Opera Omnia." In *Patrologiae cursus completus,* Series Graeca, edited by J. P. Migne. Paris: Garnier, 1857–1866.

Dahood, Mitchell, SJ. *Psalms I.* Garden City, NY: Doubleday & Co., Inc., 1966.

Davis, C. "Summary." *Clergy Review* (London), 41 (1956): 545–546 and 701–703.

Dershowitz, Idan. "The Secret History of Leviticus." *The New York Times.* July 21, 2018.

Dettloff, W., OFM. "Virgo-Mater: Kirchenväter und moderne Biologie zur jungfraülichen Mutterschaft Mariens." *Wissenschaft und Weisheit* 20 (1957).

Dewey, John. *A Common Faith*. New Haven: Yale University Press, 1934.

Dickinson, Emily. *Final Harvest: Emily Dickinson's Poems*, selected and introduced by Thomas H. Johnson. Boston: Little, Brown, & Co., 1961.

Dodds, E. R. *Pagans and Christians in an Age of Anxiety*. Cambridge: Cambridge University Press, 1965.

Donne, John. *The Complete Poetry and Selected Prose*, edited by Charles M. Coffin. New York: The Modern Library, 1952.

Dorrien, Gary. "American Liberal Theology," *Cross Currents* 55, 4 (Winter 2006).

Dostoevsky, Fyodor. *The Brothers Karamazov*. Chicago: Encyclopaedia Britannica, 1952.

Drijvers, J. W. *Helena Augusta: The Mother of Constantine the Great and the Legend of Her Finding the True Cross*. Leiden: Brill, 1991.

Dungan, David Laird. *A History of the Synoptic Problem*. New York: Doubleday, 1999.

Duns Scotus, John. *Opera Omnia*. 2$^{nd}$ ed., 26 vols. Paris: Vivès, 1891–1895.

Dupré, Louis. *Kierkegaard as Theologian*. New York: Sheed & Ward, 1963.

Durant, Will. *The Age of Faith*. Simon and Schuster, 1950.

Dwight Goddard, ed. "Tao-Te Ching." In *A Buddhist Bible*. Boston: Beacon Press, 1970.

Ehrman, Bart D. *Peter, Paul, and Mary Magdalene*. New York: Oxford University Press, 2006.

——. *How Jesus Became God*. New York: Harper One, 2014.

——. *Jesus, Apocalyptic Prophet of the New Millennium*. New York: Oxford University Press, 1999.

——. *Jesus, Interrupted*. New York: Harper One, 2009.

——. *Lost Christianities*. New York: Oxford University Press, 2003.

——. *Misquoting Jesus*. San Francisco: HarperSanFrancisco, 2005.

——. *The Triumph of Christianity*. New York: Simon & Schuster, 2018.

Eiseley, Loren. *The Immense Journey*. New York: Vintage, 1957.

Ephraem the Syrian, Saint. *Sancti Ephraem Syri Hymni et Sermones,* edited by T. J. Lamy. 4 vols. Mechliniae, 1902.

Epiphanius. *Panarion Haeresium,* edited by K. Holl. Leipzig, 1915–1931.

Erasmus of Rotterdam, Desiderius. *In Praise of Folly.* Baltimore, MD: Penguin Books, 1973.

Erikson, Erik H. *Young Man Luther.* New York: Norton, 1958.

Eusebius. *Historia Ecclesiastica.* New York: Barnes & Noble, 1995.

Farley, Edward. "Fundamentalism: A Theory." *Cross Currents* 55: 3 (Fall 2005).

Farley, Margaret A. *Just Love.* New York: Continuum, 2008.

Fideler, David. *Jesus Christ, Sun of God.* Wheaton, IL: Quest Books, 1993.

Filoramo, Giovanni. *A History of Gnosticism.* Oxford: Blackwell, 1990.

Fitzmyer, Joseph A. *The Acts of the Apostles.* New York: Doubleday, 1998.

———. *First Corinthians.* New Haven, CT: Anchor Bible, 2008.

———. *The Letter to Philemon.* New York: Doubleday, 2000.

Friedman, David M. *A Mind of Its Own: A Cultural History of the Penis.* New York: The Free Press, 2001.

Fromm, Erich. *Escape from Freedom.* New York: Rinehart, 1941.

Gensler, Harry J. *Gödel's Theorem Simplified.* Lanham: University Press of America, 1984.

Gerson, John. *Opera Omnia.* Antwerp, 1706.

Gibbon, Edward. *The Decline and Fall of the Roman Empire.* Chicago: Encyclopaedia Britannica, 1952.

Gittins, Anthony J. "Grains of wheat: culture, agriculture, and spirituality." *Spirituality Today* 42:3 (Autumn 1990): 196–208.

Gödel, Kurt. "Über formal unentscheidbare Sätze der *Principia Mathematica und* verwandter Systeme, I." *Monatshefte für Mathematik und Physik* 38 (1931): 173–198.

Gold, Penny S. "The Marriage of Mary and Joseph in the Twelfth-Century Ideology of Marriage." In *Sexual Practices and the Medieval Church* by Vern L. Bullough and James Brundage. Buffalo: Prometheus Books, 1982.

Götz, Ignacio L. *Faith, Humor, and Paradox*. Westport, CT: Praeger, 2002.

———. *Manners and Violence*. Westport, CO: Praeger, 2000.

———. *The Culture of Sexism*. Westport, CT: Praeger, 1999.

Grant, Robert M. *Gnosticism and Early Christianity*. 2nd ed. New York: Columbia University Press, 1966.

Green, Christopher C. and David I. Starling, eds. *Revelation and Reason in Christian Theology*. Bellingham, WA: Lexham Press, 2018.

Gregory of Nazianzus. "Opera." In *Patrologiae cursus completus*, Series Graeca, edited by J. P. Migne. Paris: Garnier, 1857–1866.

Griffith, Ralph T. H., trans. *The Hymns of the Rigveda*. 2 vols. Benares: E. J. Lazarus & Co., 1920.

Grossouw, W. K. *Spirituality of the New Testament*. St. Louis, MO: Herder, 1961.

Gutiérrez, Gustavo. *A Theology of Liberation*. Rev. Ed. New York: Orbis Books, 1988.

Habermas, Jürgen. *Communication and the Evolution of Society*. Boston: Beacon Press, 1979.

Hare, Richard. *Freedom and Reason*. New York: Oxford University Press, 1965.

Harris, Paul, ed. *The Fire of Silence and Stillness*. Springfield, IL: Templegate Publishers, 1997.

Hearon, Holly E. *The Mary Magdalene Tradition*. Collegeville, MN: Liturgical Press, 2004.

Heidegger, Martin. *Basic Writings*. New York: Harper & Row, 1977.

———. *Existence and Being*. Chicago: Regnery, 1949.

Hennecke, Edgar and Wilhelm Schneemelcher, eds. *New Testament Aprocrypha*. Philadelphia, PA: The Westminster Press, 1964.

Hennecke, Edgar and Wilhelm Schneemelcher, eds. "Protoevangelium of James." In *New Testament Aprocrypha*. Philadelphia, PA: The Westminster Press, 1964.

Hennecke, Edgar and Wilhelm Schneermelcher, ed. *Acts of John*, in *New Testament Aprocrypha*. Philadelphia, PA: The Westminster Press, 1964.

Hermas. "The Shepherd." In *The Apostolic Fathers*, translated by J. B. Lightfoot. Grand Rapids, MI: Baker Book House, 1965.

Hesse, Hermann. *The Journey to the East*. New York: Bantam, 1970.

Hezser, Catherine. *Jewish Literacy in Roman Palestine*. Tübingen: Mohr Siebeck, 2001.

Hippolytus. "Refutatio omnium haeresiarum." In *Patrologiae cursus completus*, Series Graeca, edited J. P. Migne. Paris: Garnier, 1857–1866.

Hofstadter, Richard. *Anti-Intellectualism in American Life*. New York: Vintage, 1963.

Hölderlin, Friedrich. *Werke*. Berlin: Propyläen-Verlag, 1914.

Homer. *Odyssey*. Chicago: Encyclopaedia Britannica, 1952.

———. *Iliad*. Chicago: Encyclopaedia Britannica, 1952.

Hopkins, Gerard Manley. *Poems and Prose*. New York: Alfred A Knopf, 1995.

Horsley, Richard A. and John S. Hanson. *Bandits, Prophets, and Messiahs*. San Francisco: Harper & Row, 1985.

Ignatius of Antioch. "Epistles of S. Ignatius." In *The Apostolic Fathers*, translated and edited by J. B. Lightfoot. Grand Rapids, MI: Baker Book House, 1965.

Irenaeus of Lyons. "Adversus Haereses," translated by A. Cleveland Coxe. In *The Ante-Nicene Fathers*. Grand Rapids, MI: Eerdmans, 1885 [1979].

James Rendel Harris, ed. *Odes of Solomon*. Cambridge: The University Press, 1909.

James, M. R., ed. "Gospel of James." In *The Apocryphal New Testament*. Oxford: Oxford University Press, 1924.

James, William. *Varieties of Religious Experience*. New York: Mentor, 1964.

Jeremias, Joachim. *The Eucharistic Words of Jesus*. New York: Scribner's, 1966.

———. *The Prayers of Jesus*. Philadelphia, PA: Fortress Press, 1978.

John Chrysostom, Saint. *Homilies on the Gospel of Matthew*. New York: Catholic University of America Press, 1998.

John of the Cross, Saint. *Spiritual Canticle*, translated by W. Allison Peers. Garden City, NY: Doubleday & Co., 1961.

Jonas, Hans. *The Gnostic Religion.* 2nd ed. Boston: Beacon Press, 1963.

Jones, Prudence and Nigel Pennick. *A History of Pagan Europe.* London: Routledge, 1995.

Jordan, Mark. *The Silence of Sodom: Homosexuality and Modern Catholicism.* Chicago: The University of Chicago Press, 2000.

———. *The Invention of Sodomy in Christian Theology.* Chicago: The University of Chicago Press, 1997.

Josephus, Flavius. *Works,* translated and edited by Henry St. John Thackeray et al. 10 vols. Cambridge, MA: Harvard University Press, 1926–1965.

Joyce, James. *A Portrait of the Artist as a Young Man.* New York: The Viking Press, 1958.

Justinian. *The Digest of Justinian,* translated by Charles H. Monro and W. W. Buckland. Cambridge: Cambridge University Press, 1904–1909 and 1993.

Juvenal. *The Satires of Juvenal,* translated by Rolfe Humphries. Bloomington, IN: Indiana University Press, 1958.

Kant, Immanuel. *Immanuel Kants Werke,* edited by Ernst Cassirer. Berlin: Bruno Cassirer, 1922–1923.

Kasser, Rudolphe, Marvin Meyer, and Gregor Wurst, eds. *Gospel of Judas.* Washington, DC: National Geographic, 2006.

Kaufmann, Walter. *Without Guilt and Justice.* New York: Dell Publishing Co., Inc., 1973.

Kazantzakis, Nikos. *Christ Recrucified.* London: Faber and Faber, 1954.

Keen, Sam. *To a Dancing God.* New York: Harper & Row, 1970.

Keith, Chris. *The Pericope Adulterae, the Gospel of John, and the Literacy of Jesus.* Leiden: Brill, 2009.

Kiefer, Otto. *Sexual Life in Ancient Rome.* London: Routledge & Kegan Paul, Ltd., 1953.

Kierkegaard, Søren. *The Present Age.* New York: Harper & Row, 1962.

———. "Concerning the Dedication to 'The Individual.'" In *The Point of View of My Work as an Author.* New York: Harper & Row, 1962.

King, Karen L. *What Is Gnosticism?* Cambridge, MA: Harvard University Press, 2003.

Klijn, A. F. J. "The 'Single One' in the Gospel of Thomas." *Journal of Biblical Literature* 81:3 (1962).

Kripal, Jeffrey J. "Heroic Heretical Homosexuality." *Cross Currents* 54, 3 (Fall 2004).

Labalme, Patricia H., ed. *Beyond Their Sex.* New York: New York University Press, 1984.

Laude, Patrick. "An Eternal Perfume." *Parabola* 30: 4 (Winter 2005).

Leach, Edmund R. "Magical Hair." In *Myth and Cosmos*, edited by John Middleton. Austin: Texas University Press, 1967.

Lehman, Paul. *Ethics in a Christian Context.* New York: Harper & Row, 1963.

Lewis, C. S. *The Screwtape Letters & Screwtape Proposes a Toast.* New York: Macmillan, 1962.

LiDonnici, Lynn R. *The Epidaurian Miracle Inscriptions: Text, Translation, and Commentary.* SBL Texts and Translations 36. Atlanta: Scholars Press, 1995.

Lightfoot, J. B., trans. and ed. "2 Clement." In *The Apostolic Fathers.* Grand Rapids, MI: Baker Book House, 1965.

Lowrie, Walter. *Kierkegaard.* New York: Harper Torchbooks, 1962.

Lutyens, Mary. *Krishnamurti.* 2 vols. New York: Avon Books, 1975, 1983.

MacDermott, Violet, trans. *Pistis Sophia.* Nag Hammadi Studies 9. Leiden: E. J. Brill, 1978.

Macdonald, Dennis R. "Corinthian Veils and Gnostic Androgynes." In *Images of Feminism in Gnosticism*, edited by Karen L. King. Philadelphia: Fortress Press, 1988.

———. *There Is No Male and Female: The Fate of a Dominical Saying in Paul and Gnosticism.* Philadelphia: Fortress Press, 1987.

Maimonides. "Essay on Resurrection" (1191). In *Epistles of Maimonides: Crisis and Leadership*, translated and edited by Abraham Halkin. Philadelphia: The Jewish Publication Society, 1985.

Marty, Martin, ed. *Fundamentalism and Evangelicalism.* New York: K. G. Saur, 1993.

Martyn, J. Kouis. *History and Theology in the Fourth Gospel.* New York: Harper & Row, 1968.

Massignon, Louis. *The Passion of al-Hallāj.* 4 vols. Princeton: Princeton University Press, 1982.

Mayotte, Ricky Alan. *The Complete Jesus.* South Royalton, VT: Steerforth Press, 1997.

Mcpherson Oliver, Mary Anne. "Conjugal Spirituality (or Radical Proximity): A New Form of Con-templ-ation." *Spirituality Today* 43, 1 (Spring 1991): 53–67.

Meeks, Wayne A. *The Origins of Christian Morality.* New Haven, CT: Yale University Press, 1993.

———. "The Image of the Androgyne: Some Uses of a Symbol in Earliest Christianity." *History of Religions* 13:3 (1974).

Meier, John P. *A Marginal Jew.* 3 vols. New York: Doubleday, 1994.

Mendels, Doron. *The Rise and Fall of Jewish Nationalism.* New York: Doubleday, 1992.

Merton, Thomas. *Day of a Stranger.* Salt Lake City: Gibbs M. Smith, 1981.

Meyer, Marvin W. *The Unknown Sayings of Jesus.* Boston: New Seeds, 2005.

———. ed. *The Ancient Mysteries: A Sourcebook.* New York: Harper & Row, 1987.

———. "Making Mary Male: The Categories 'Male' and 'Female' in the Gospel of Thomas." *New Testament Studies* 31:4 (October 1985).

Miles, Jack. *God: A Biography.* New York: Vintage, 1995.

Milgrom, Jacob. *Leviticus: A New Translation with Introduction and Commentary.* 3 vols. New York: The Anchor Bible, 2000.

Miller, Robert J. "Gospel of the Nazoreans." In *The Complete Gospels.* San Francisco: HarperSanFrancisco, 1994.

Miller, Robert J. "Infancy Gospel of Thomas." In *The Complete Gospels.* San Francisco: HarperSanFrancisco, 1994.

Miller, Robert J. *The Complete Gospels.* San Francisco: HarperSanFrancisco, 1994.

Migne, J. P., ed. "Physiologos." In *Patrologiae cursus completus,* Series Graeca. Paris: Garnier, 1844–1855.

Mitamura, Taisuke. *Chinese Eunuchs.* Rutland, VT: Charles E. Tuttle Co., Inc., 1970.

Mitterer, A. Dogma und Biologie der heiligen Familie nach dem Welt bild des h. Thomas von Aquin und dem Gegenwart. Wien, 1952.

Montaigne, Michel de. *Journal de Voyage en Italie par la Suisse et l'Allemagne en 1580–1581,* edited by Charles Dédéyan. Paris, 1946.

Murray, Robert, SJ. *Symbols of Church and Kingdom: A Study in Early Syriac Tradition.* Piscataway, NJ: Gorgias Press, 2004.

Myers, Charles D. Jr. "What the Bible Really Says about Homosexuality." *Anima* 19: 1 (Fall 1992): 47–53.

Nasr, Seyyed Hossein. "The Sacred World of the Other." *Parabola* 30: 4 (Winter 2005).

Neill, Stephen. *A History of Christianity in India.* Cambridge: Cambridge University Press, 1984.

Neusner, Jacob. *Judaism: The Evidence of the Mishnah.* Chicago: The University of Chicago Press, 1981.

Newman, John Henry. *The Idea of a University.* Garden City, NY: Doubleday & Co., 1959.

Nicolau, Michaele, SJ. *De revelatione Cristiana.* Madrid: Biblioteca de Autores Cristianos, 1958.

Niebuhr, H. Richard. *The Responsible Self.* New York: Harper & Row, 1963.

Nietzsche, Friedrich. *The Gay Science.* New York: Vintage, 1974.

———. *On the Genealogy of Morals* and *Ecce Homo,* translated by Walter Kaufmann. New York: Vintage, 1967.

———. *Thus Spoke Zarathustra.* New York: The Viking Press, 1966.

Nissinen, Martin. *Homoeroticism in the Biblical World.* Minneapolis, MN: Fortress Press, 1998.

Norris, Kathleen. *The Cloister Walk.* New York: Riverhead Books, 1996.

O'Connor, Michael Patrick. "Controlling Men: Eunuchs in the Bible and the Ancient Near East." *Mid-Atlantic Society for Biblical Literature.* Meeting, Baltimore (March 2006).

O'Flaherty, Wendy Doniger. "Inside and Outside the Mouth of God: the Boundary between Myth and Reality." *Daedalus* 109, No. 2 (1980).

O'Sullivan, Owen. "The Silent Schism." *Cross Currents* 44: 4 (Winter 1994–95).

Orbe, Antonio, SJ. *Estudios valentinianos*. Rome: Gregorian University, 1958–1966.

Origen. "Contra Celsum." In *Patrologiae cursus completus*, Series Graeca, edited by J. P. Migne. Paris: Garnier, 1857–1866.

Ovid. *Metamorphoses*, translated by Rolfe Humphries. Bloomington, IN: Indiana University Press, 1964.

Pagels, Elaine and Karen L. King. *Reading Judas*. New York: Penguin Books, 2007.

Pagels, Elaine. *Adam, Eve, and the Serpent*. New York: Random House, 1988.

———. *The Gnostic Gospels*. New York: Random House, 1979.

Parrot, Douglas M., trans. "The Sophia of Jesus Christ." In *The Nag Hammadi Library*, edited by James M. Robinson. San Francisco: Harper & Row, 1978.

*Passio Sanctarum Perpetuae et Felicitatis*. CJMJ. Bonn: Hanstein, 1938.

Pauly, A. and G. Wissowa. *Real-Encyclopädie der classischen Altestums-wissenschaften*. 2nd ser. Stuttgart.

Phillips, John A. *Eve: The History of an Idea*. New York: Harper & Row, 1984.

Philo of Alexandria. *Works of Philo, Complete and Unabridged*, translated by C. D. Yonge. Peabody, MA: Hendrickson Publ., 1993.

Phipps, William E. *The Sexuality of Jesus*. Cleveland, OH: Pilgrim Press, 1996.

Piaget, Jean. *The Moral Judgment of the Child*. New York: The Free Press, 1965.

Plato. *Plato's Works*. Chicago: Encyclopaedia Britannica, 1952.

Plotinus. *The Six Enneads*. Chicago: Encyclopaedia Britannica, 1952.

Plutarch. *The Lives of the Noble Grecians and Romans*. Chicago: Encyclopaedia Britannica, 1952.

Porphyry. "Life of Plotinus." In *Plotin: Ennéades*, translated and edited by E. Bréhier. Paris, 1924.

Prat, Ferdinand, SJ. *Jesus Christ.* Milwaukee: The Bruce Publishing Co., 1950.

Prestige, G. L. *Fathers and Heretics.* London, 1940.

Prothero, Stephen. *American Jesus.* New York: Farrar, Straus & Giroux, 2003.

Puhl, Louis J., SJ, trans. *The Spiritual Exercises of Saint Ignatius.* Allahabad, India: St Paul Publication, 1962.

Quesnell, Quentin, SJ. "Made Themselves Eunuchs for the Kingdom of Heaven," *Catholic Biblical Quarterly*, 30:3 (July 1968).

Radford Ruether, Rosemary. *Sexism and God-Talk.* Boston: Beacon Press, 1983.

Radhakrishnan, S., ed. *The Bhagavadgîtâ.* London: George Allen & Unwin, 1960.

Rahner, Hugo, SJ. *The Spirituality of St. Ignatius Loyola.* Westminster, MD: The Newman Press, 1953.

Rahner, Karl. "Zur Theologie der Menschwerdung." *Catholica* 12 (1958): 1–16.

Randall Jr., John Herman. *Hellenistic Ways of Deliverance and the Making of the Christian Synthesis.* New York: Columbia University Press, 1970.

Ranke-Heinemann, Uta. *Eunuchs for the Kingdom of Heaven.* New York: Doubleday, 1990.

Rashkover, Randi. "Cultivating Theology." *Cross Currents* 55, 2 (Summer 2005).

Renan, Ernest. *The Life of Jesus.* New York: The Modern Library, 1927.

Reps, Paul. *Zen Flesh, Zen Bones.* Garden City, NY: Doubleday Anchor, n. d.

Robinson, James M. "Apocalypse of Peter." In *The Nag Hammadi Library in English.* San Francisco: Harper & Row, 1978.

Robinson, James M., ed. "Gospel of Mary." In *The Nag Hammadi Library.* San Francisco: Harper & Row, 1978.

Robinson, James M., ed. "Gospel of Philip." In *The Nag Hammadi Library.* San Francisco: Harper & Row, 1978.

Robinson, James M., ed. "Gospel of the Egyptians." In *The Nag Hammadi Library*. San Francisco: Harper & Row, 1978.

Robinson, James M., ed. "Gospel of Thomas." In *The Nag Hammadi Library*. San Francisco: Harper & Row, 1978.

Robinson, James M., ed. "Second Discourse of the Great Seth." In *The Nag Hammadi Library*. San Francisco: Harper & Row, 1978.

Robinson, James M., ed. "The Thunder, Perfect Mind." In *The Nag Hammadi Library*. New York: Harper & Row, 1981.

Robinson, James M., ed. *The Nag Hammadi Library*. San Francisco: Harper & Row, 1978.

Rodríguez, Alonso, SJ. *Ejercicios de perfeccion y virtudes cristianas*. 7th ed. Madrid: Apostolado de la Prensa, 1950.

Rosser, Barkcly. "An informal exposition of proofs of Gödel's theorems and Church's theorem." *The Journal of Symbolic Logic* 4:2 (June 1939): 53–60.

Roth, Philip. "The Conversion of the Jews." In *Goodbye, Columbus*. New York: The Modern Library, 1959.

Rousselle, Aline. *Porneia: On Desire and the Body in Antiquity*. London: Basil Blackwell, 1988.

Ruether, Rosemary Radford. *Sexism and God-Talk*. Boston: Beacon Press, 1983.

Rûmî, Jelaludîn. *Mathnawî*, translated and edited by R. A. Nicholson. London: Luzac, 1925–1940.

Ruskin, John. *Modern Painters III*. Chicago & New York: Bedford, Clarke and Co., 1873.

Schaberg, Jane. *The Resurrection of Mary Magdalene Legends, Apocrypha, and the New Testament*. New York: Continuum, 2002.

———. *The Illegitimacy of Jesus*. San Francisco: Harper & Row, 1987.

Scholem, Gershom. *Jewish Gnosticism, Merkabah Mysticism, and Talmudic Tradition*. New York: Jewish Theological Seminary of America, 1960.

Schüssler Fiorenza, Elisabeth. *Jesus: Miriam's Child, Sophia's Prophet*. New York: Continuum, 1994.

Sells, Michael A., ed. *Early Islamic Mysticism*. New York: Paulist Press, 1996.

Shakespeare, William. *A Midsummer-night's Dream*. Chicago: Encyclopaedia Britannica, 1952.

Sheehan, Thomas. *The First Coming*. New York: Random House, 1986.

Spong, John Shelby. *A New Christianity for a New World*. San Francisco, CA: HarperSanFrancisco, 2002.

Staal, Frits. *Exploring Mysticism*. Berkeley, CA: University of California Press, 1975.

Steiner, Rudolf. *The Gospel of St. John*. New York: Anthroposophic Press, 1962.

———. *Christianity as Mystical Fact* and *the Mysteries of Christianity*. West Nyack, NY: R. Steiner Publications, Inc., 1961.

Steinsaltz, Adin. "What is the right way to make a cake?" *Parabola* 31: 1 (Spring 2006).

———. *The Essential Talmud*. New York: Bantam Books, 1976.

Stone, Merlin. *When God Was a Woman*. New York: Harcourt Brace Jovanovich, 1976.

Suarez, Mimi. "Did you hear the one about the Christian comedian?" *The New York Times Sunday Magazine*. February 24, 2008.

Suetonius. *The Twelve Caesars*. London: Penguin Books, 1972.

Suzuki, Daisetz T. *Manual of Zen Buddhism*. New York: Grove Press, Inc., 1960.

Synesius of Cyrene. "Opera Omnia." In vol. 66 of *Patrologiae Cursus Completus, Series Graeca*, edited by J. P. Migne. Paris, 1857–1880.

Tabor, James D. *The Jesus Dynasty*. New York: Simon & Schuster, 2006.

Teresa de Jesús, Santa. *Obras Completas*, edited by Efrén de la Madre de Dios, OCD and O. Carm Otger Steggink. Madrid: Biblioteca de Autores Cristianos, 1967.

Tertullian. *Tertulliani opera. Corpus Christianorum, series Latina*. Turnhout: Brepols, 1954.

*The Hymns of Zarathustra*. Boston: Beacon Press, 1963.

Thomas à Kempis. *The Imitation of Christ*. London: Burns & Oates, 1957.

Thomas, D. Winton, ed. *Documents from Old Testament Times*. New York: Harper Torch-books, 1958.

Thompson, Thomas L. *The Mythic Past*. New York: Basic Books, 1999.

Tisserant, E. "Ascensio Isaiae." In *Ascension d'Isaie*. Paris, 1909.

Tolkien, J. R. R. *The Lord of the Rings*. 2nd ed. Boston: Houghton Mifflin Co., 1965.

Tompkins, Peter. *The Eunuch and the Virgin*. New York: Breamhall House, 1962.

Tresmontant, Claude. *Saint Paul and the Mystery of Christ*. New York: Harper & Brothers, 1962.

Twitty, Anne. "Lines in the Sand," *Parabola* 30: 4 (Winter 2005).

Unamuno, Miguel de. *The Tragic Sense of Life*. New York: Dover Publications, Inc., 1954.

Valmiki. *Ramayana*. Baroda: Oriental Institute, 1960–1975.

Van Der Leeuw, Gerardus. *Sacred and Profane Beauty: The Holy in Art*. New York: Holt, Rinehart and Winston, 1963.

Van Kaam, Adrian, C. S. Sp. *Spirituality and the Gentle Life*. Denville, NJ: Dimension Books, Inc., 1974.

Van Zeller, Hubert, OSB. *The Inner Search*. Garden City, NY: Image Books, 1957.

Vermes, Geza. *The Resurrection*. New York: Doubleday, 2008.

Virgil. *The Aeneid*. Chicago: Encyclopaedia Britannica, 1952.

Walsh, James, SJ, trans. and ed. *The Cloud of Unknowing*. New York: Paulist Press, 1981.

Ward, Benedicta. *Harlots of the Desert*. Kalamazoo, MI: Cistercian Publications, 1987.

Weems, Mason Locke. *The Life of George Washington the Great*. Reprint, Augusta, GA: G. F. Randolph, 1806.

Weininger, Otto. *Sex and Character*. New York: A. L. Burt Co., *ca.* 1906.

Wiesel, Elie. *Souls on Fire*. New York: Random House, 1972.

———. *All Rivers Run to the Sea: Memoirs*. New York: Knopf, 1995.

Williams, Michael A. "Uses of Gender Imagery in Ancient Gnostic Texts." In *Gender and Religion*, edited by Caroline W. Bynum et al. Boston: Beacon Press, 1986.

Wilson, A. N. *Paul: The Mind of the Apostle*. New York: W. W. Norton, 1997.

Wink, Walter. *The Human Being*. Minneapolis, MN: Fortress Press, 2002.

Wisdom, John. "Gods." In *Religion from Tolstoy to Camus*, edited by Walter Kaufmann. New York: Harper Torchbooks, 1964.

Wise, Michael, Martin Abegg, and Edward Cook, eds. *The Dead Sea Scrolls*. San Francisco: HarperSan Francisco, 1996.

Wittgenstein, Ludwig. *Tractatus Logico-Philosophicus*. London: Routledge & Kegan Paul, 1961.

Zeno of Verona. "Opera." In *Patrologiae cursus completus*, Series Latina, edited by J. P. Migne. Paris: Garnier, 1857–1866.

# ABOUT THE AUTHOR

Ignacio L. Götz is Lawrence A. Stessin Distinguished Professor Emeritus at New College of Hofstra University, where he taught for thirty-five years. He was ordained a priest in 1962. He is the author of many books and scholarly articles in philosophy and religion, including *Technology and the Spirit* (2001); *Faith, Humor, and Paradox* (2002); *Conceptions of Happiness: Revised Edition* (2010); *Knowing My Faith* (2018); and *Meditations on Living My Faith* (2018). He lives in Point Harbor, North Carolina.

CPSIA information can be obtained
at www.ICGtesting.com
Printed in the USA
BVHW071429120122
625993BV00002B/200